BEDTIME GAMES ™

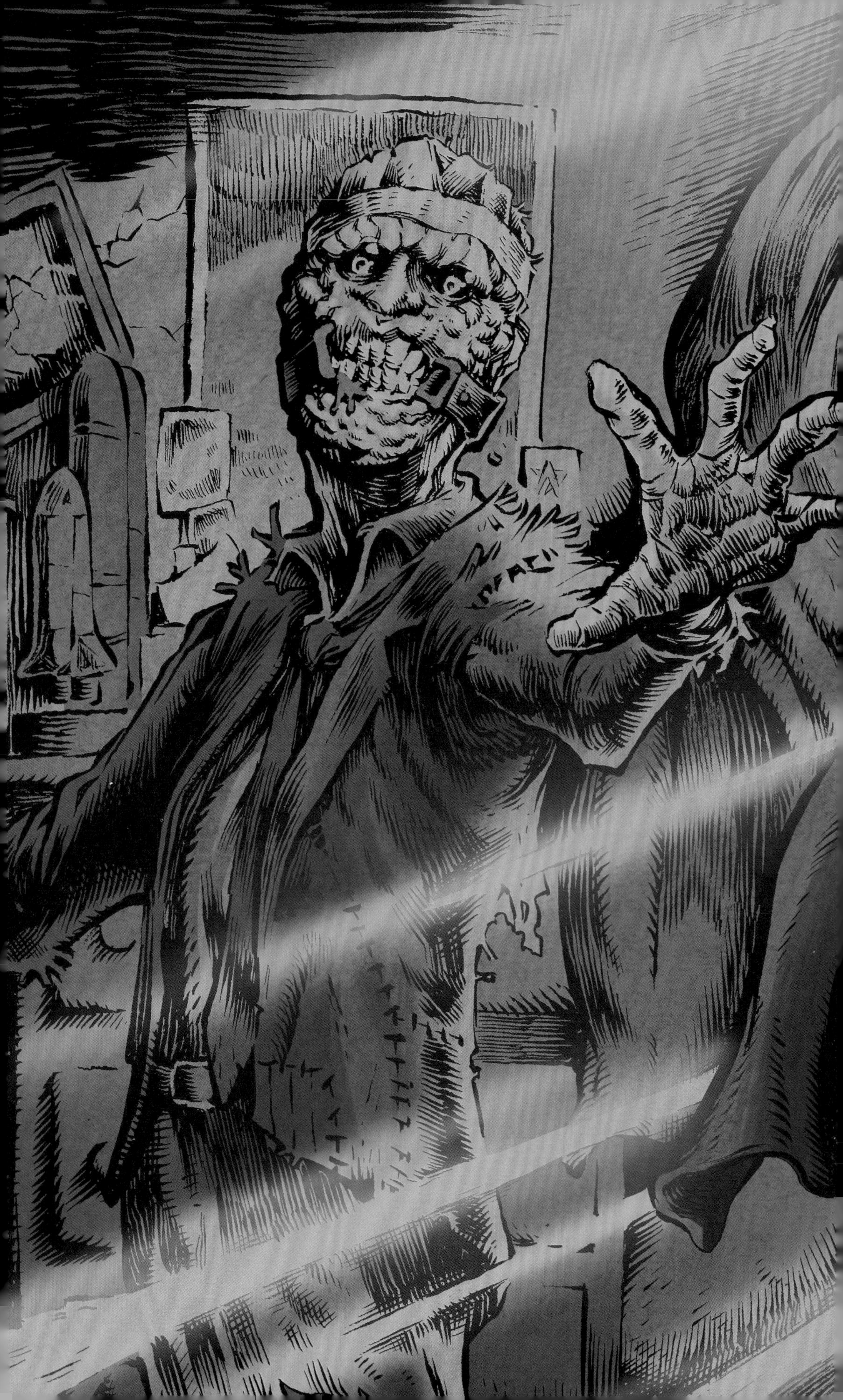

BEDTIME GAMES ™

STORY BY
NICK KELLER

ART BY
CONOR NOLAN

COLORS BY
KELLY FITZPATRICK

LETTERS BY
JOHN J. HILL

COVER AND CHAPTER BREAK ART BY
CONOR NOLAN

PUBLISHER **MIKE RICHARDSON**   EDITOR **KATII O'BRIEN**

ASSISTANT EDITOR **JENNY BLENK**   DESIGNER **JASON RALL**

DIGITAL ART TECHNICIAN **JOSIE CHRISTENSEN**

DARK HORSE BOOKS

EXECUTIVE VICE PRESIDENT **NEIL HANKERSON**
CHIEF FINANCIAL OFFICER **TOM WEDDLE**
VICE PRESIDENT OF PUBLISHING **RANDY STRADLEY**
CHIEF BUSINESS DEVELOPMENT OFFICER **NICK MCWHORTER**
VICE PRESIDENT OF MARKETING **MATT PARKINSON**
VICE PRESIDENT OF INFORMATION TECHNOLOGY **DALE LaFOUNTAIN**
VICE PRESIDENT OF PRODUCTION AND SCHEDULING **CARA NIECE**
VICE PRESIDENT OF BOOK TRADE AND DIGITAL SALES **MARK BERNARDI**
GENERAL COUNSEL **KEN LIZZI**
EDITOR IN CHIEF **DAVE MARSHALL**
EDITORIAL DIRECTOR **DAVEY ESTRADA**
SENIOR BOOKS EDITOR **CHRIS WARNER**
DIRECTOR OF SPECIALTY PROJECTS **CARY GRAZZINI**
ART DIRECTOR **LIA RIBACCHI**
DIRECTOR OF PRINT PURCHASING **VANESSA TODD-HOLMES**
DIRECTOR OF DIGITAL ART AND PREPRESS **MATT DRYER**
DIRECTOR OF INTERNATIONAL PUBLISHING AND LICENSING **MICHAEL GOMBOS**
DIRECTOR OF CUSTOM PROGRAMS **KARI YADRO**
DIRECTOR OF INTERNATIONAL LICENSING **KARI TORSON**

Published by Dark Horse Books
A division of Dark Horse Comics, Inc.
10956 SE Main Street
Milwaukie, OR 97222

DarkHorse.com
Facebook.com/DarkHorseComics
Twitter.com/DarkHorseComics

First edition: February 2019
ISBN 978-1-50670-901-7

1 3 5 7 9 10 8 6 4 2
Printed in China

This volume collects *Bedtime Games* #1–#4, published by Dark Horse Comics.

Library of Congress Cataloging-in-Publication Data

Names: Keller, Nick, author. | Nolan, Conor, artist. | Fitzpatrick, Kelly,
   1988- colourist. | Hill, John J. (Letterer), letterer.
Title: Bedtime games / story by Nick Keller ; art by Conor Nolan ; colors by
   Kelly Fitzpatrick ; letters by John J. Hill ; chapter break art by Conor
   Nolan.
Description: First edition. | Milwaukie, OR : Dark Horse Books, February
   2019. | "This volume collects Bedtime Games #1-#4."
Identifiers: LCCN 2018042778 | ISBN 9781506709017
Subjects: LCSH: Graphic novels.
Classification: LCC PN6728.B377 K45 2019 | DDC 741.5/973--dc23
LC record available at https://lccn.loc.gov/2018042778

CHAPTER ONE

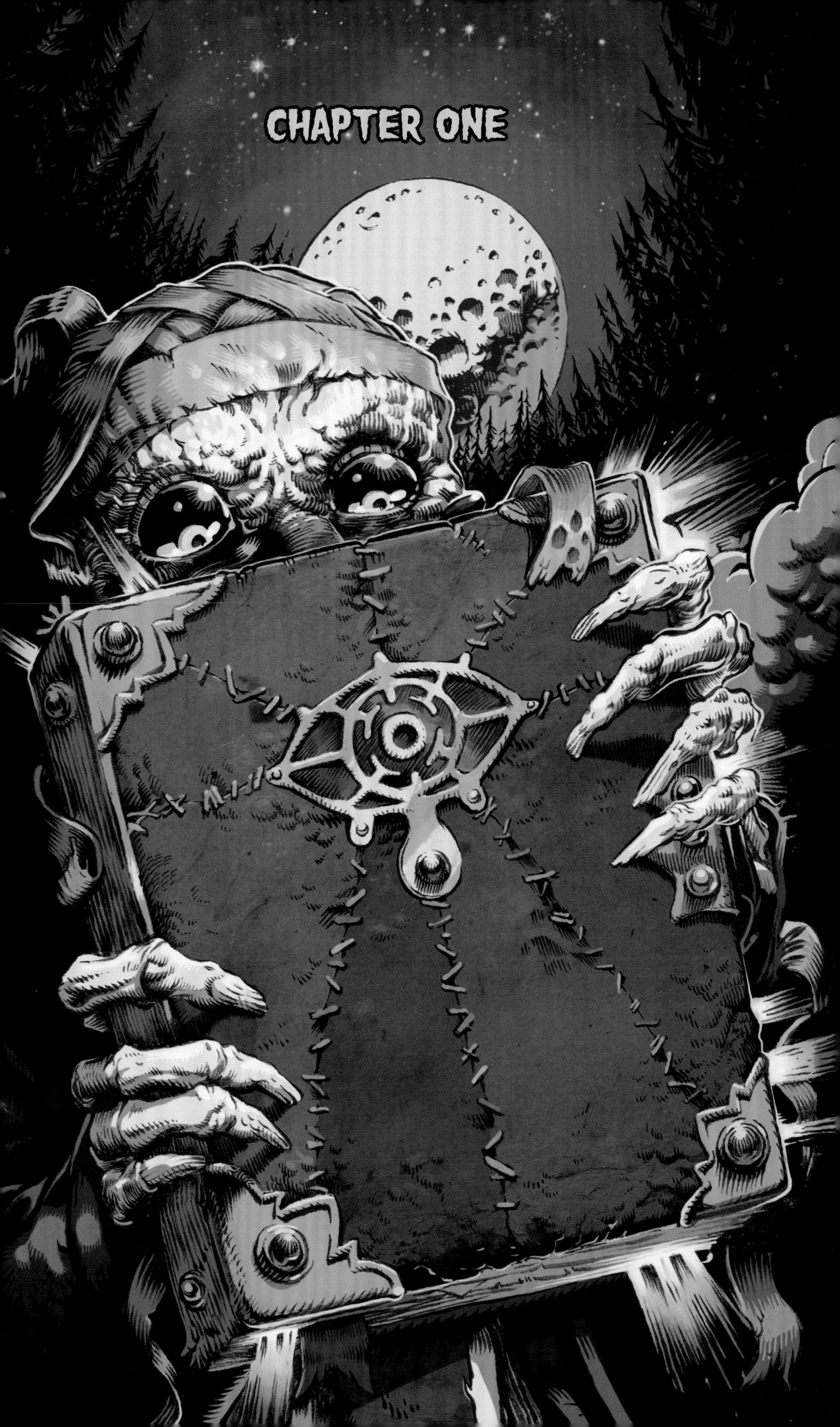

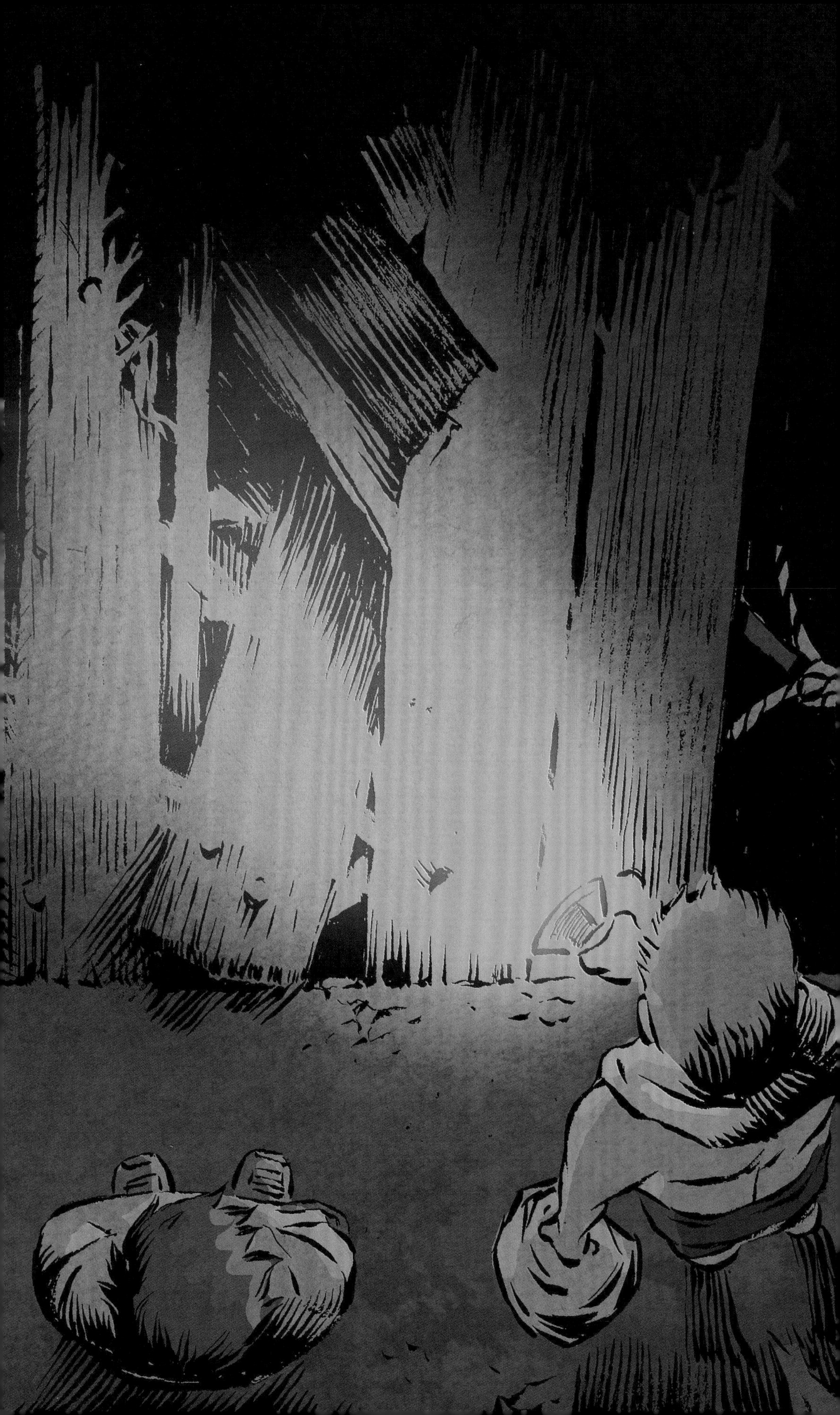

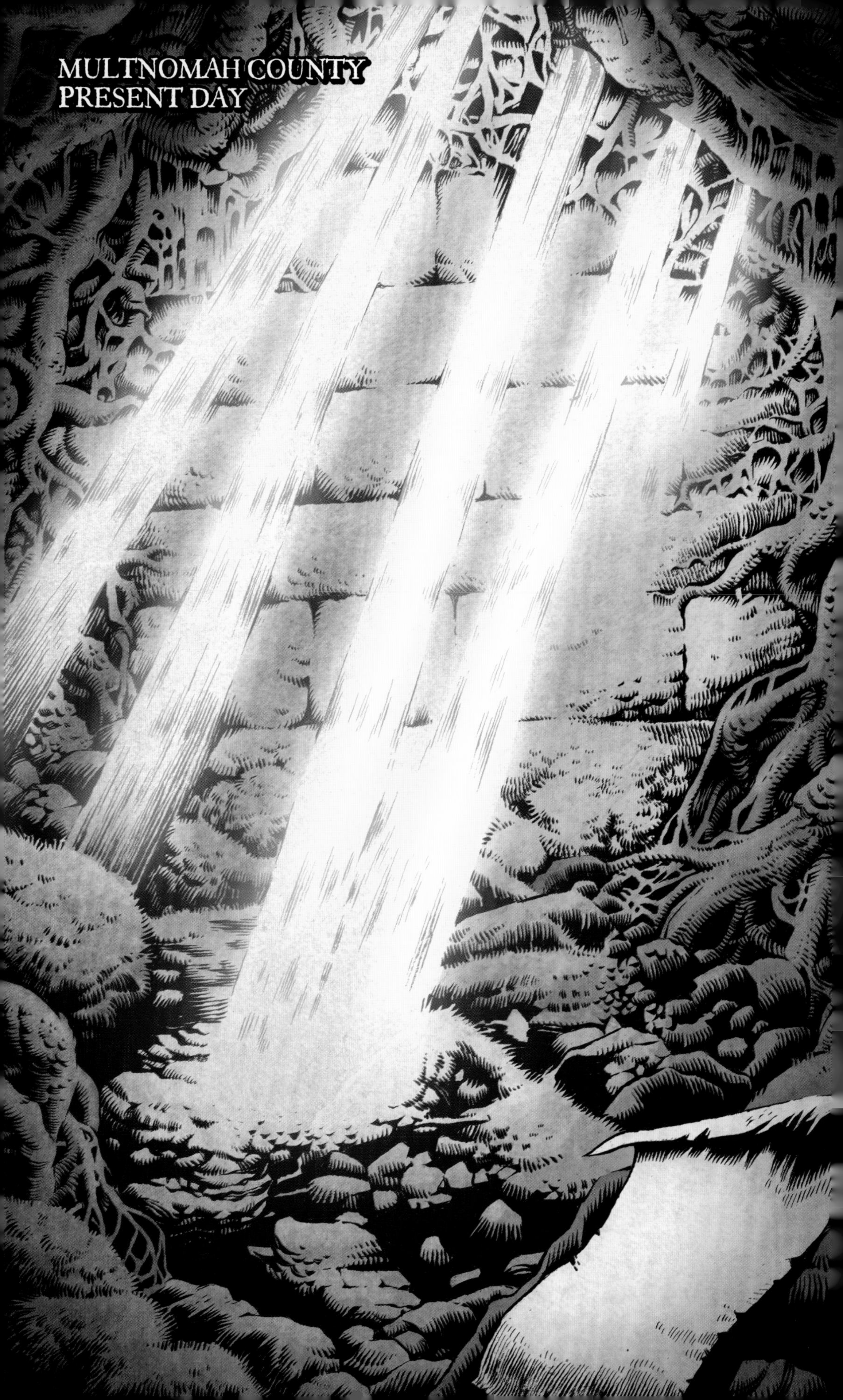
MULTNOMAH COUNTY
PRESENT DAY

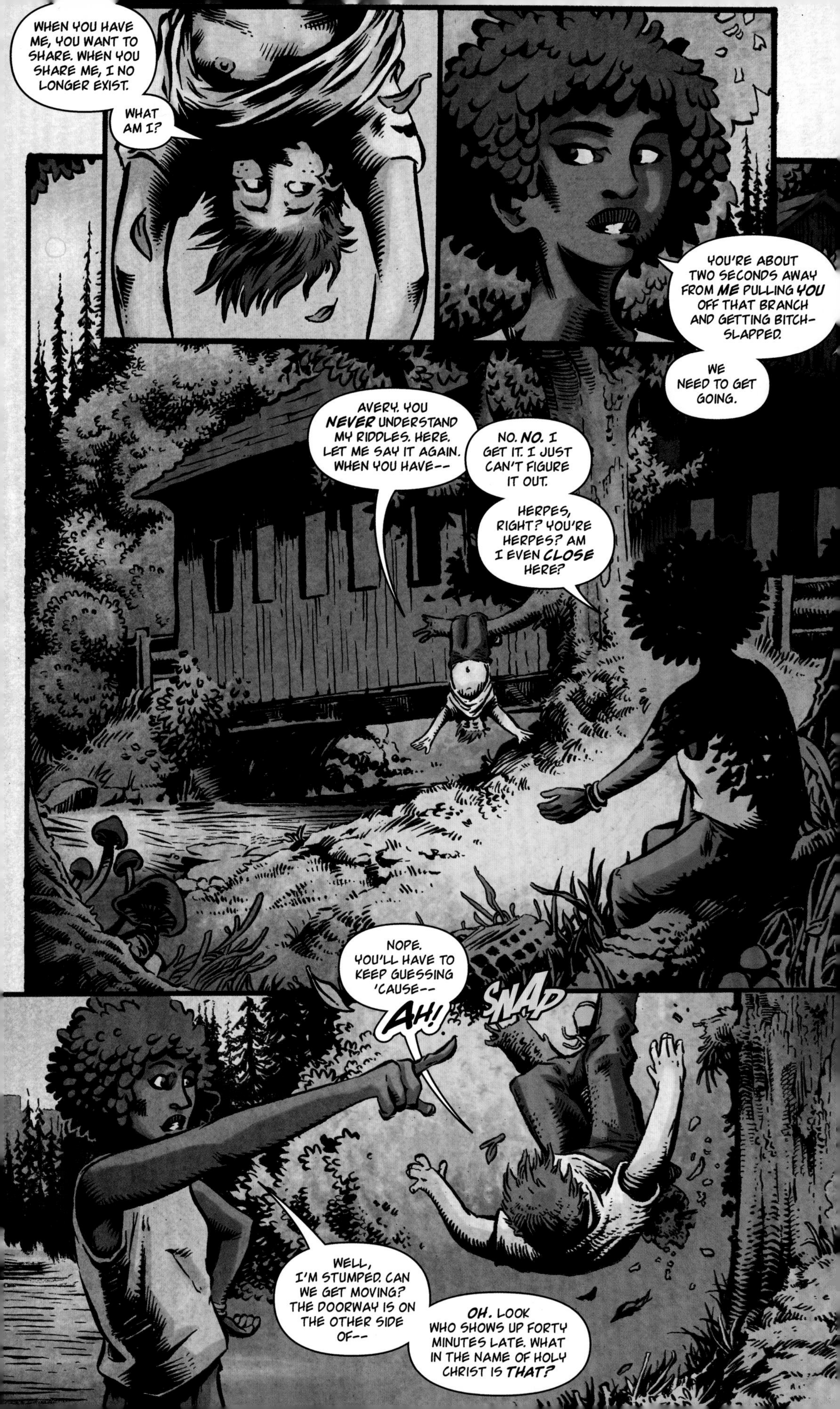

WHEN YOU HAVE ME, YOU WANT TO SHARE. WHEN YOU SHARE ME, I NO LONGER EXIST.
WHAT AM I?
YOU'RE ABOUT TWO SECONDS AWAY FROM ME PULLING YOU OFF THAT BRANCH AND GETTING BITCH-SLAPPED.
WE NEED TO GET GOING.
AVERY. YOU NEVER UNDERSTAND MY RIDDLES. HERE. LET ME SAY IT AGAIN. WHEN YOU HAVE--
NO. NO. I GET IT. I JUST CAN'T FIGURE IT OUT.
HERPES, RIGHT? YOU'RE HERPES? AM I EVEN CLOSE HERE?
NOPE. YOU'LL HAVE TO KEEP GUESSING 'CAUSE--
AH!
SNAP
WELL, I'M STUMPED. CAN WE GET MOVING? THE DOORWAY IS ON THE OTHER SIDE OF--
OH. LOOK WHO SHOWS UP FORTY MINUTES LATE. WHAT IN THE NAME OF HOLY CHRIST IS THAT?

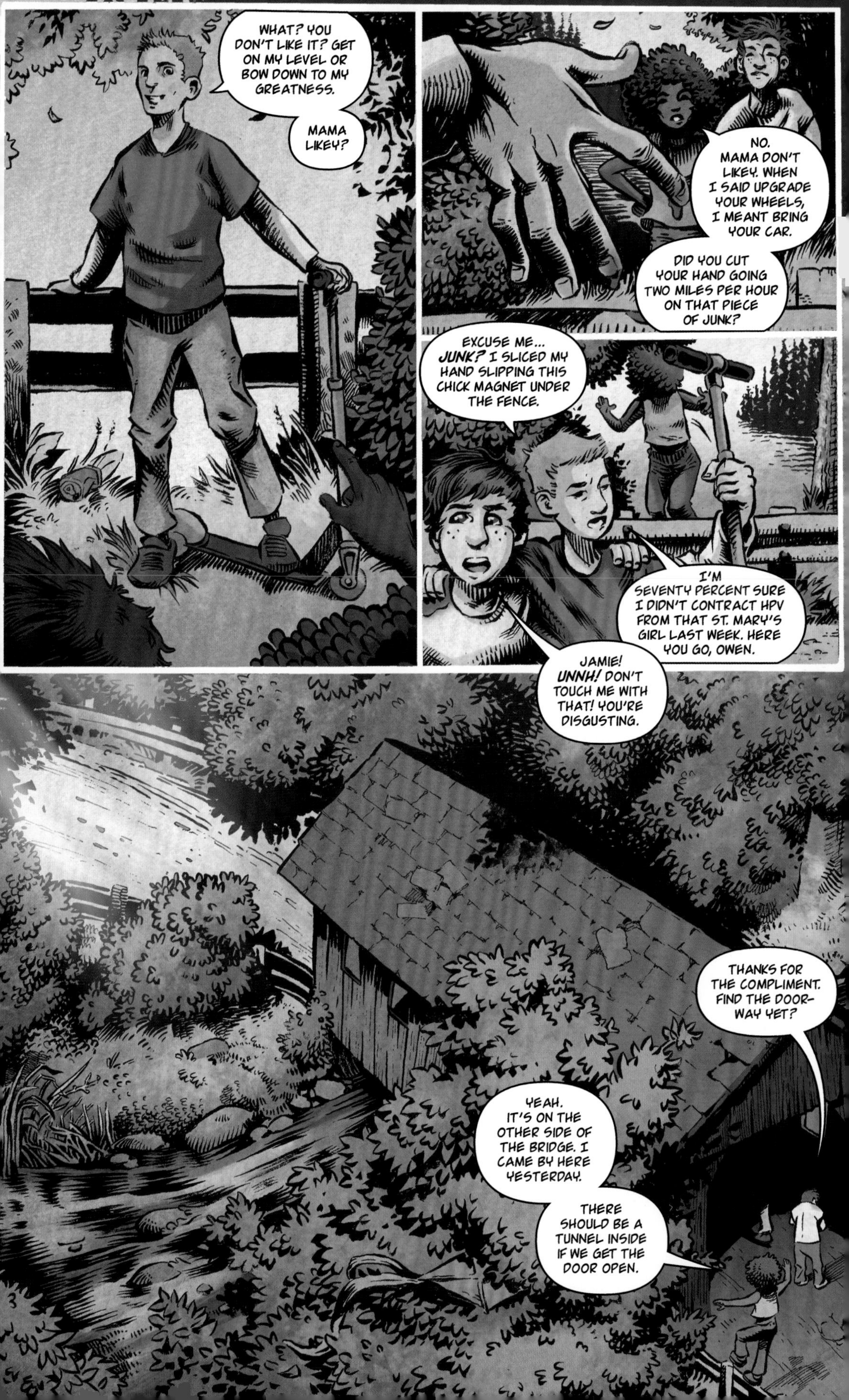

WHAT? YOU DON'T LIKE IT? GET ON MY LEVEL OR BOW DOWN TO MY GREATNESS.
MAMA LIKEY?
NO. MAMA DON'T LIKEY. WHEN I SAID UPGRADE YOUR WHEELS, I MEANT BRING YOUR CAR.
DID YOU CUT YOUR HAND GOING TWO MILES PER HOUR ON THAT PIECE OF JUNK?
EXCUSE ME... JUNK? I SLICED MY HAND SLIPPING THIS CHICK MAGNET UNDER THE FENCE.
I'M SEVENTY PERCENT SURE I DIDN'T CONTRACT HPV FROM THAT ST. MARY'S GIRL LAST WEEK. HERE YOU GO, OWEN.
JAMIE! UNNH! DON'T TOUCH ME WITH THAT! YOU'RE DISGUSTING.
THANKS FOR THE COMPLIMENT. FIND THE DOOR-WAY YET?
YEAH. IT'S ON THE OTHER SIDE OF THE BRIDGE. I CAME BY HERE YESTERDAY.
THERE SHOULD BE A TUNNEL INSIDE IF WE GET THE DOOR OPEN.

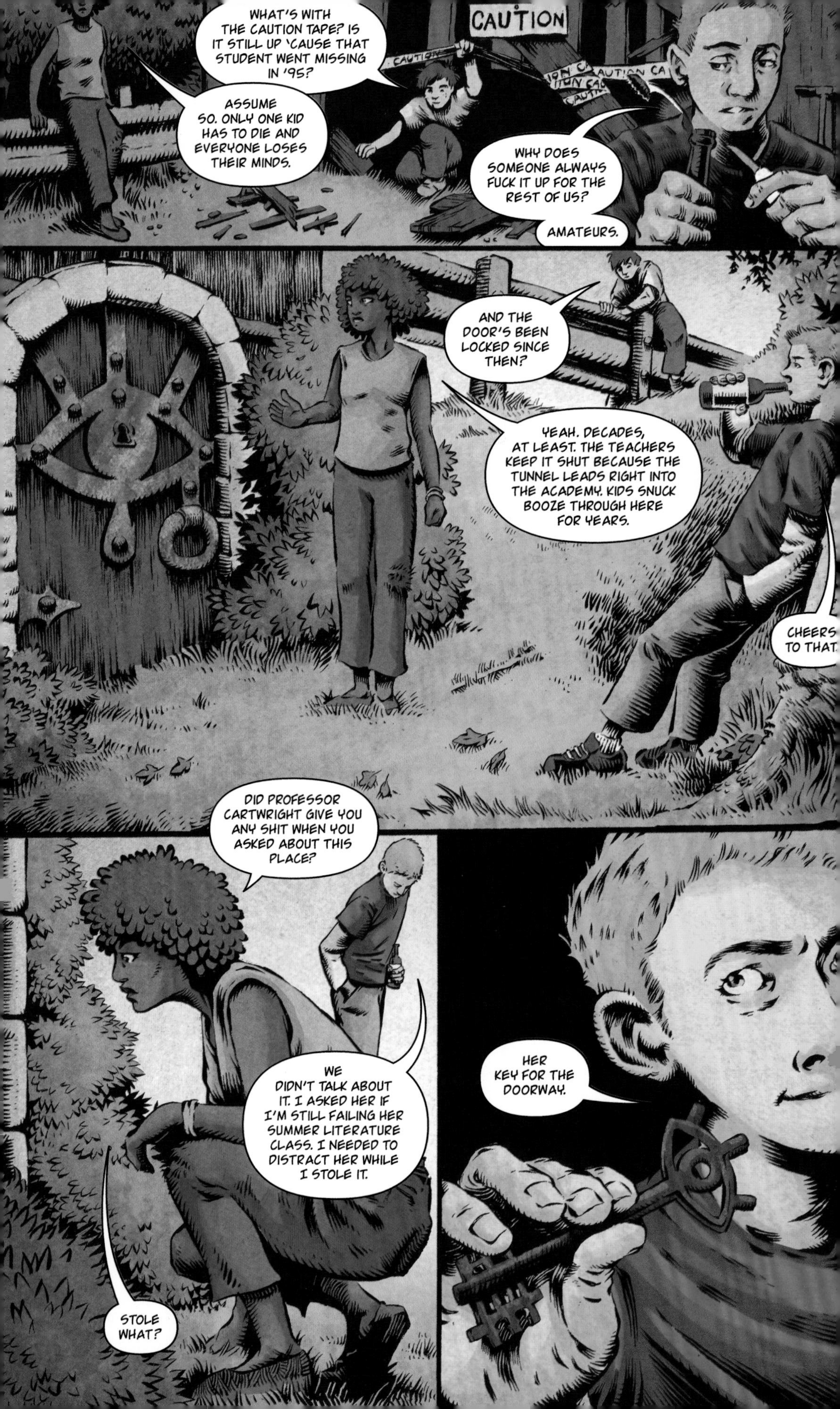
CAUTION
WHAT'S WITH THE CAUTION TAPE? IS IT STILL UP 'CAUSE THAT STUDENT WENT MISSING IN '95?
ASSUME SO. ONLY ONE KID HAS TO DIE AND EVERYONE LOSES THEIR MINDS.
WHY DOES SOMEONE ALWAYS FUCK IT UP FOR THE REST OF US?
AMATEURS.
AND THE DOOR'S BEEN LOCKED SINCE THEN?
YEAH. DECADES, AT LEAST. THE TEACHERS KEEP IT SHUT BECAUSE THE TUNNEL LEADS RIGHT INTO THE ACADEMY. KIDS SNUCK BOOZE THROUGH HERE FOR YEARS.
CHEERS TO THAT.
DID PROFESSOR CARTWRIGHT GIVE YOU ANY SHIT WHEN YOU ASKED ABOUT THIS PLACE?
WE DIDN'T TALK ABOUT IT. I ASKED HER IF I'M STILL FAILING HER SUMMER LITERATURE CLASS. I NEEDED TO DISTRACT HER WHILE I STOLE IT.
STOLE WHAT?
HER KEY FOR THE DOORWAY.

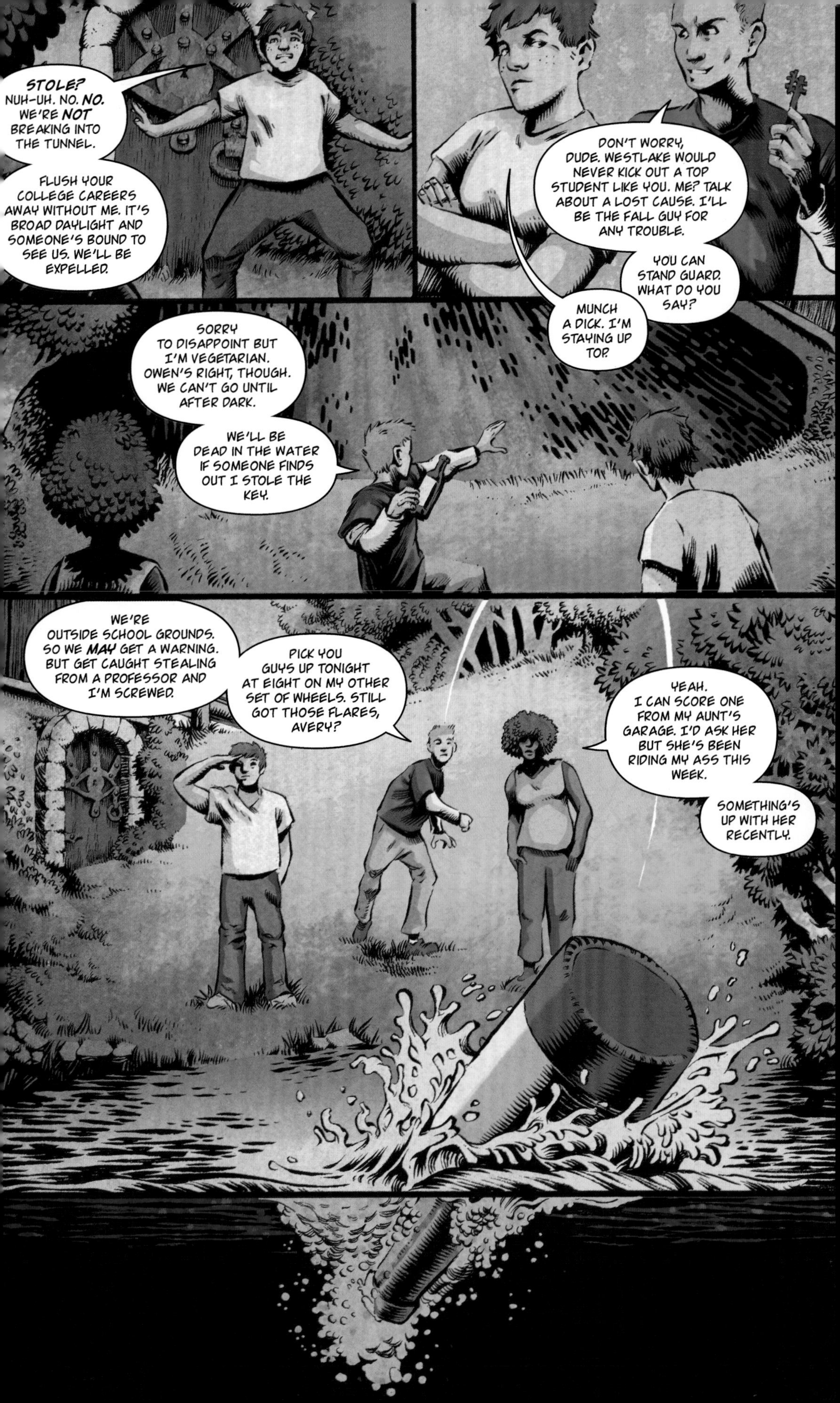
STOLE? NUH-UH. NO. NO. WE'RE NOT BREAKING INTO THE TUNNEL.
FLUSH YOUR COLLEGE CAREERS AWAY WITHOUT ME. IT'S BROAD DAYLIGHT AND SOMEONE'S BOUND TO SEE US. WE'LL BE EXPELLED.
DON'T WORRY, DUDE. WESTLAKE WOULD NEVER KICK OUT A TOP STUDENT LIKE YOU. ME? TALK ABOUT A LOST CAUSE. I'LL BE THE FALL GUY FOR ANY TROUBLE.
YOU CAN STAND GUARD. WHAT DO YOU SAY?
MUNCH A DICK. I'M STAYING UP TOP.
SORRY TO DISAPPOINT BUT I'M VEGETARIAN. OWEN'S RIGHT, THOUGH. WE CAN'T GO UNTIL AFTER DARK.
WE'LL BE DEAD IN THE WATER IF SOMEONE FINDS OUT I STOLE THE KEY.
WE'RE OUTSIDE SCHOOL GROUNDS. SO WE MAY GET A WARNING. BUT GET CAUGHT STEALING FROM A PROFESSOR AND I'M SCREWED.
PICK YOU GUYS UP TONIGHT AT EIGHT ON MY OTHER SET OF WHEELS. STILL GOT THOSE FLARES, AVERY?
YEAH. I CAN SCORE ONE FROM MY AUNT'S GARAGE. I'D ASK HER BUT SHE'S BEEN RIDING MY ASS THIS WEEK.
SOMETHING'S UP WITH HER RECENTLY.

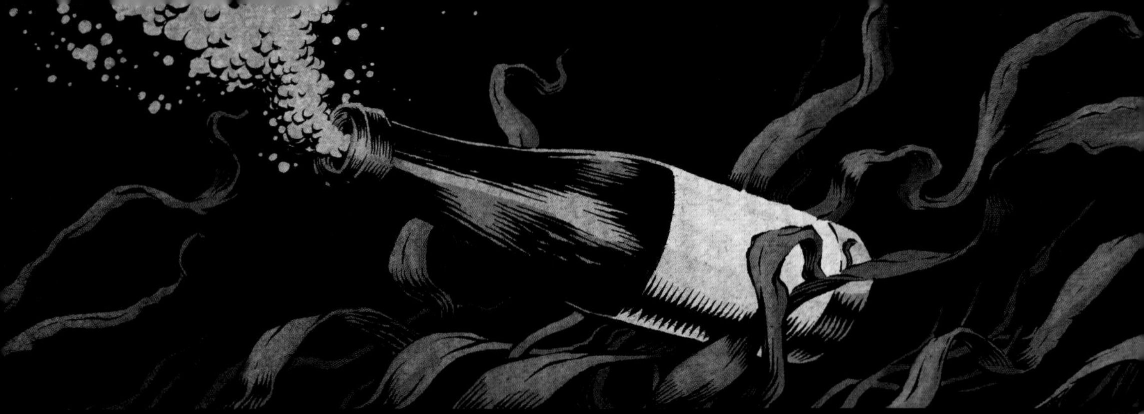

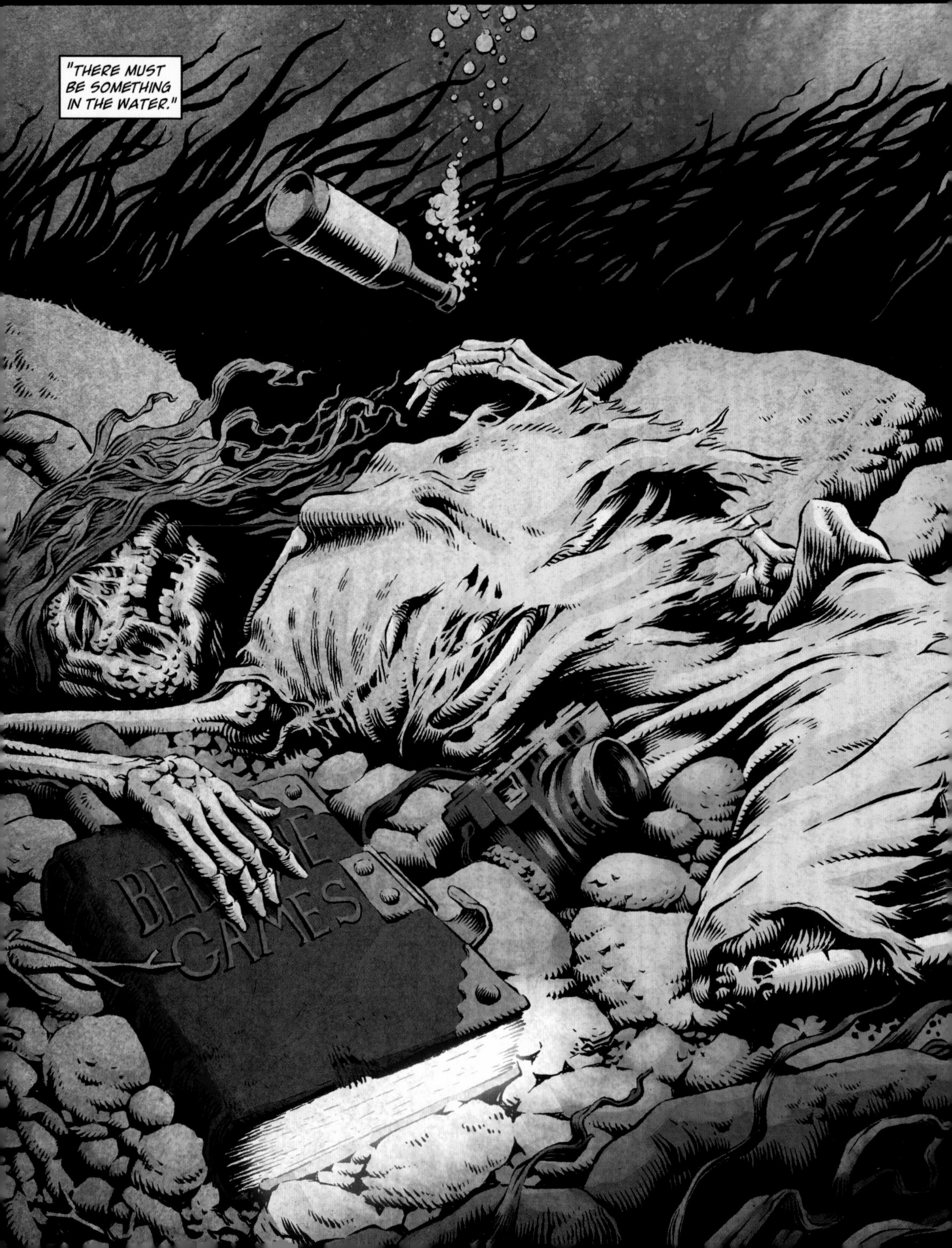
"THERE MUST BE SOMETHING IN THE WATER."

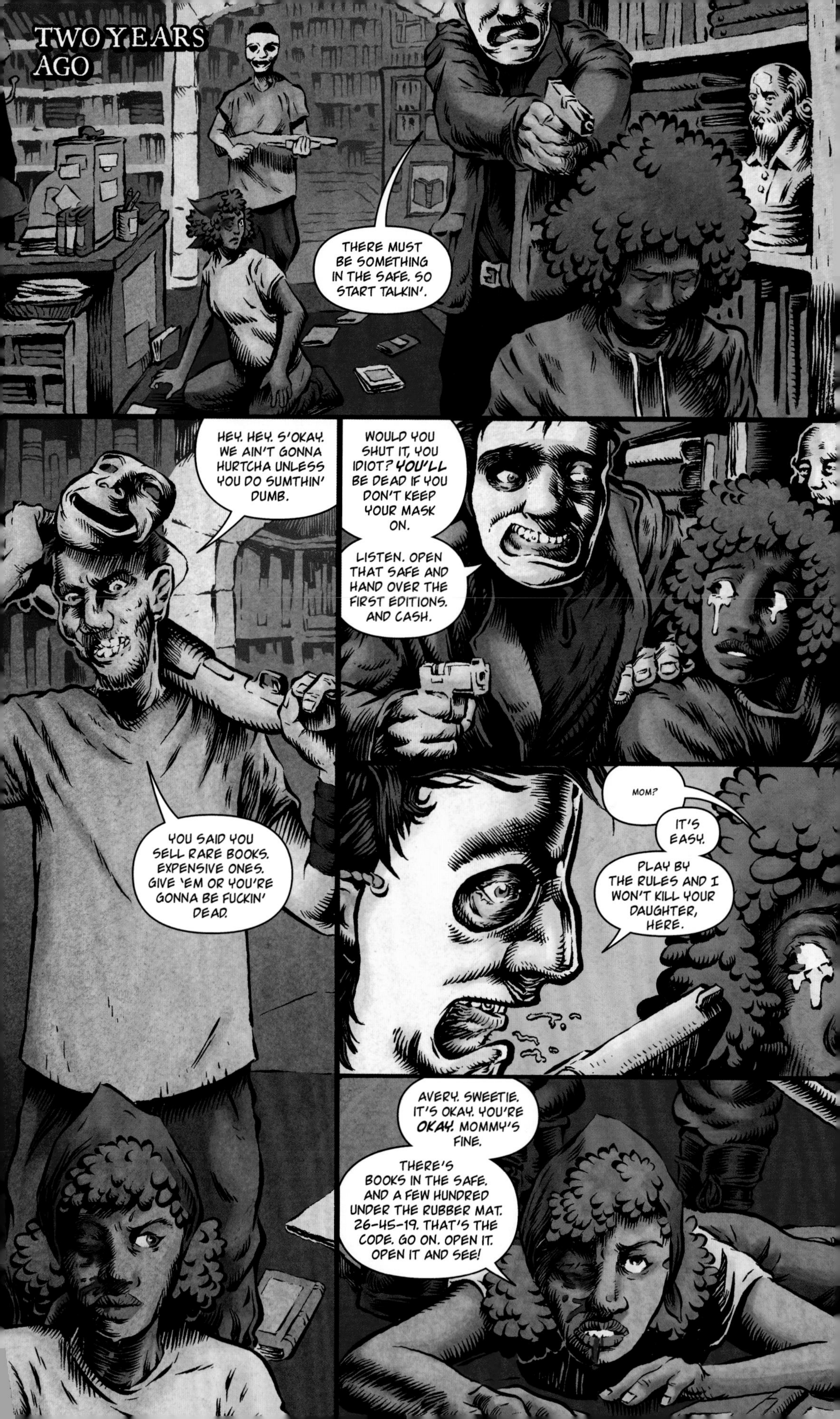
TWO YEARS AGO
THERE MUST BE SOMETHING IN THE SAFE. SO START TALKIN'.
HEY. HEY. S'OKAY. WE AIN'T GONNA HURTCHA UNLESS YOU DO SUMTHIN' DUMB.
WOULD YOU SHUT IT, YOU IDIOT? YOU'LL BE DEAD IF YOU DON'T KEEP YOUR MASK ON.
LISTEN. OPEN THAT SAFE AND HAND OVER THE FIRST EDITIONS. AND CASH.
YOU SAID YOU SELL RARE BOOKS. EXPENSIVE ONES. GIVE 'EM OR YOU'RE GONNA BE FUCKIN' DEAD.
MOM?
IT'S EASY.
PLAY BY THE RULES AND I WON'T KILL YOUR DAUGHTER, HERE.
AVERY. SWEETIE. IT'S OKAY. YOU'RE OKAY. MOMMY'S FINE.
THERE'S BOOKS IN THE SAFE. AND A FEW HUNDRED UNDER THE RUBBER MAT. 26-45-19. THAT'S THE CODE. GO ON. OPEN IT. OPEN IT AND SEE!

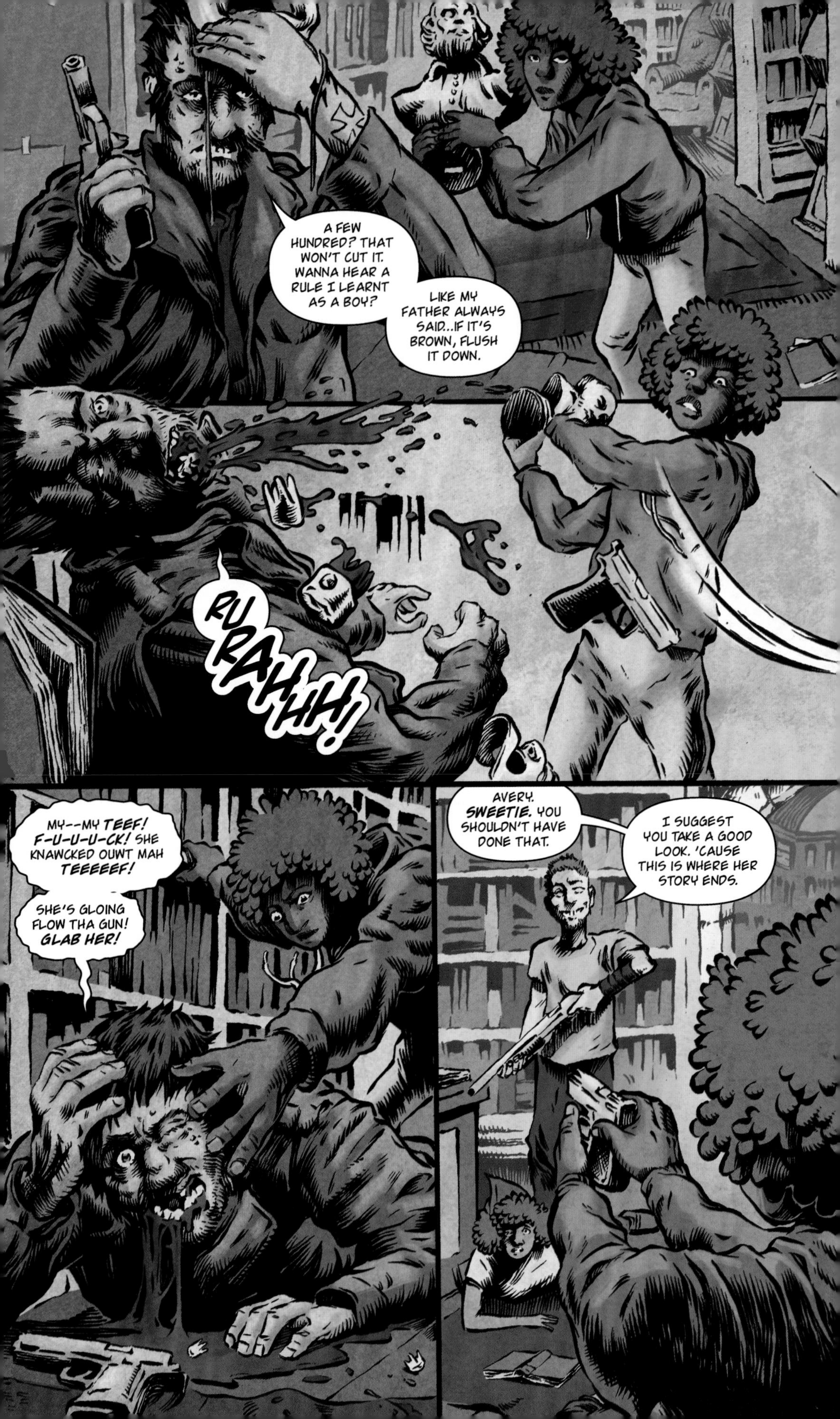
A FEW HUNDRED? THAT WON'T CUT IT. WANNA HEAR A RULE I LEARNT AS A BOY?
LIKE MY FATHER ALWAYS SAID...IF IT'S BROWN, FLUSH IT DOWN.
RU RAHHH!
MY--MY **TEEF!** **F-U-U-U-CK!** SHE KNAWCKED OUWT MAH **TEEEEEF!**
SHE'S GLOING FLOW THA GUN! **GLAB HER!**
AVERY. **SWEETIE.** YOU SHOULDN'T HAVE DONE THAT.
I SUGGEST YOU TAKE A GOOD LOOK. 'CAUSE THIS IS WHERE HER STORY ENDS.

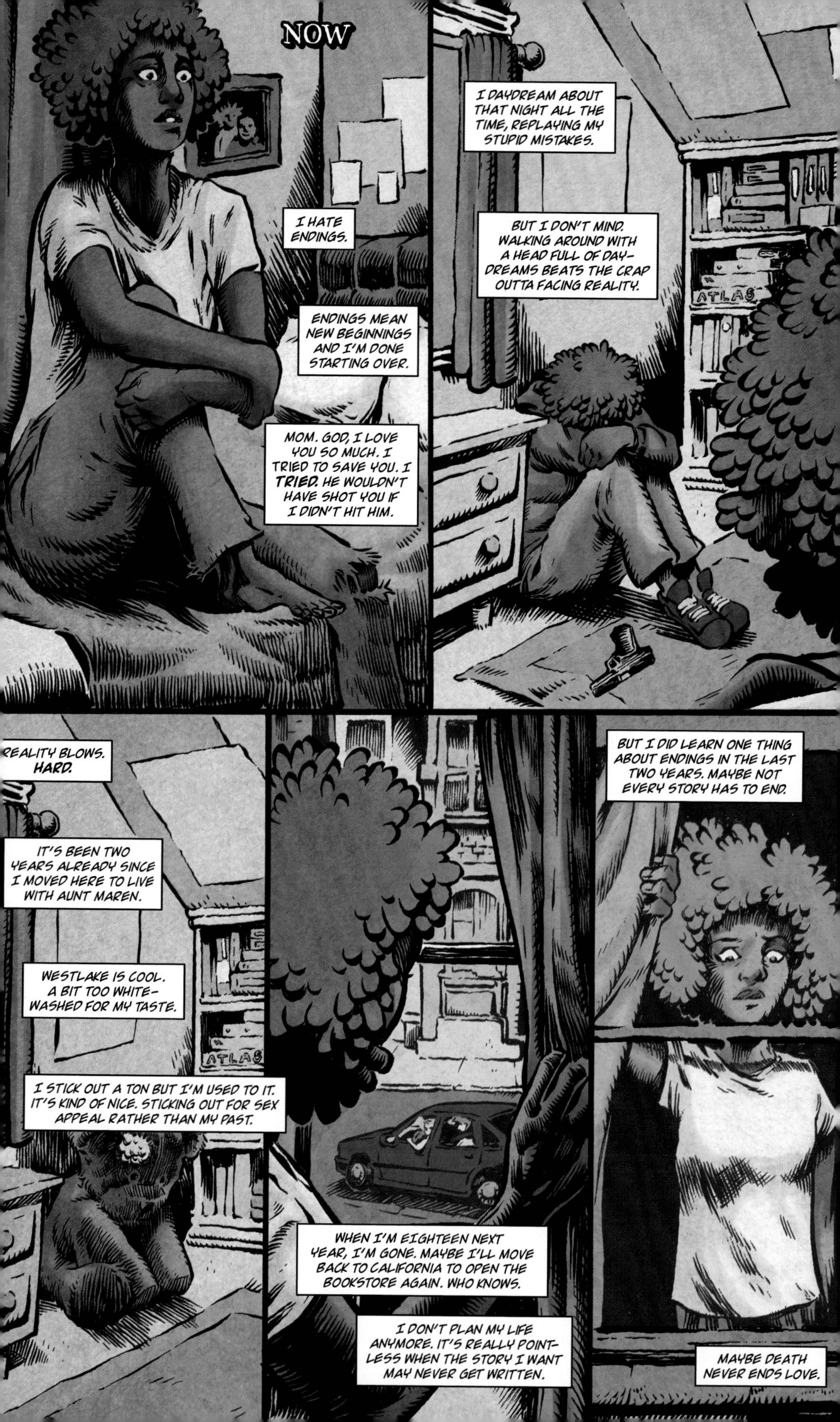
NOW
I HATE ENDINGS.
ENDINGS MEAN NEW BEGINNINGS AND I'M DONE STARTING OVER.
MOM. GOD, I LOVE YOU SO MUCH. I TRIED TO SAVE YOU. I **TRIED**. HE WOULDN'T HAVE SHOT YOU IF I DIDN'T HIT HIM.
I DAYDREAM ABOUT THAT NIGHT ALL THE TIME, REPLAYING MY STUPID MISTAKES.
BUT I DON'T MIND. WALKING AROUND WITH A HEAD FULL OF DAY-DREAMS BEATS THE CRAP OUTTA FACING REALITY.
ATLAS
REALITY BLOWS. **HARD.**
IT'S BEEN TWO YEARS ALREADY SINCE I MOVED HERE TO LIVE WITH AUNT MAREN.
WESTLAKE IS COOL. A BIT TOO WHITE-WASHED FOR MY TASTE.
ATLAS
I STICK OUT A TON BUT I'M USED TO IT. IT'S KIND OF NICE. STICKING OUT FOR SEX APPEAL RATHER THAN MY PAST.
WHEN I'M EIGHTEEN NEXT YEAR, I'M GONE. MAYBE I'LL MOVE BACK TO CALIFORNIA TO OPEN THE BOOKSTORE AGAIN. WHO KNOWS.
I DON'T PLAN MY LIFE ANYMORE. IT'S REALLY POINT-LESS WHEN THE STORY I WANT MAY NEVER GET WRITTEN.
BUT I DID LEARN ONE THING ABOUT ENDINGS IN THE LAST TWO YEARS. MAYBE NOT EVERY STORY HAS TO END.
MAYBE DEATH NEVER ENDS LOVE.

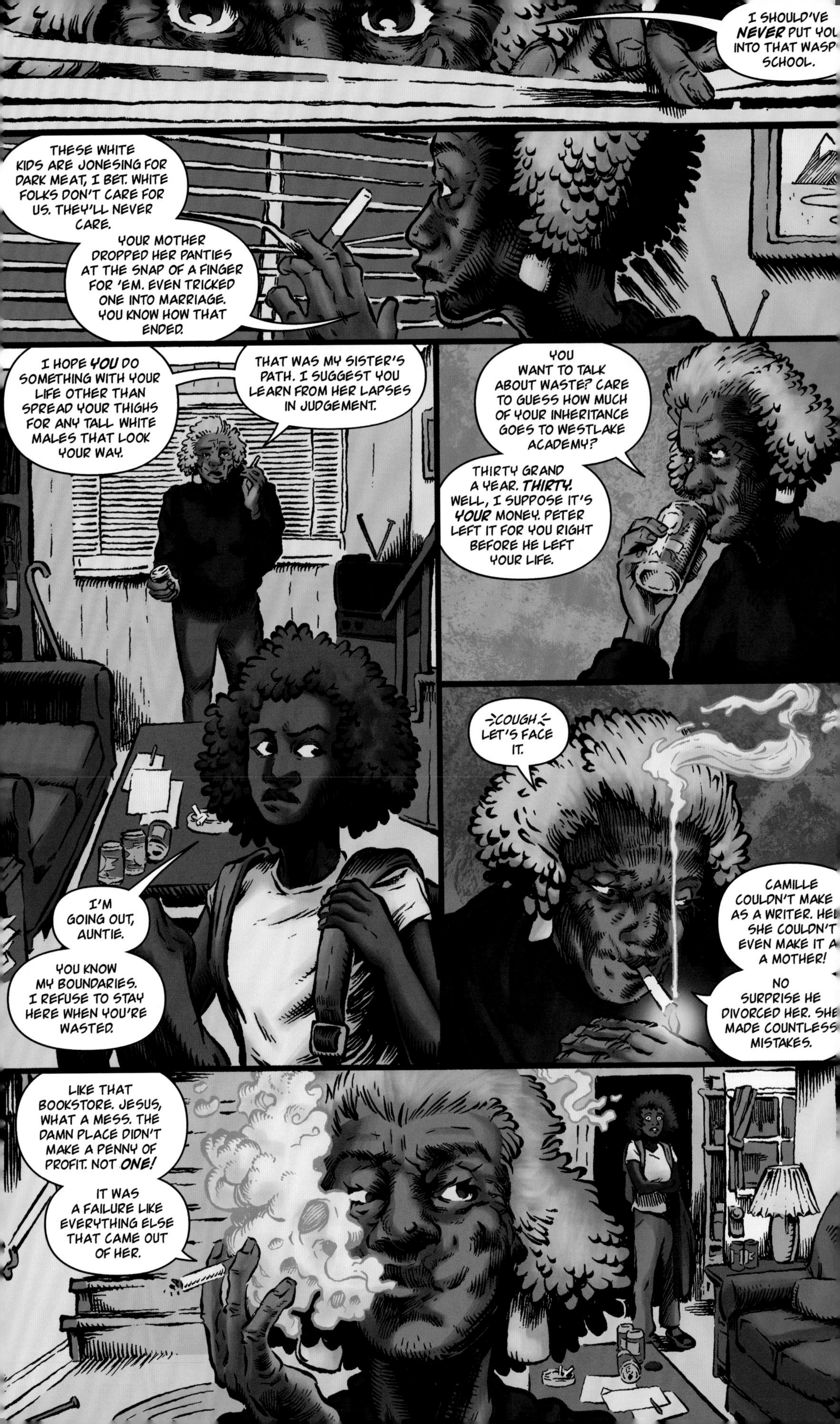

I SHOULD'VE NEVER PUT YOU INTO THAT WASP SCHOOL.
THESE WHITE KIDS ARE JONESING FOR DARK MEAT, I BET. WHITE FOLKS DON'T CARE FOR US. THEY'LL NEVER CARE.
YOUR MOTHER DROPPED HER PANTIES AT THE SNAP OF A FINGER FOR 'EM. EVEN TRICKED ONE INTO MARRIAGE. YOU KNOW HOW THAT ENDED.
I HOPE YOU DO SOMETHING WITH YOUR LIFE OTHER THAN SPREAD YOUR THIGHS FOR ANY TALL WHITE MALES THAT LOOK YOUR WAY.
THAT WAS MY SISTER'S PATH. I SUGGEST YOU LEARN FROM HER LAPSES IN JUDGEMENT.
YOU WANT TO TALK ABOUT WASTE? CARE TO GUESS HOW MUCH OF YOUR INHERITANCE GOES TO WESTLAKE ACADEMY?
THIRTY GRAND A YEAR. THIRTY. WELL, I SUPPOSE IT'S YOUR MONEY. PETER LEFT IT FOR YOU RIGHT BEFORE HE LEFT YOUR LIFE.
COUGH LET'S FACE IT.
I'M GOING OUT, AUNTIE.
YOU KNOW MY BOUNDARIES. I REFUSE TO STAY HERE WHEN YOU'RE WASTED.
CAMILLE COULDN'T MAKE AS A WRITER. HE SHE COULDN'T EVEN MAKE IT A A MOTHER!
NO SURPRISE HE DIVORCED HER. SHE MADE COUNTLESS MISTAKES.
LIKE THAT BOOKSTORE. JESUS, WHAT A MESS. THE DAMN PLACE DIDN'T MAKE A PENNY OF PROFIT. NOT ONE!
IT WAS A FAILURE LIKE EVERYTHING ELSE THAT CAME OUT OF HER.

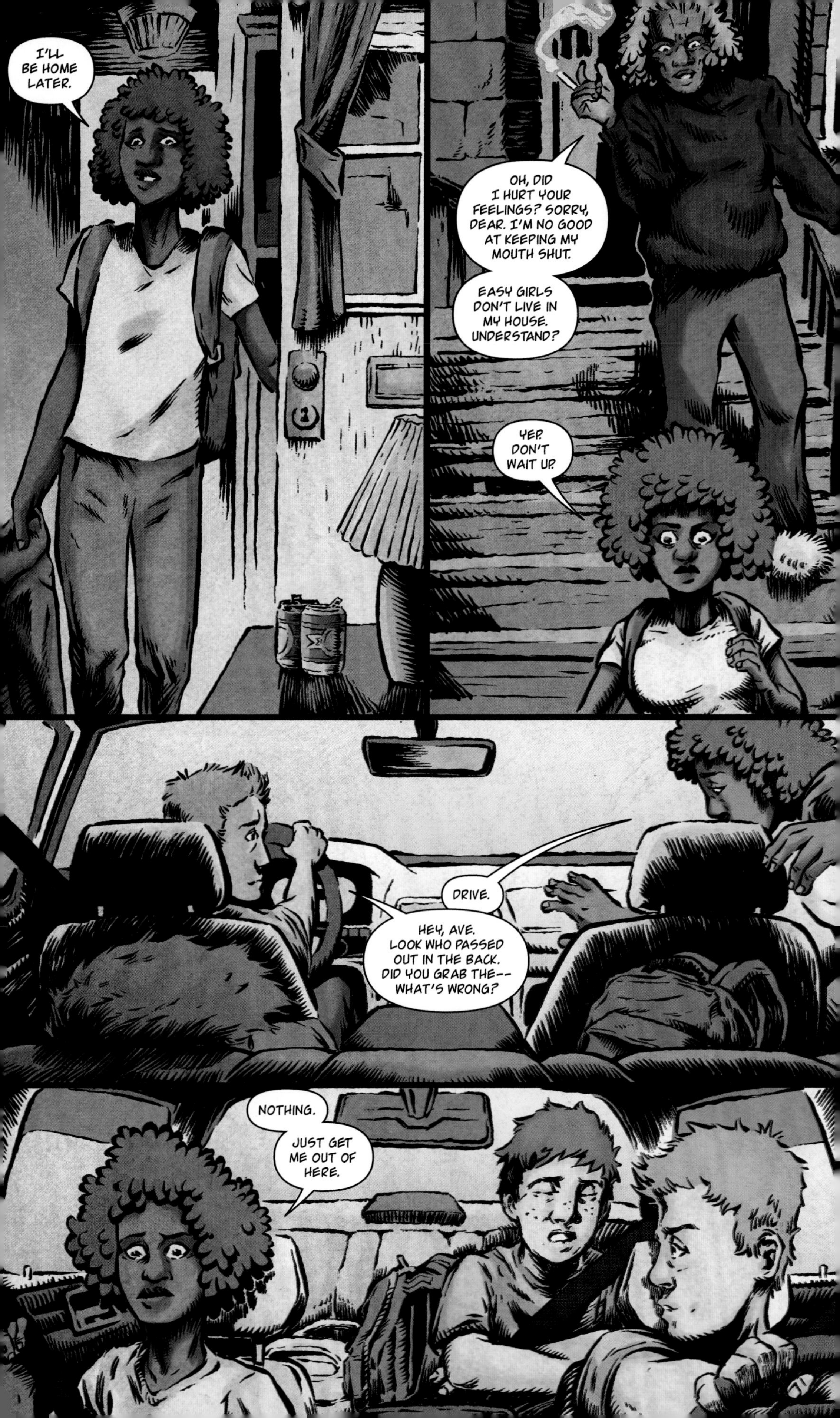
I'LL BE HOME LATER.
OH, DID I HURT YOUR FEELINGS? SORRY, DEAR. I'M NO GOOD AT KEEPING MY MOUTH SHUT.
EASY GIRLS DON'T LIVE IN MY HOUSE. UNDERSTAND?
YEP. DON'T WAIT UP.
HEY, AVE. LOOK WHO PASSED OUT IN THE BACK. DID YOU GRAB THE-- WHAT'S WRONG?
DRIVE.
NOTHING.
JUST GET ME OUT OF HERE.

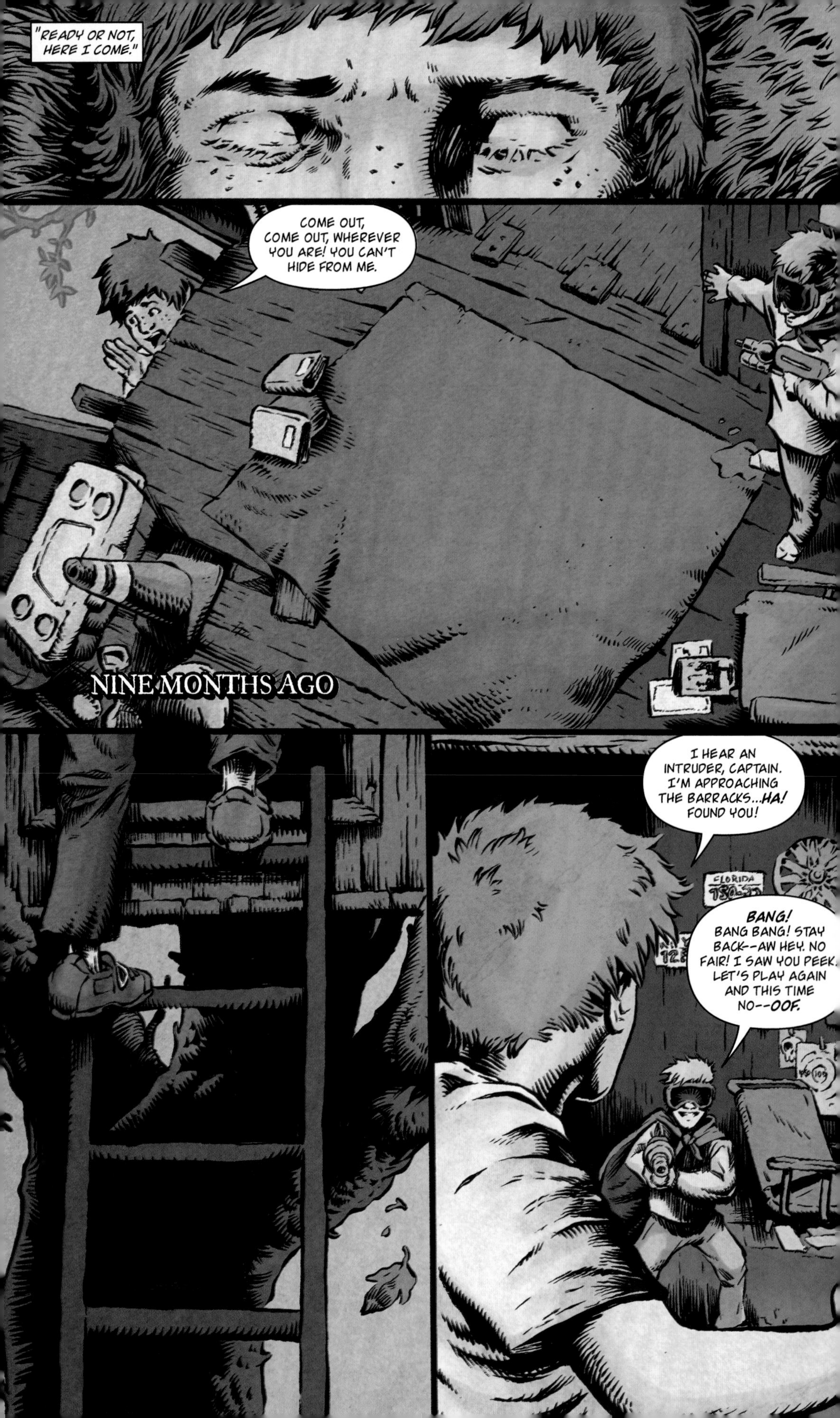
"READY OR NOT, HERE I COME."
COME OUT, COME OUT, WHEREVER YOU ARE! YOU CAN'T HIDE FROM ME.
NINE MONTHS AGO
I HEAR AN INTRUDER, CAPTAIN. I'M APPROACHING THE BARRACKS...HA! FOUND YOU!
FLORIDA
BANG! BANG BANG! STAY BACK--AW HEY. NO FAIR! I SAW YOU PEEK. LET'S PLAY AGAIN AND THIS TIME NO--OOF.

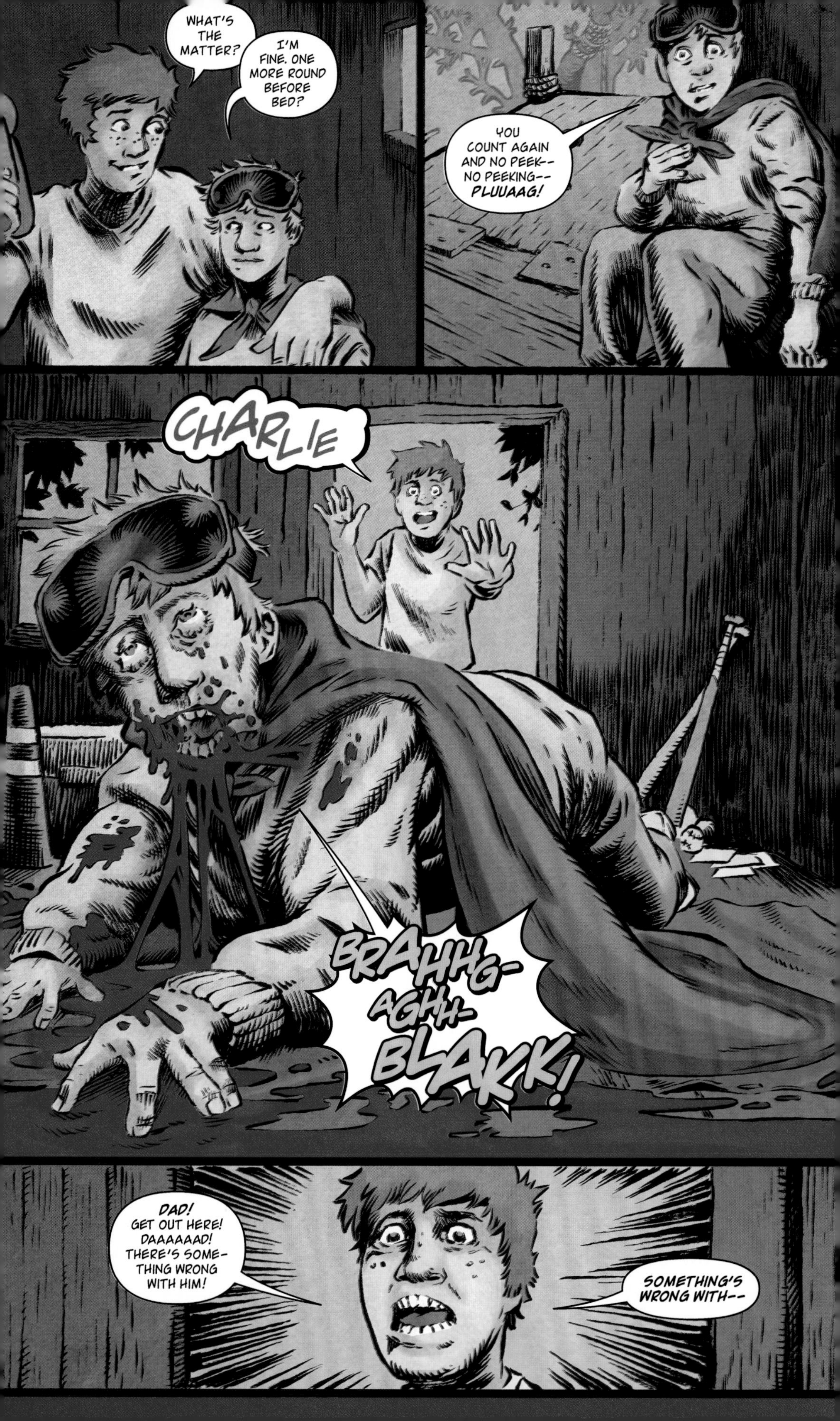
WHAT'S THE MATTER?
I'M FINE. ONE MORE ROUND BEFORE BED?
YOU COUNT AGAIN AND NO PEEK-- NO PEEKING-- PLUUAAG!
CHARLIE
BRAHHG-AGHH-BLAKK!
DAD! GET OUT HERE! DAAAAAAD! THERE'S SOME-THING WRONG WITH HIM!
SOMETHING'S WRONG WITH--

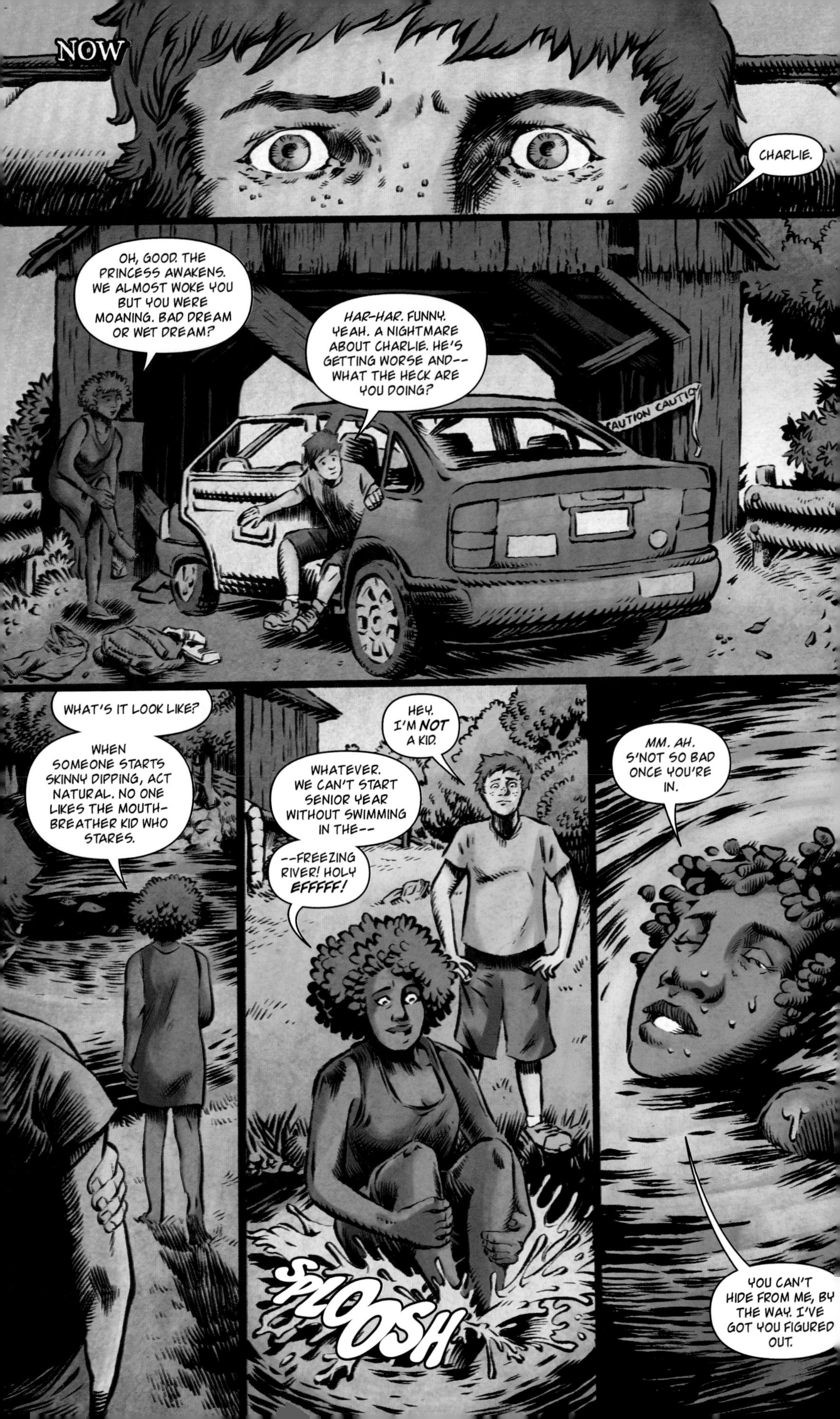
NOW
CHARLIE.
OH, GOOD. THE PRINCESS AWAKENS. WE ALMOST WOKE YOU BUT YOU WERE MOANING. BAD DREAM OR WET DREAM?
HAR-HAR. FUNNY. YEAH. A NIGHTMARE ABOUT CHARLIE. HE'S GETTING WORSE AND-- WHAT THE HECK ARE YOU DOING?
CAUTION CAUTIO
WHAT'S IT LOOK LIKE?
WHEN SOMEONE STARTS SKINNY DIPPING, ACT NATURAL. NO ONE LIKES THE MOUTH-BREATHER KID WHO STARES.
HEY. I'M NOT A KID.
WHATEVER. WE CAN'T START SENIOR YEAR WITHOUT SWIMMING IN THE--
--FREEZING RIVER! HOLY EFFFFF!
SPLOOSH
MM. AH. S'NOT SO BAD ONCE YOU'RE IN.
YOU CAN'T HIDE FROM ME, BY THE WAY. I'VE GOT YOU FIGURED OUT.

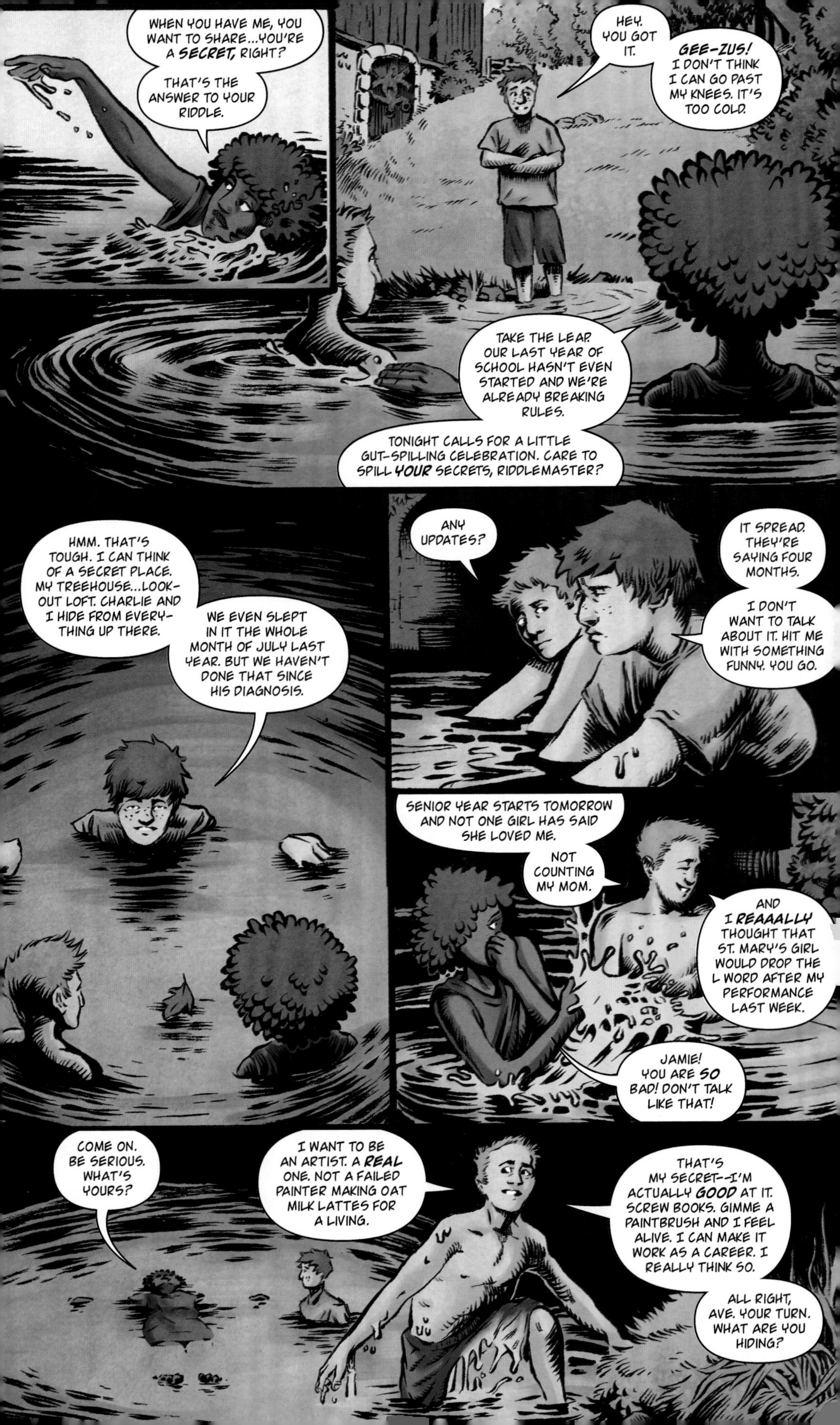
WHEN YOU HAVE ME, YOU WANT TO SHARE...YOU'RE A **SECRET,** RIGHT?
THAT'S THE ANSWER TO YOUR RIDDLE.
HEY. YOU GOT IT.
GEE-ZUS! I DON'T THINK I CAN GO PAST MY KNEES. IT'S TOO COLD.
TAKE THE LEAP. OUR LAST YEAR OF SCHOOL HASN'T EVEN STARTED AND WE'RE ALREADY BREAKING RULES.
TONIGHT CALLS FOR A LITTLE GUT-SPILLING CELEBRATION. CARE TO SPILL **YOUR** SECRETS, RIDDLEMASTER?
HMM. THAT'S TOUGH. I CAN THINK OF A SECRET PLACE. MY TREEHOUSE...LOOK-OUT LOFT. CHARLIE AND I HIDE FROM EVERY-THING UP THERE.
WE EVEN SLEPT IN IT THE WHOLE MONTH OF JULY LAST YEAR. BUT WE HAVEN'T DONE THAT SINCE HIS DIAGNOSIS.
ANY UPDATES?
IT SPREAD. THEY'RE SAYING FOUR MONTHS.
I DON'T WANT TO TALK ABOUT IT. HIT ME WITH SOMETHING FUNNY. YOU GO.
SENIOR YEAR STARTS TOMORROW AND NOT ONE GIRL HAS SAID SHE LOVED ME.
NOT COUNTING MY MOM.
AND I **REAAALLY** THOUGHT THAT ST. MARY'S GIRL WOULD DROP THE L WORD AFTER MY PERFORMANCE LAST WEEK.
JAMIE! YOU ARE **SO** BAD! DON'T TALK LIKE THAT!
COME ON. BE SERIOUS. WHAT'S YOURS?
I WANT TO BE AN ARTIST. A **REAL** ONE. NOT A FAILED PAINTER MAKING OAT MILK LATTES FOR A LIVING.
THAT'S MY SECRET--I'M ACTUALLY **GOOD** AT IT. SCREW BOOKS. GIMME A PAINTBRUSH AND I FEEL ALIVE. I CAN MAKE IT WORK AS A CAREER. I REALLY THINK SO.
ALL RIGHT, AVE. YOUR TURN. WHAT ARE YOU HIDING?

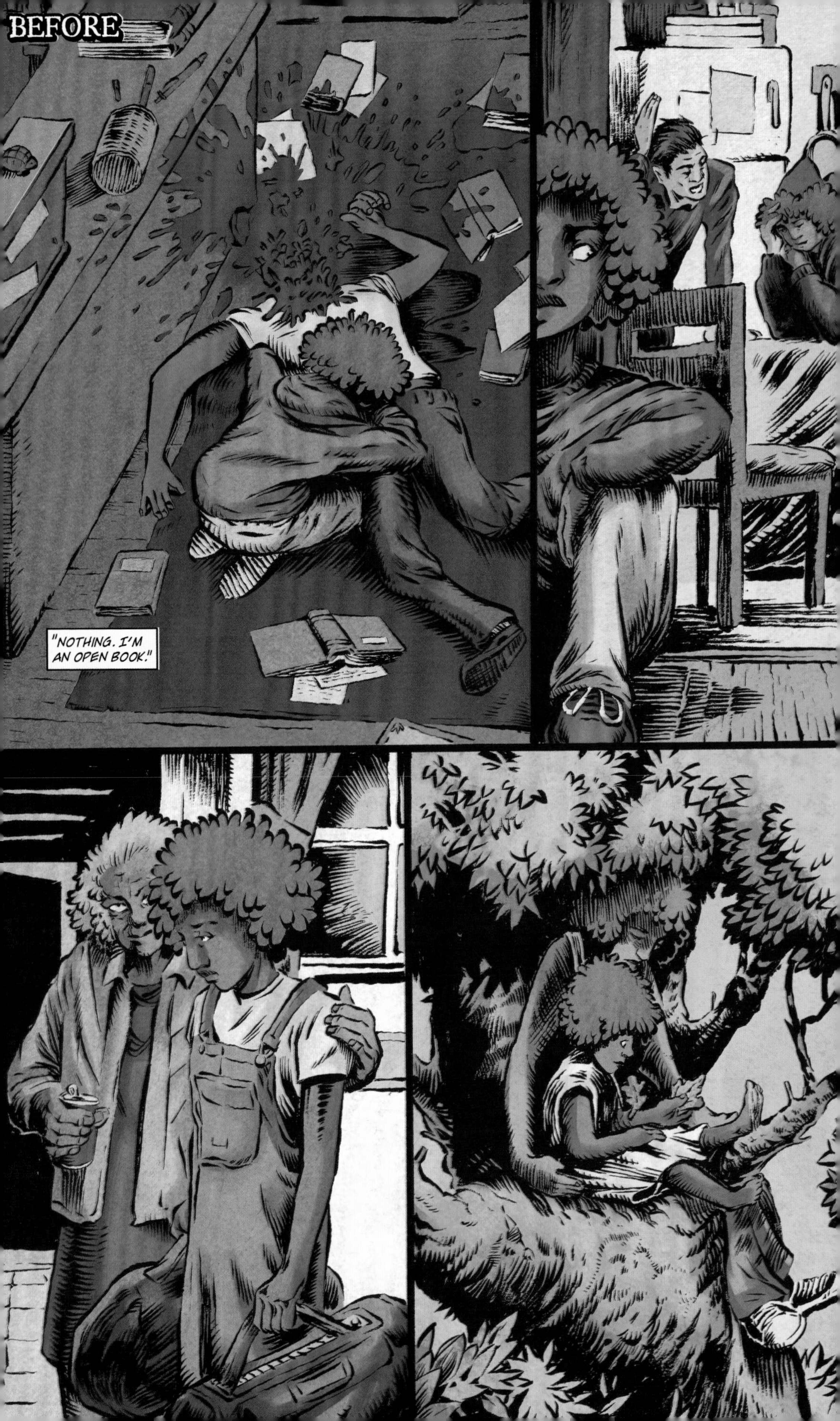
BEFORE
"NOTHING. I'M AN OPEN BOOK."

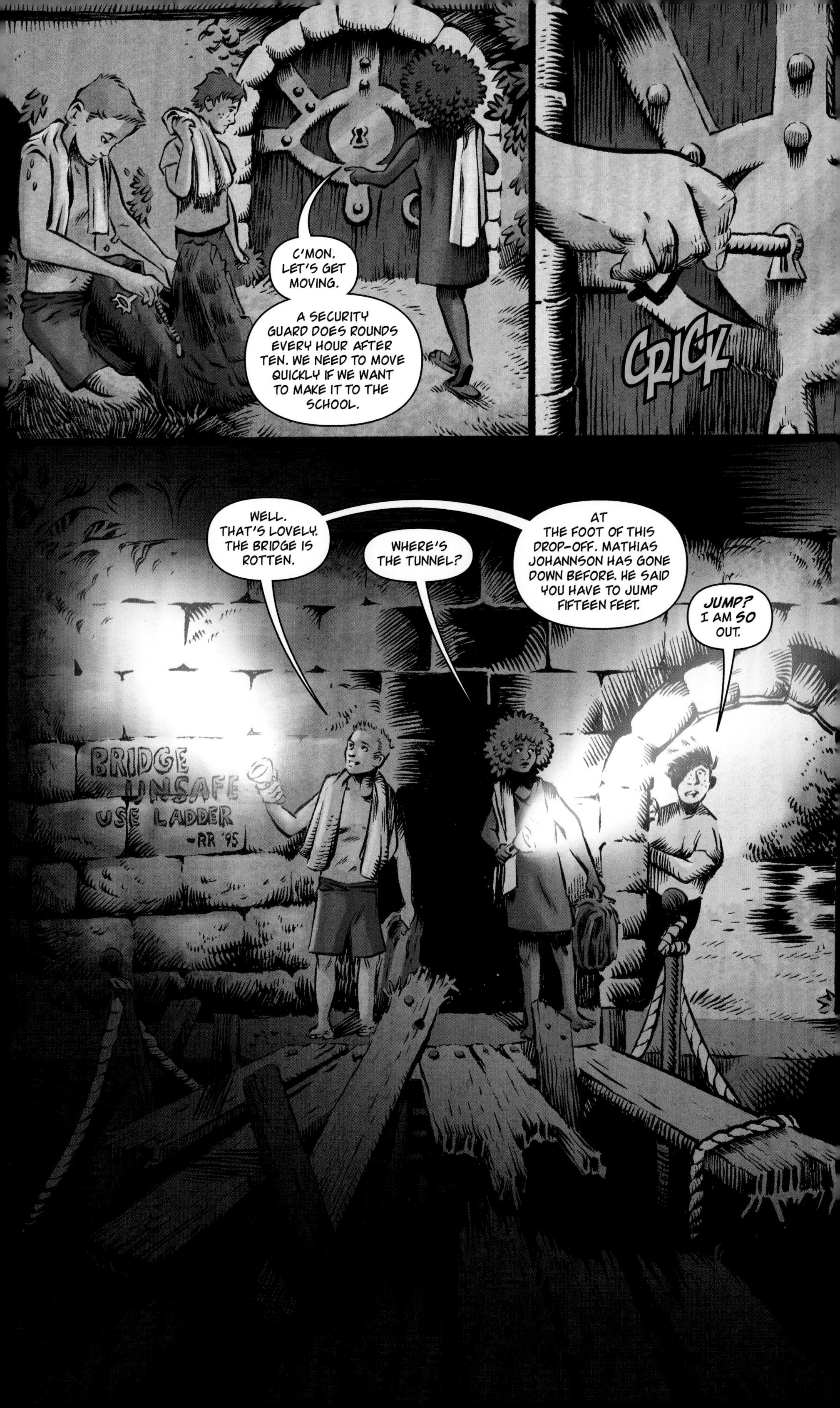

C'MON. LET'S GET MOVING.
A SECURITY GUARD DOES ROUNDS EVERY HOUR AFTER TEN. WE NEED TO MOVE QUICKLY IF WE WANT TO MAKE IT TO THE SCHOOL.
CRICK
WELL. THAT'S LOVELY. THE BRIDGE IS ROTTEN.
WHERE'S THE TUNNEL?
AT THE FOOT OF THIS DROP-OFF. MATHIAS JOHANNSON HAS GONE DOWN BEFORE. HE SAID YOU HAVE TO JUMP FIFTEEN FEET.
JUMP? I AM SO OUT.
BRIDGE UNSAFE USE LADDER -RR '95

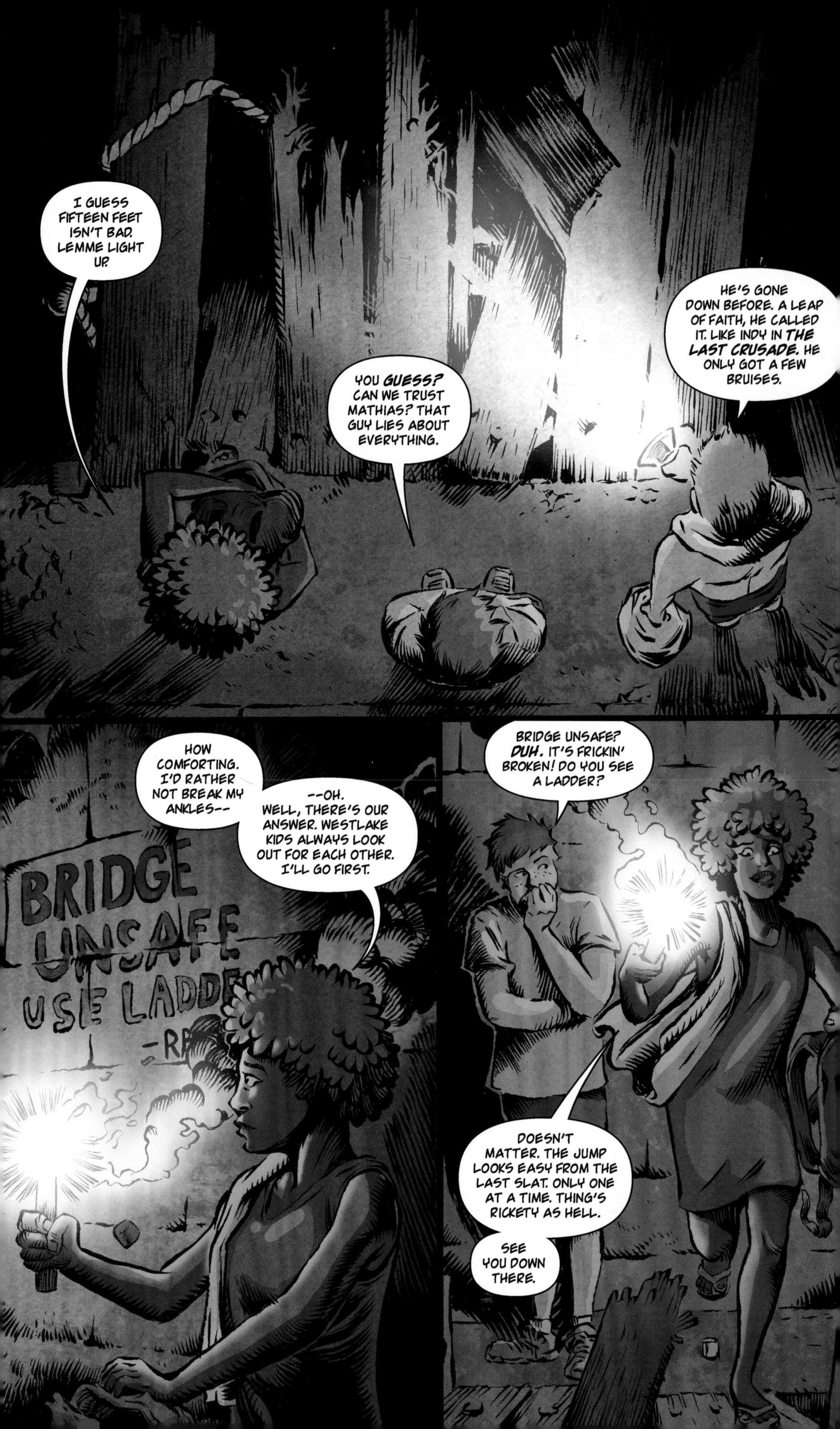
I GUESS FIFTEEN FEET ISN'T BAD. LEMME LIGHT UP.
YOU *GUESS?* CAN WE TRUST MATHIAS? THAT GUY LIES ABOUT EVERYTHING.
HE'S GONE DOWN BEFORE. A LEAP OF FAITH, HE CALLED IT. LIKE INDY IN *THE LAST CRUSADE.* HE ONLY GOT A FEW BRUISES.
HOW COMFORTING. I'D RATHER NOT BREAK MY ANKLES--
--OH. WELL, THERE'S OUR ANSWER. WESTLAKE KIDS ALWAYS LOOK OUT FOR EACH OTHER. I'LL GO FIRST.
BRIDGE UNSAFE USE LADDE
BRIDGE UNSAFE? *DUH.* IT'S FRICKIN' BROKEN! DO YOU SEE A LADDER?
DOESN'T MATTER. THE JUMP LOOKS EASY FROM THE LAST SLAT. ONLY ONE AT A TIME. THING'S RICKETY AS HELL.
SEE YOU DOWN THERE.

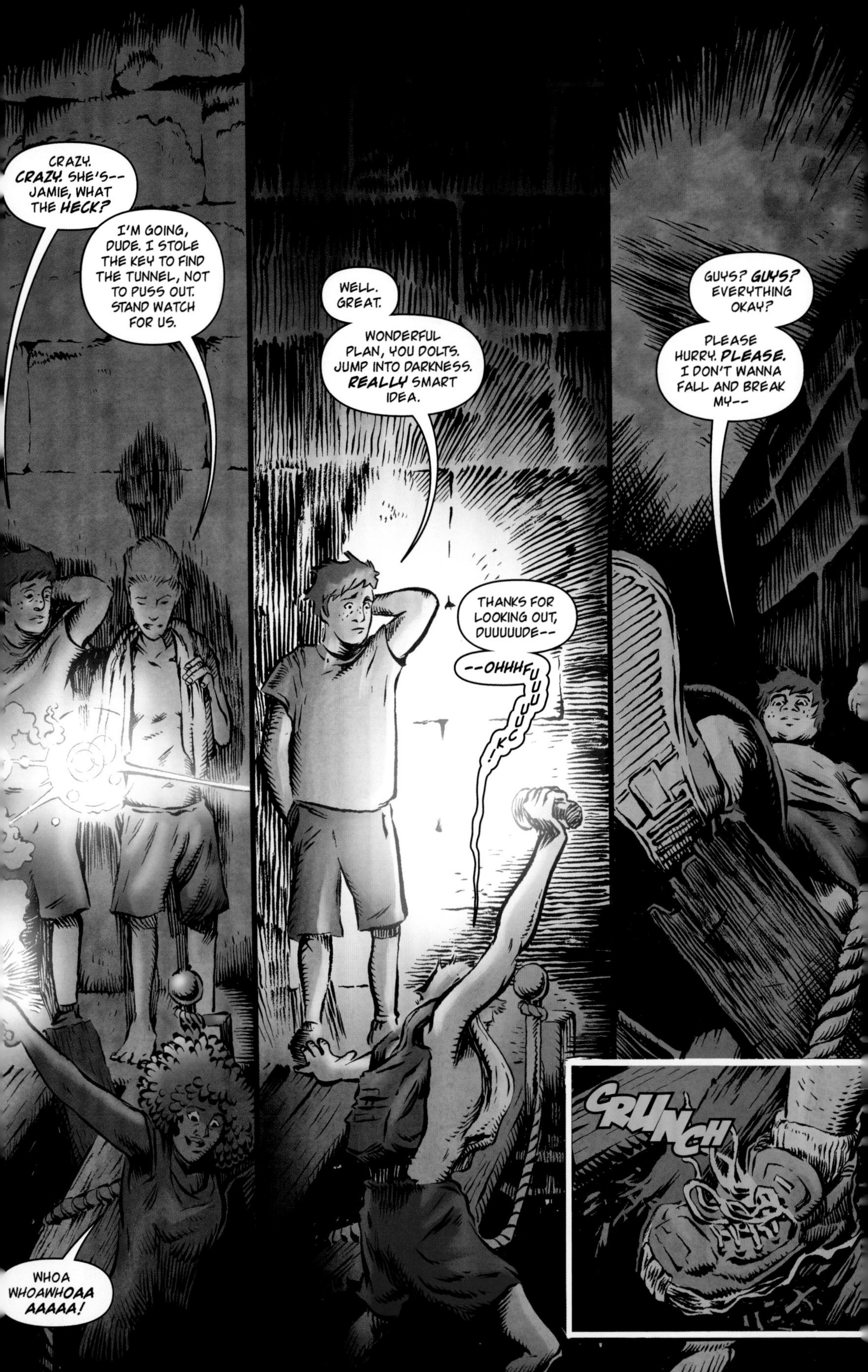
CRAZY. **CRAZY.** SHE'S-- JAMIE, WHAT THE **HECK?**
I'M GOING, DUDE. I STOLE THE KEY TO FIND THE TUNNEL, NOT TO PUSS OUT. STAND WATCH FOR US.
WHOA WHOAWHOAA AAAAA!
WELL. GREAT.
WONDERFUL PLAN, YOU DOLTS. JUMP INTO DARKNESS. **REALLY** SMART IDEA.
THANKS FOR LOOKING OUT, DUUUUUDE--
--OHHHFUUUUUUUCK!
GUYS? **GUYS?** EVERYTHING OKAY?
PLEASE HURRY. **PLEASE.** I DON'T WANNA FALL AND BREAK MY--
CRUNCH

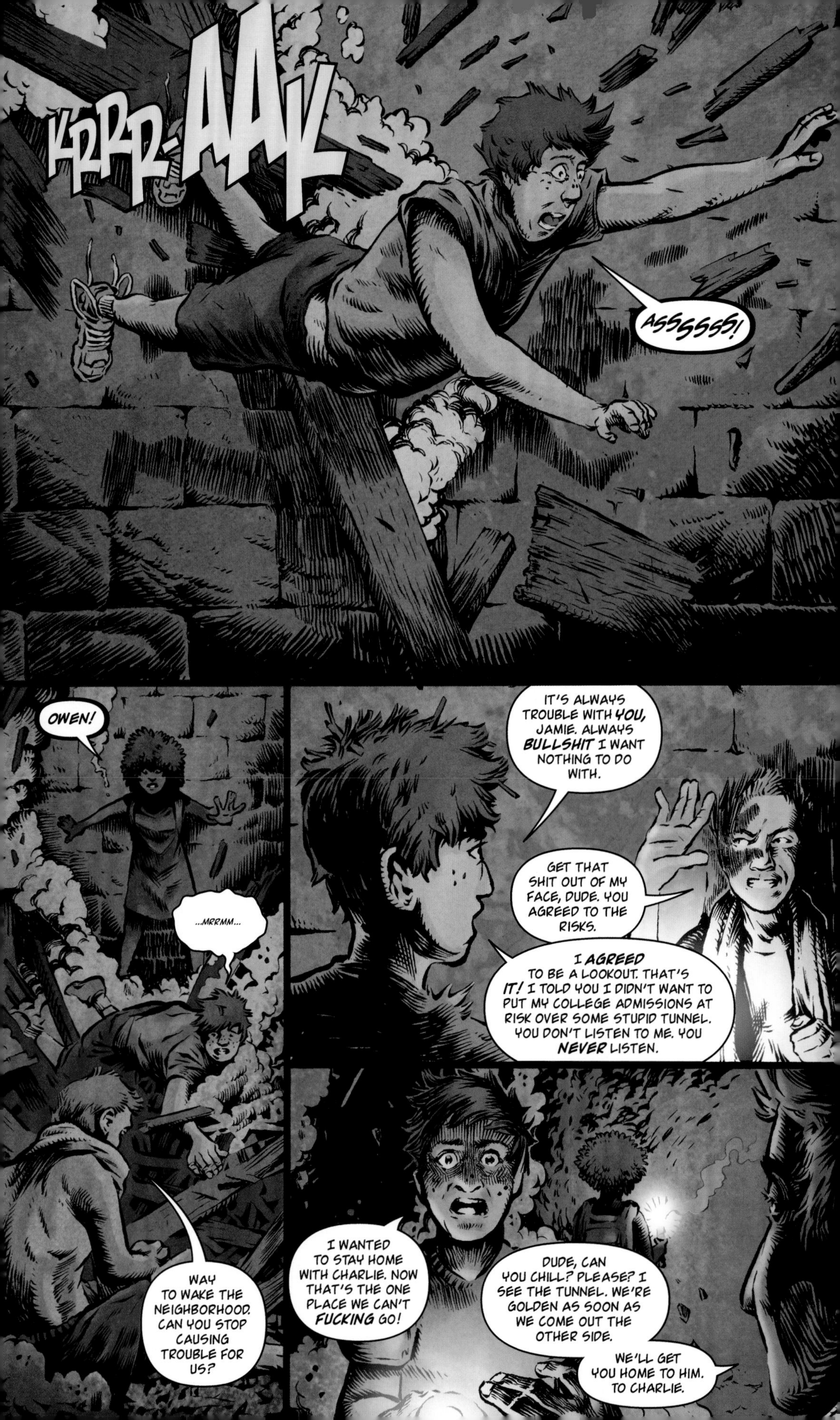
KRRR-AAAK
ASSSSSS!
OWEN!
...MRRMM...
WAY TO WAKE THE NEIGHBORHOOD. CAN YOU STOP CAUSING TROUBLE FOR US?
IT'S ALWAYS TROUBLE WITH YOU, JAMIE. ALWAYS BULLSHIT I WANT NOTHING TO DO WITH.
GET THAT SHIT OUT OF MY FACE, DUDE. YOU AGREED TO THE RISKS.
I AGREED TO BE A LOOKOUT. THAT'S IT! I TOLD YOU I DIDN'T WANT TO PUT MY COLLEGE ADMISSIONS AT RISK OVER SOME STUPID TUNNEL. YOU DON'T LISTEN TO ME. YOU NEVER LISTEN.
I WANTED TO STAY HOME WITH CHARLIE. NOW THAT'S THE ONE PLACE WE CAN'T FUCKING GO!
DUDE, CAN YOU CHILL? PLEASE? I SEE THE TUNNEL. WE'RE GOLDEN AS SOON AS WE COME OUT THE OTHER SIDE.
WE'LL GET YOU HOME TO HIM. TO CHARLIE.

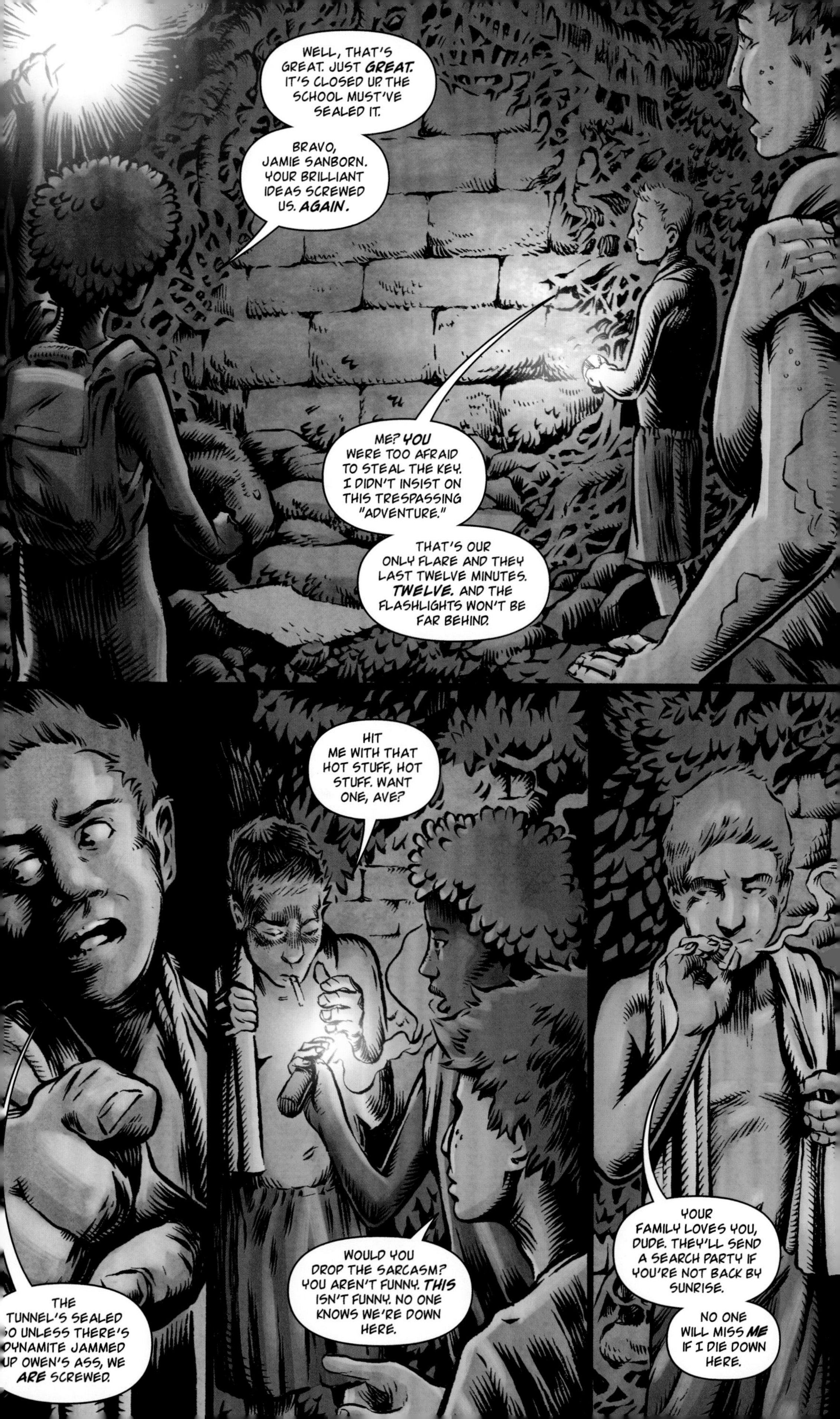
WELL, THAT'S GREAT. JUST GREAT. IT'S CLOSED UP. THE SCHOOL MUST'VE SEALED IT.
BRAVO, JAMIE SANBORN. YOUR BRILLIANT IDEAS SCREWED US. AGAIN.
ME? YOU WERE TOO AFRAID TO STEAL THE KEY. I DIDN'T INSIST ON THIS TRESPASSING "ADVENTURE."
THAT'S OUR ONLY FLARE AND THEY LAST TWELVE MINUTES. TWELVE. AND THE FLASHLIGHTS WON'T BE FAR BEHIND.
THE TUNNEL'S SEALED SO UNLESS THERE'S DYNAMITE JAMMED UP OWEN'S ASS, WE ARE SCREWED.
HIT ME WITH THAT HOT STUFF, HOT STUFF. WANT ONE, AVE?
WOULD YOU DROP THE SARCASM? YOU AREN'T FUNNY. THIS ISN'T FUNNY. NO ONE KNOWS WE'RE DOWN HERE.
YOUR FAMILY LOVES YOU, DUDE. THEY'LL SEND A SEARCH PARTY IF YOU'RE NOT BACK BY SUNRISE.
NO ONE WILL MISS ME IF I DIE DOWN HERE.

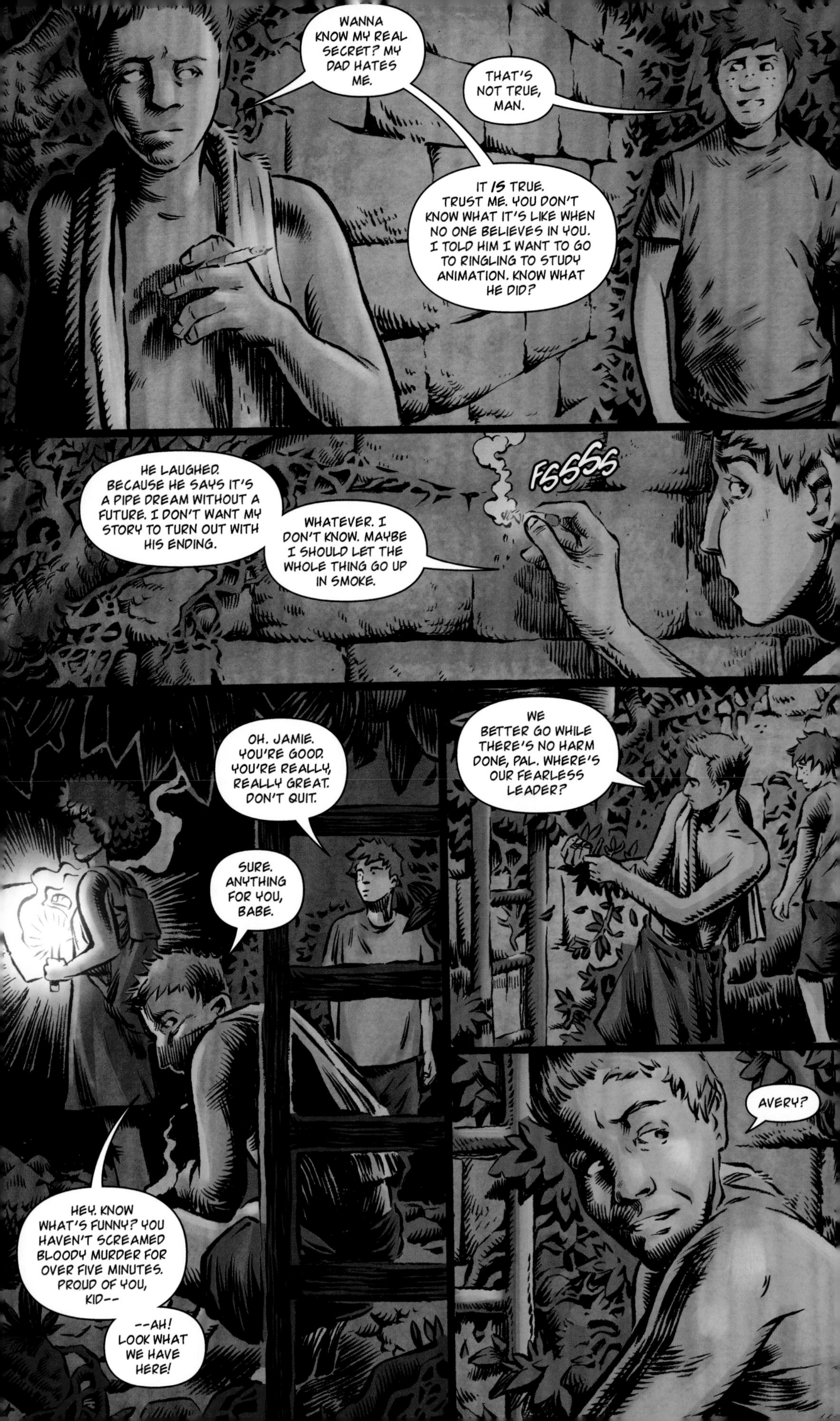

WANNA KNOW MY REAL SECRET? MY DAD HATES ME.
THAT'S NOT TRUE, MAN.
IT IS TRUE. TRUST ME. YOU DON'T KNOW WHAT IT'S LIKE WHEN NO ONE BELIEVES IN YOU. I TOLD HIM I WANT TO GO TO RINGLING TO STUDY ANIMATION. KNOW WHAT HE DID?
HE LAUGHED. BECAUSE HE SAYS IT'S A PIPE DREAM WITHOUT A FUTURE. I DON'T WANT MY STORY TO TURN OUT WITH HIS ENDING.
WHATEVER. I DON'T KNOW. MAYBE I SHOULD LET THE WHOLE THING GO UP IN SMOKE.
FSSSS
OH. JAMIE. YOU'RE GOOD. YOU'RE REALLY, REALLY GREAT. DON'T QUIT.
SURE. ANYTHING FOR YOU, BABE.
HEY. KNOW WHAT'S FUNNY? YOU HAVEN'T SCREAMED BLOODY MURDER FOR OVER FIVE MINUTES. PROUD OF YOU, KID--
--AH! LOOK WHAT WE HAVE HERE!
WE BETTER GO WHILE THERE'S NO HARM DONE, PAL. WHERE'S OUR FEARLESS LEADER?
AVERY?

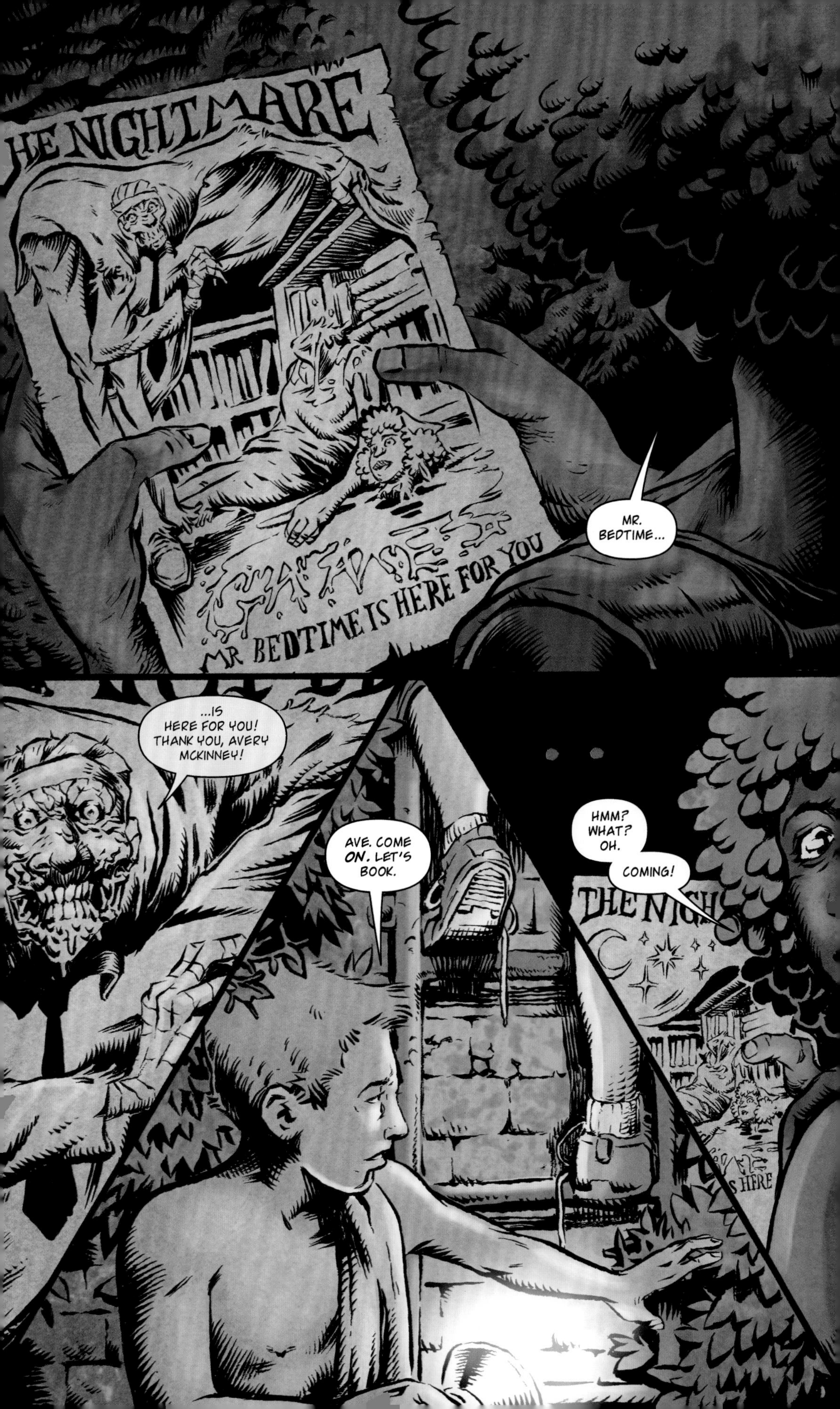
THE NIGHTMARE
MR BEDTIME IS HERE FOR YOU
MR. BEDTIME...
...IS HERE FOR YOU! THANK YOU, AVERY MCKINNEY!
AVE. COME ON. LET'S BOOK.
HMM? WHAT? OH.
COMING!
THE NIGH
S HERE

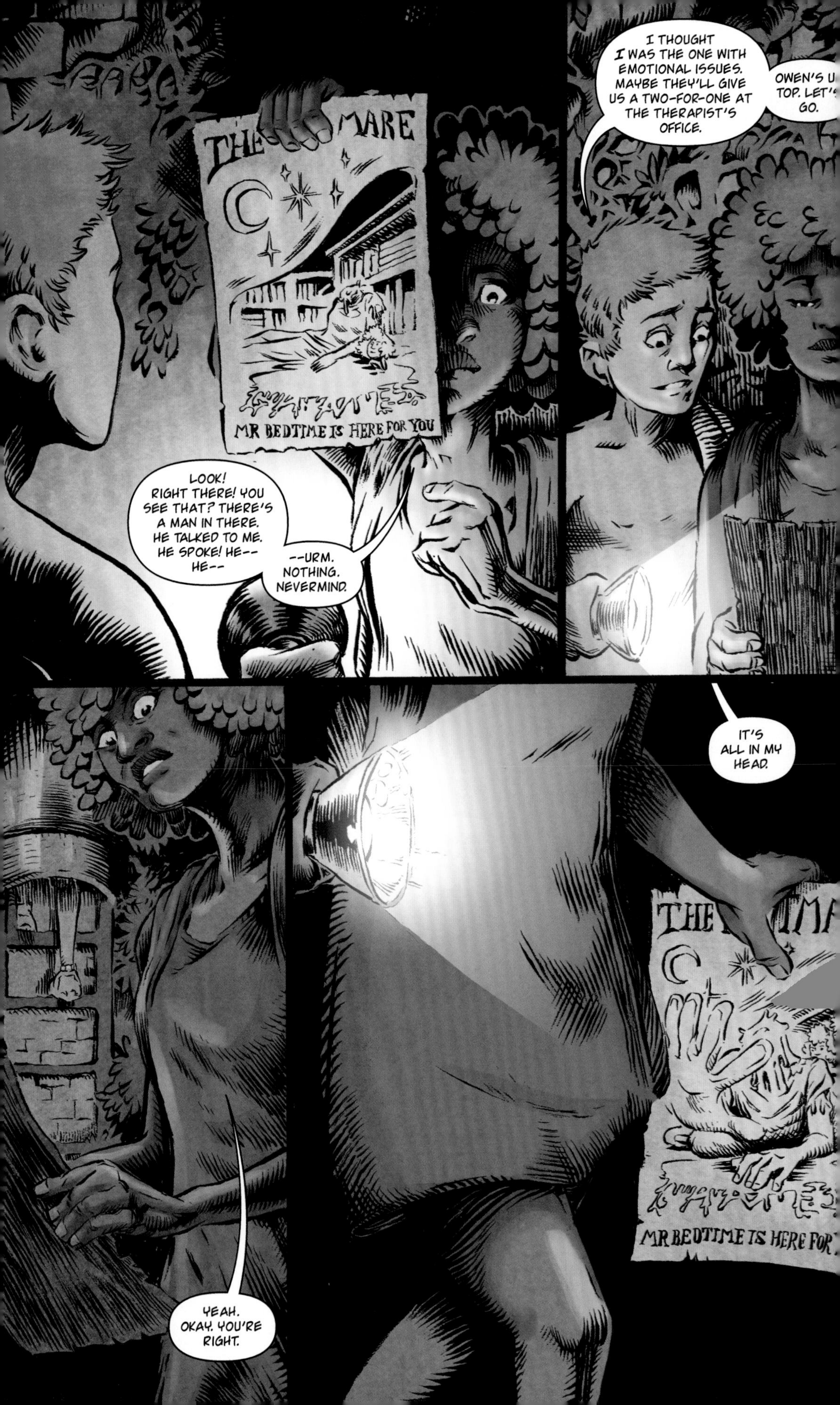

THE MARE
MR BEDTIME IS HERE FOR YOU
LOOK! RIGHT THERE! YOU SEE THAT? THERE'S A MAN IN THERE. HE TALKED TO ME. HE SPOKE! HE-- HE--
--URM. NOTHING. NEVERMIND.
I THOUGHT I WAS THE ONE WITH EMOTIONAL ISSUES. MAYBE THEY'LL GIVE US A TWO-FOR-ONE AT THE THERAPIST'S OFFICE.
OWEN'S U TOP. LET'S GO.
IT'S ALL IN MY HEAD.
YEAH. OKAY. YOU'RE RIGHT.
MR BEDTIME IS HERE FOR

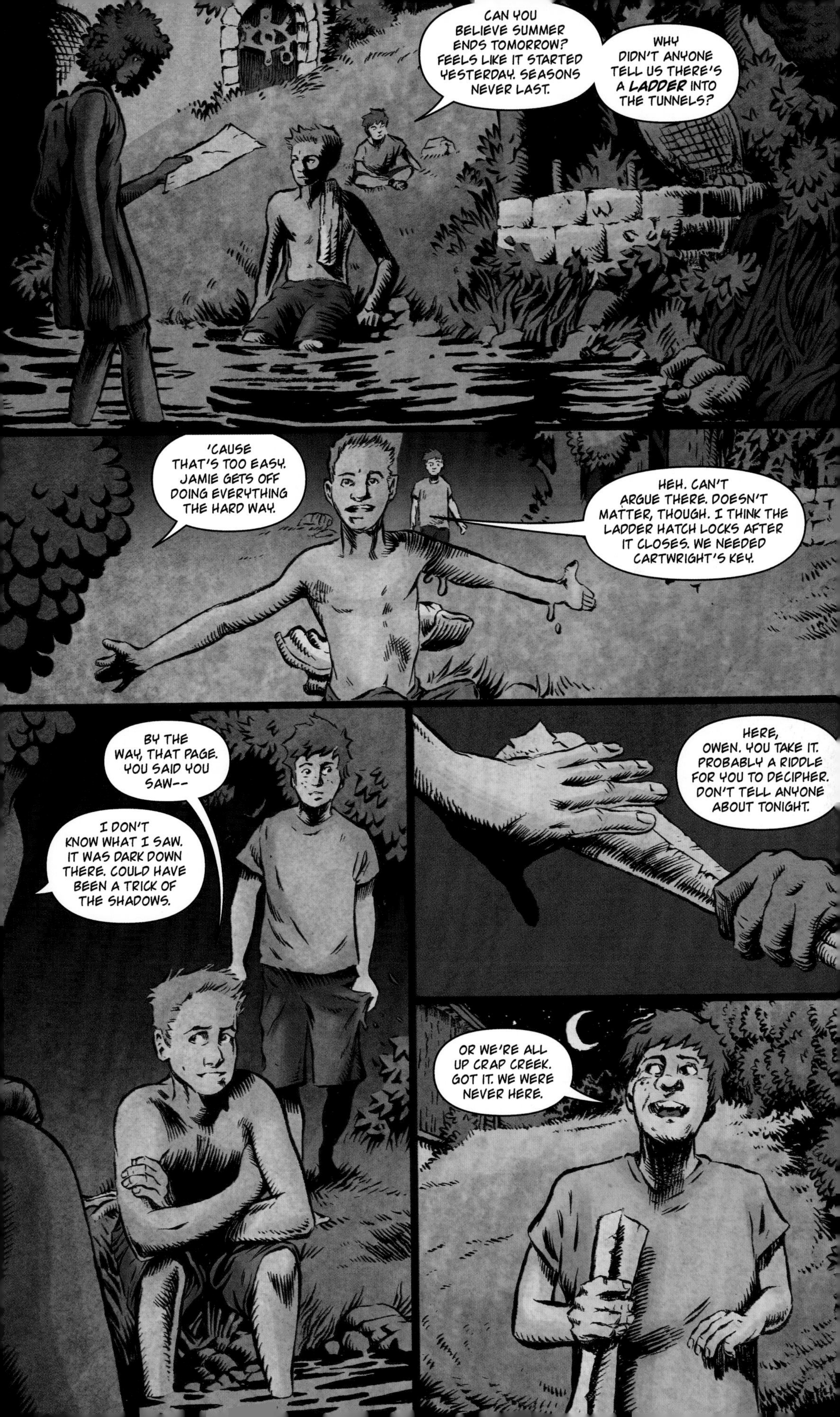
CAN YOU BELIEVE SUMMER ENDS TOMORROW? FEELS LIKE IT STARTED YESTERDAY. SEASONS NEVER LAST.
WHY DIDN'T ANYONE TELL US THERE'S A **LADDER** INTO THE TUNNELS?
'CAUSE THAT'S TOO EASY. JAMIE GETS OFF DOING EVERYTHING THE HARD WAY.
HEH. CAN'T ARGUE THERE. DOESN'T MATTER, THOUGH. I THINK THE LADDER HATCH LOCKS AFTER IT CLOSES. WE NEEDED CARTWRIGHT'S KEY.
BY THE WAY, THAT PAGE. YOU SAID YOU SAW--
I DON'T KNOW WHAT I SAW. IT WAS DARK DOWN THERE. COULD HAVE BEEN A TRICK OF THE SHADOWS.
HERE, OWEN. YOU TAKE IT. PROBABLY A RIDDLE FOR YOU TO DECIPHER. DON'T TELL ANYONE ABOUT TONIGHT.
OR WE'RE ALL UP CRAP CREEK. GOT IT. WE WERE NEVER HERE.

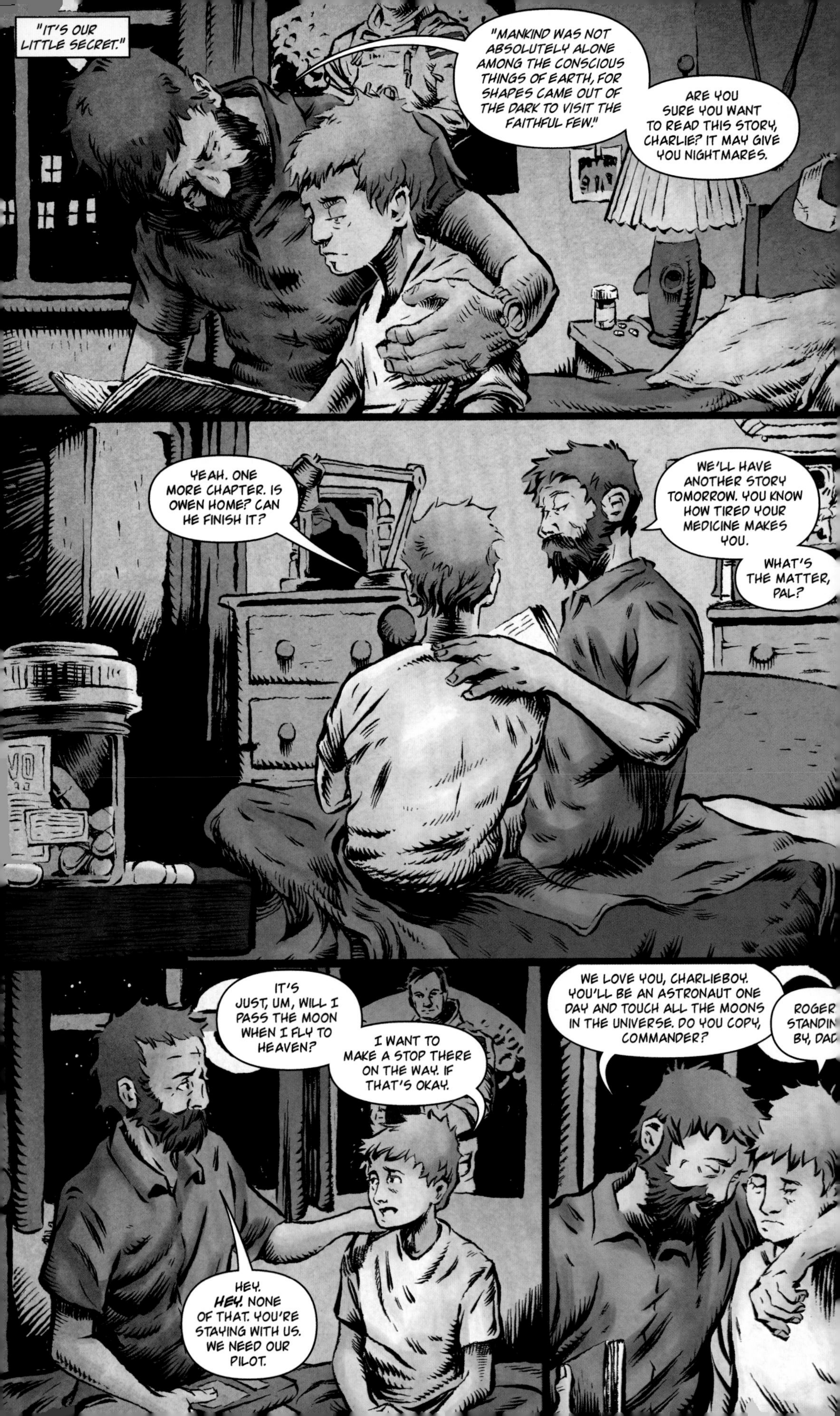

"IT'S OUR LITTLE SECRET."
"MANKIND WAS NOT ABSOLUTELY ALONE AMONG THE CONSCIOUS THINGS OF EARTH, FOR SHAPES CAME OUT OF THE DARK TO VISIT THE FAITHFUL FEW."
ARE YOU SURE YOU WANT TO READ THIS STORY, CHARLIE? IT MAY GIVE YOU NIGHTMARES.
YEAH. ONE MORE CHAPTER. IS OWEN HOME? CAN HE FINISH IT?
WE'LL HAVE ANOTHER STORY TOMORROW. YOU KNOW HOW TIRED YOUR MEDICINE MAKES YOU.
WHAT'S THE MATTER, PAL?
IT'S JUST, UM, WILL I PASS THE MOON WHEN I FLY TO HEAVEN?
I WANT TO MAKE A STOP THERE ON THE WAY. IF THAT'S OKAY.
HEY. HEY. NONE OF THAT. YOU'RE STAYING WITH US. WE NEED OUR PILOT.
WE LOVE YOU, CHARLIEBOY. YOU'LL BE AN ASTRONAUT ONE DAY AND TOUCH ALL THE MOONS IN THE UNIVERSE. DO YOU COPY, COMMANDER?
ROGER STANDIN BY, DAD

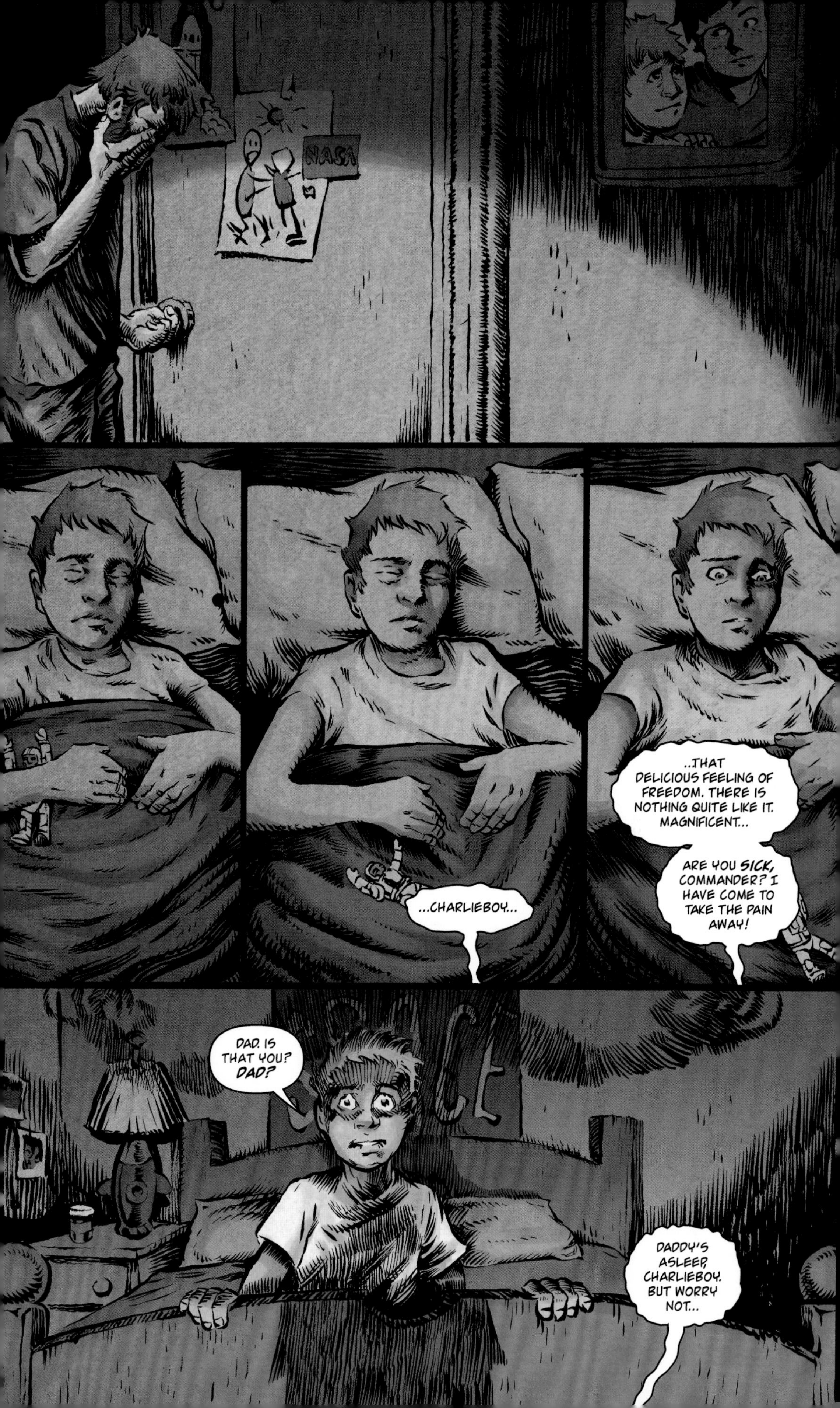

NASA
...CHARLIEBOY...
..THAT DELICIOUS FEELING OF FREEDOM. THERE IS NOTHING QUITE LIKE IT. MAGNIFICENT...
ARE YOU **SICK**, COMMANDER? I HAVE COME TO TAKE THE PAIN AWAY!
DAD. IS THAT YOU? **DAD?**
DADDY'S ASLEEP, CHARLIEBOY. BUT WORRY NOT...

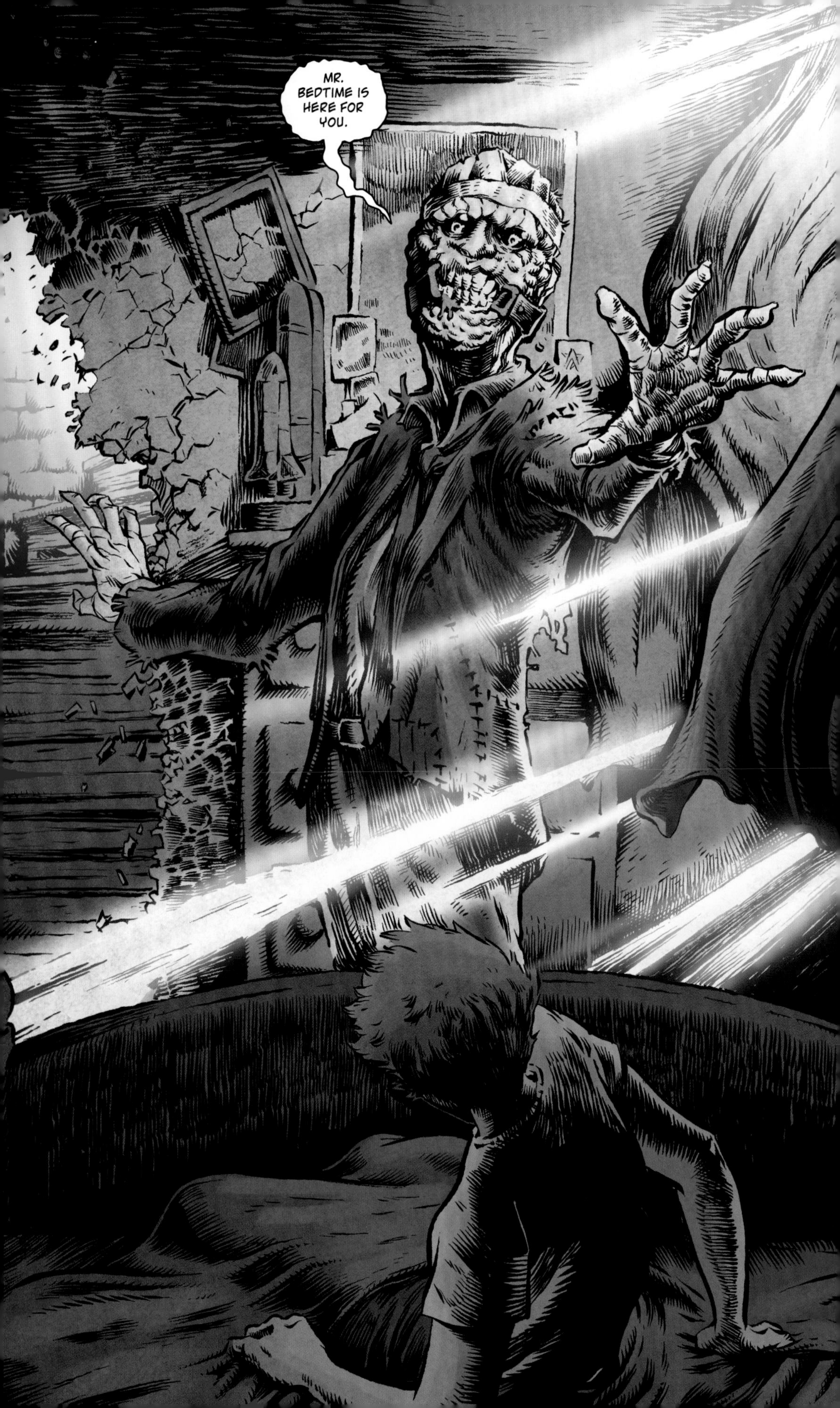
MR. BEDTIME IS HERE FOR YOU.

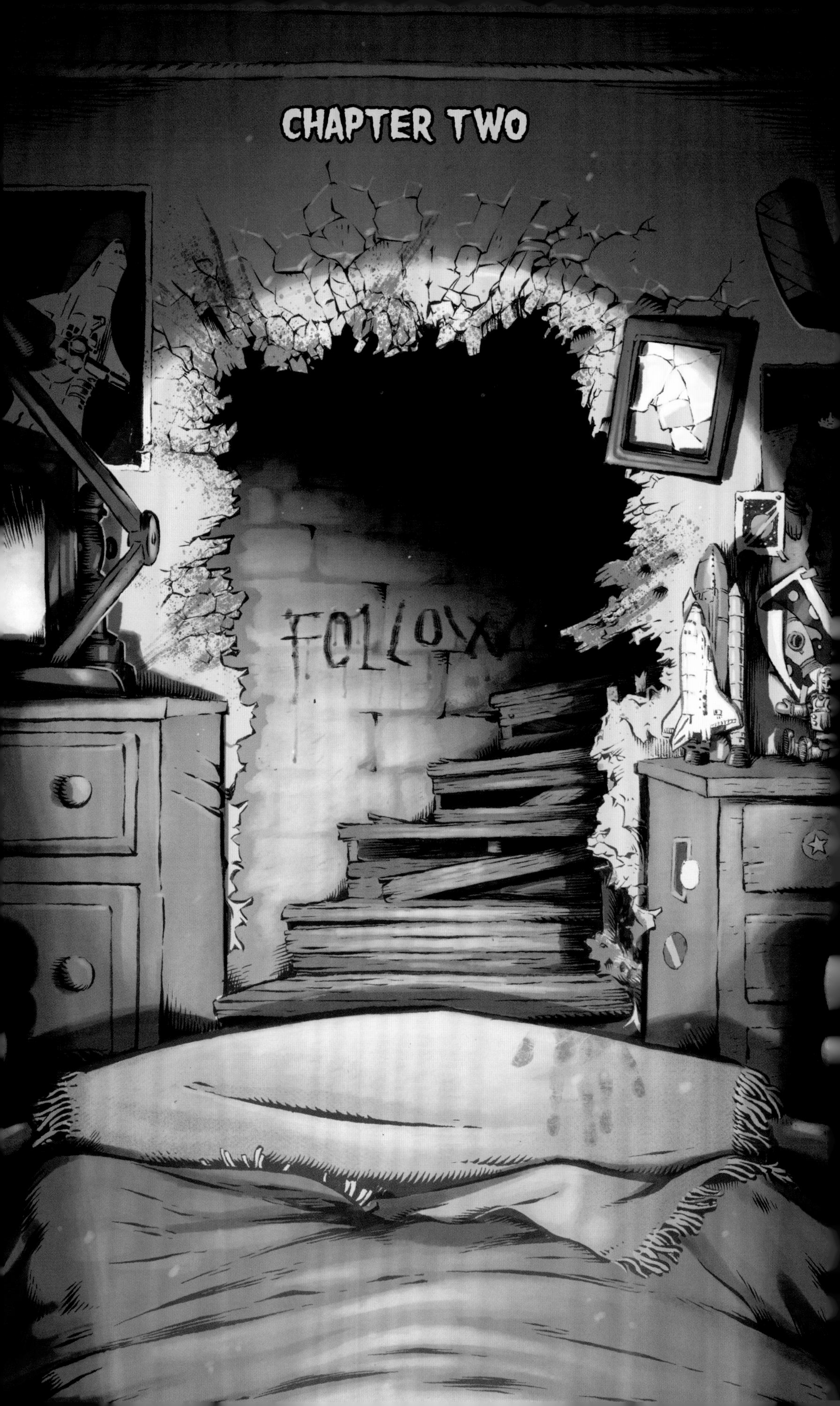
CHAPTER TWO
FOLLOW

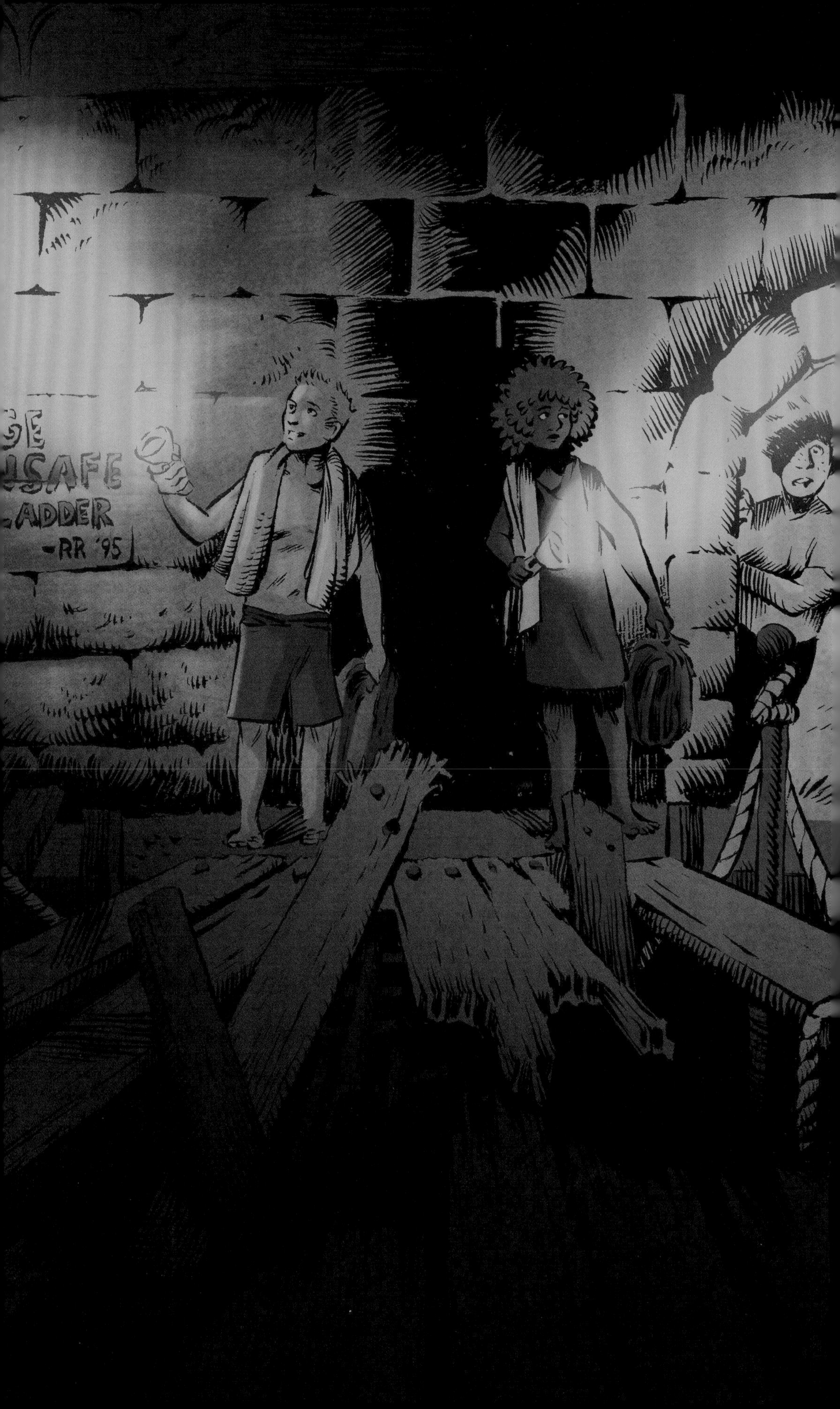
GE
ISAFE
ADDER
-RR '95

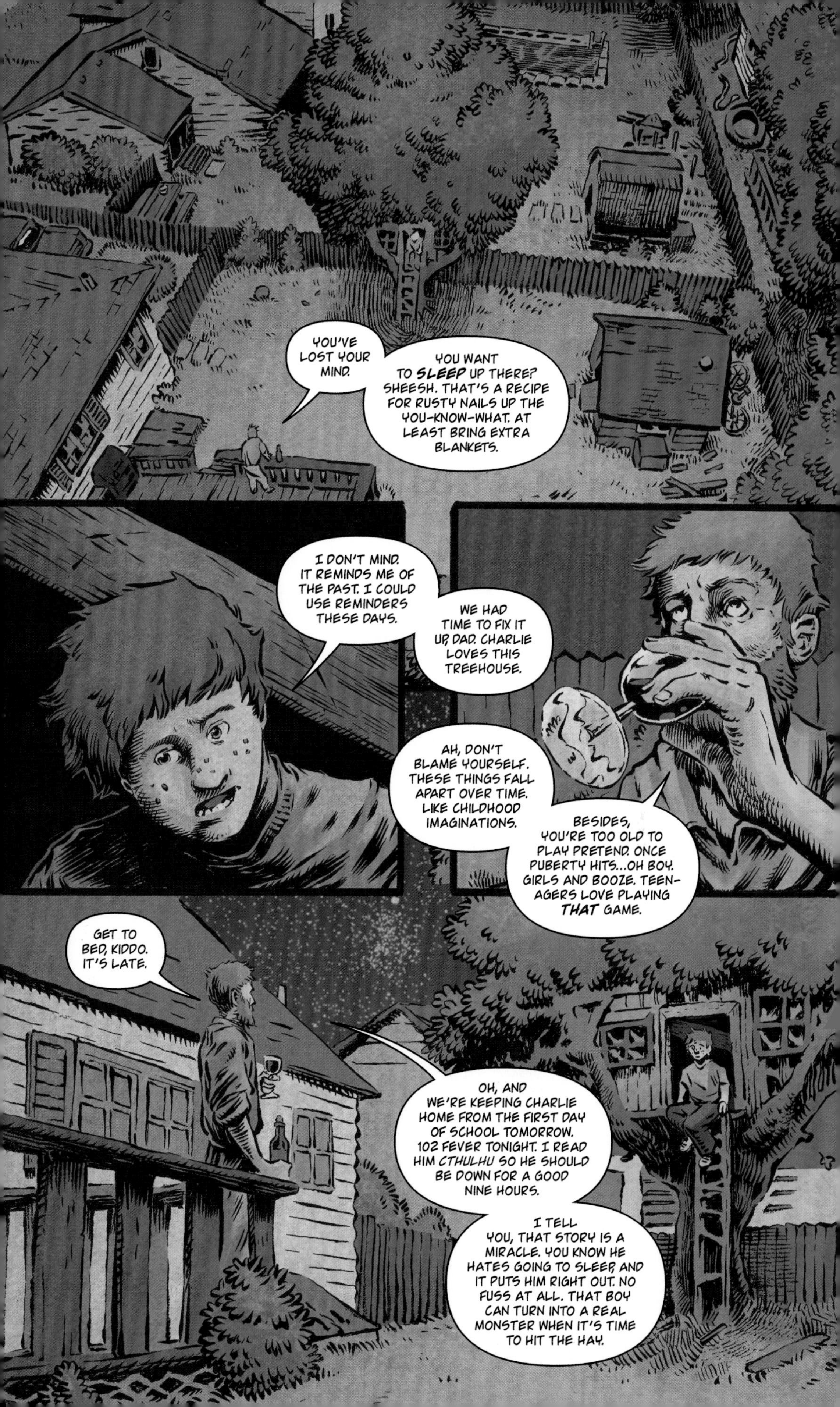

YOU'VE LOST YOUR MIND.
YOU WANT TO SLEEP UP THERE? SHEESH. THAT'S A RECIPE FOR RUSTY NAILS UP THE YOU-KNOW-WHAT. AT LEAST BRING EXTRA BLANKETS.
I DON'T MIND. IT REMINDS ME OF THE PAST. I COULD USE REMINDERS THESE DAYS.
WE HAD TIME TO FIX IT UP, DAD. CHARLIE LOVES THIS TREEHOUSE.
AH, DON'T BLAME YOURSELF. THESE THINGS FALL APART OVER TIME. LIKE CHILDHOOD IMAGINATIONS.
BESIDES, YOU'RE TOO OLD TO PLAY PRETEND. ONCE PUBERTY HITS...OH BOY. GIRLS AND BOOZE. TEEN-AGERS LOVE PLAYING THAT GAME.
GET TO BED, KIDDO. IT'S LATE.
OH, AND WE'RE KEEPING CHARLIE HOME FROM THE FIRST DAY OF SCHOOL TOMORROW. 102 FEVER TONIGHT. I READ HIM CTHULHU SO HE SHOULD BE DOWN FOR A GOOD NINE HOURS.
I TELL YOU, THAT STORY IS A MIRACLE. YOU KNOW HE HATES GOING TO SLEEP, AND IT PUTS HIM RIGHT OUT. NO FUSS AT ALL. THAT BOY CAN TURN INTO A REAL MONSTER WHEN IT'S TIME TO HIT THE HAY.

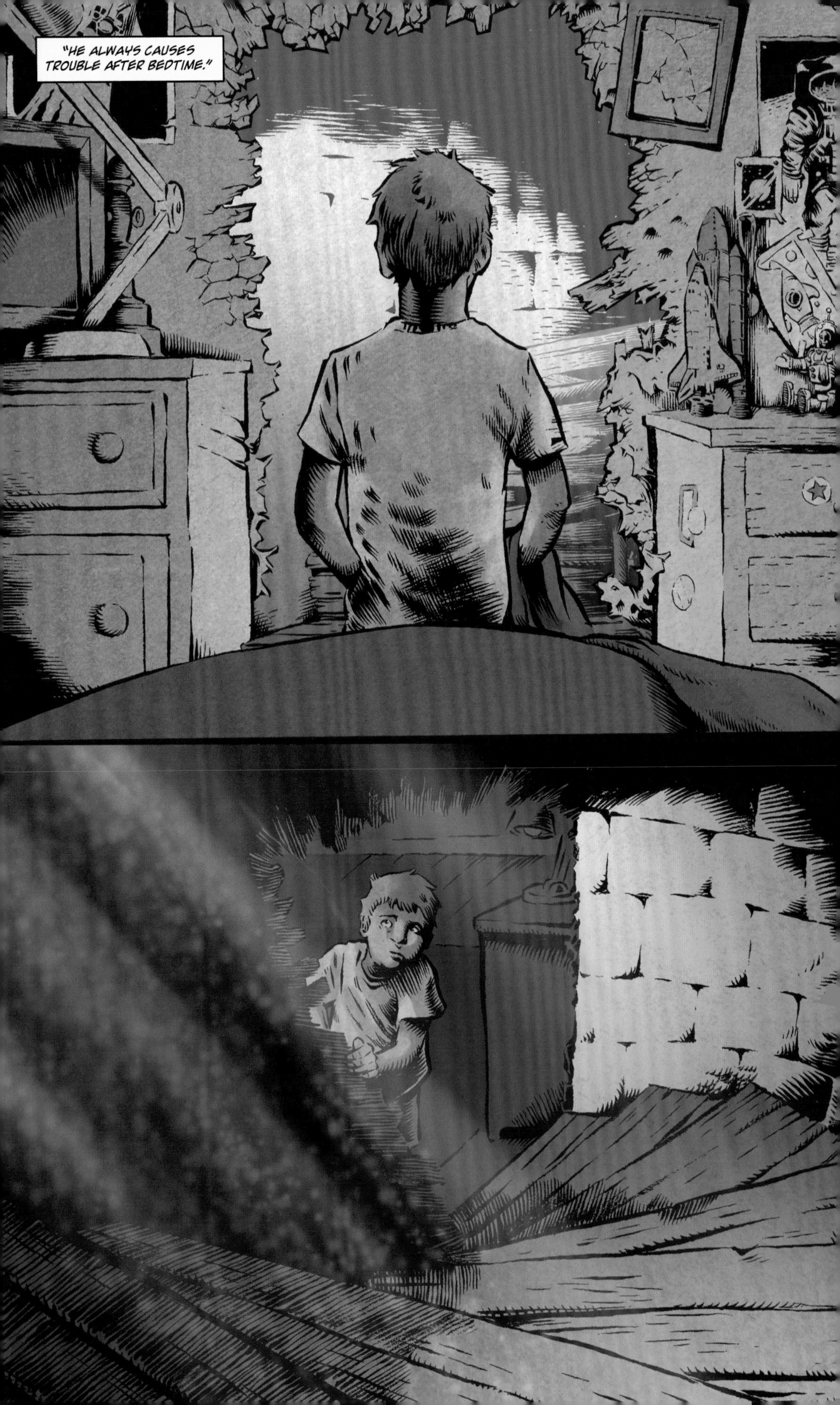
"HE ALWAYS CAUSES TROUBLE AFTER BEDTIME."

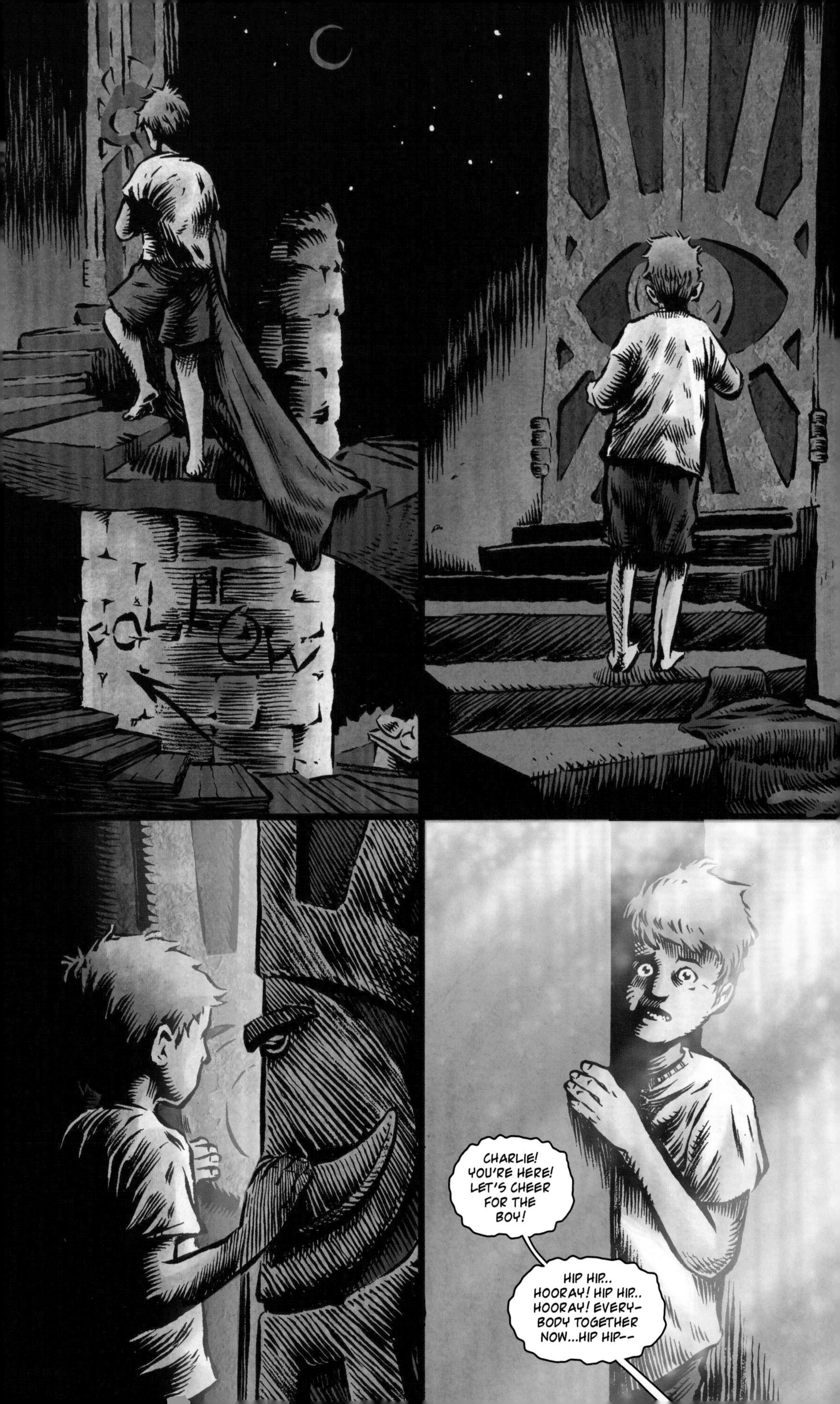
FOLLOW
CHARLIE! YOU'RE HERE! LET'S CHEER FOR THE BOY!
HIP HIP.. HOORAY! HIP HIP.. HOORAY! EVERY-BODY TOGETHER NOW...HIP HIP--

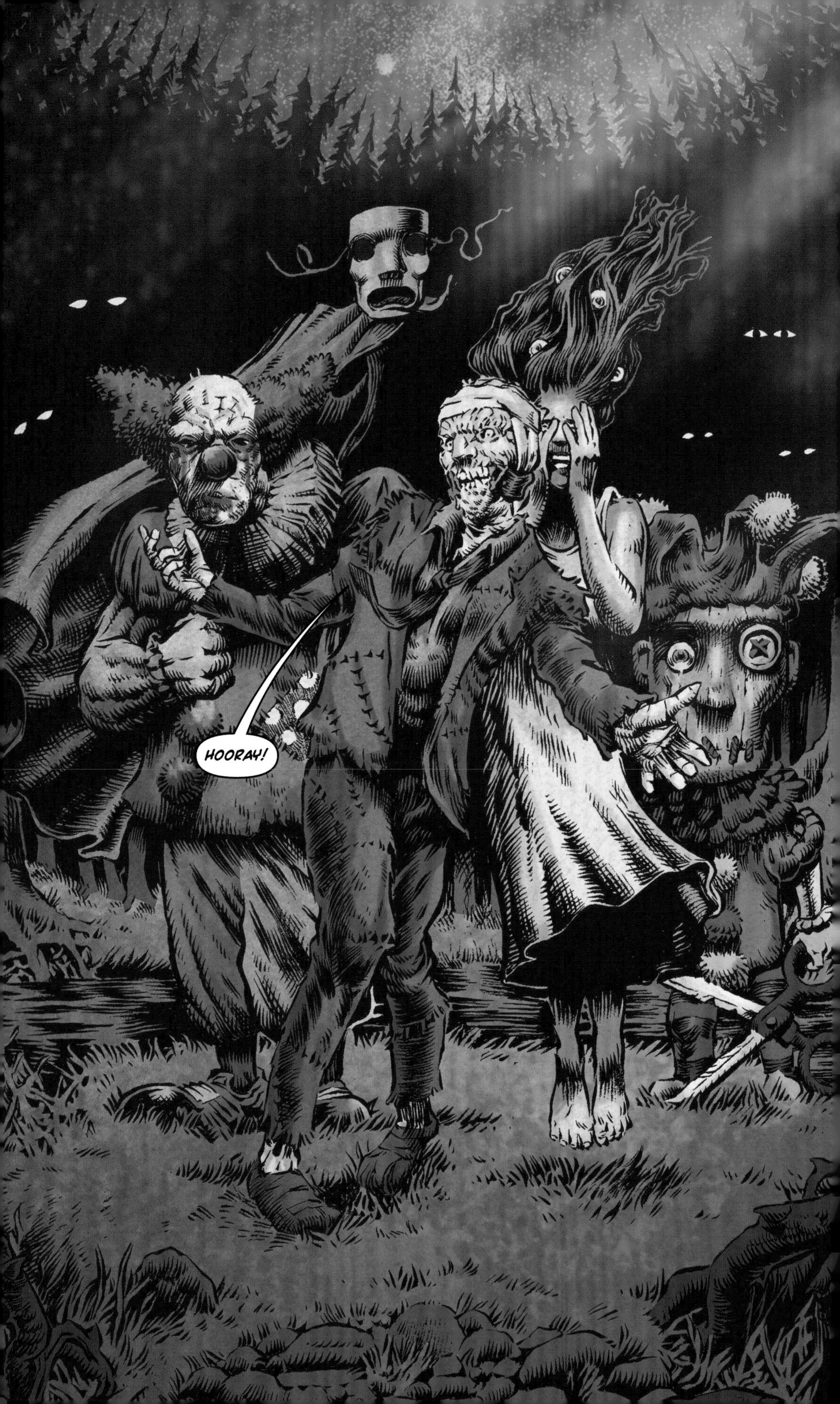
HOORAY!

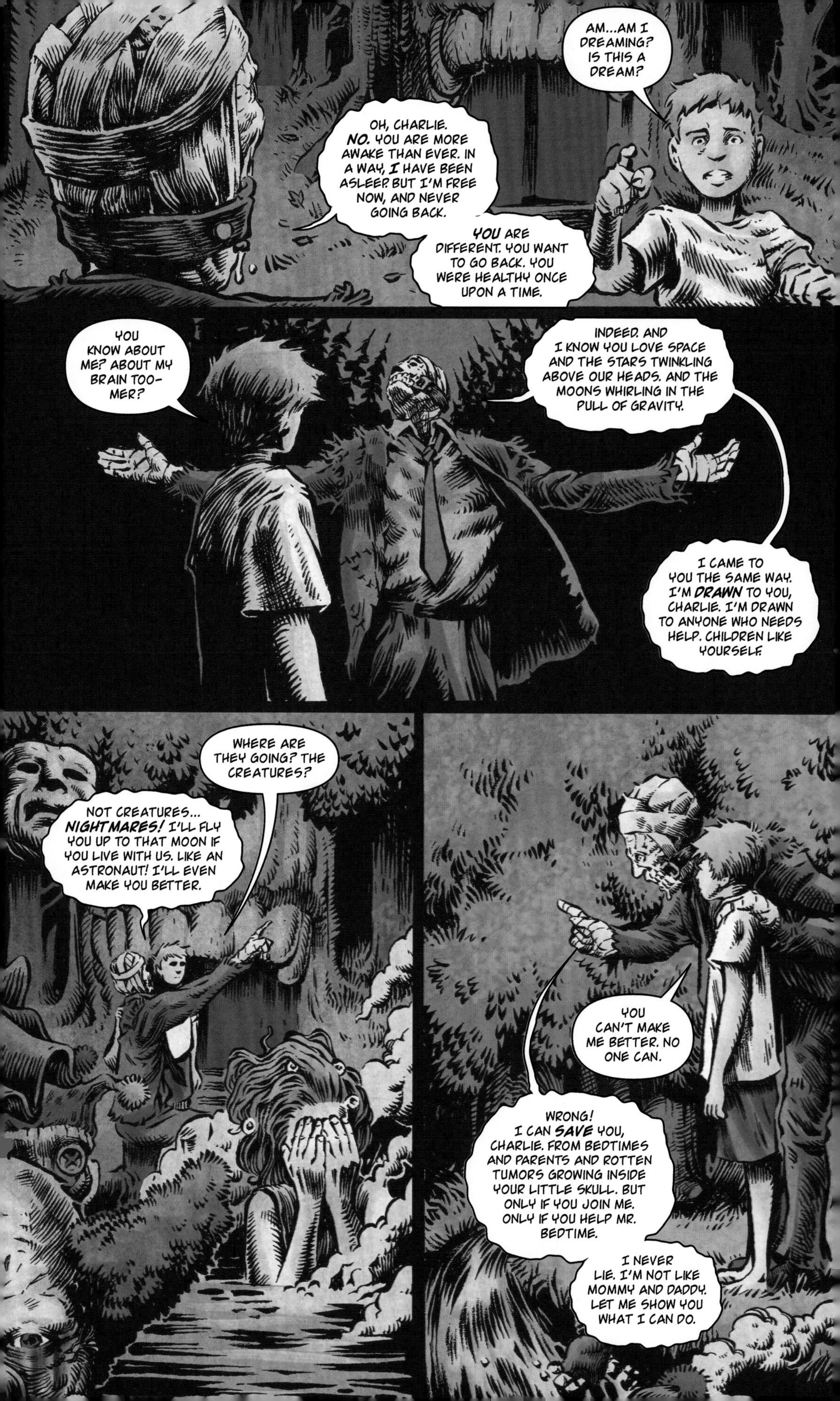

AM...AM I DREAMING? IS THIS A DREAM?
OH, CHARLIE. NO. YOU ARE MORE AWAKE THAN EVER. IN A WAY, I HAVE BEEN ASLEEP. BUT I'M FREE NOW, AND NEVER GOING BACK.
YOU ARE DIFFERENT. YOU WANT TO GO BACK. YOU WERE HEALTHY ONCE UPON A TIME.
YOU KNOW ABOUT ME? ABOUT MY BRAIN TOO-MER?
INDEED. AND I KNOW YOU LOVE SPACE AND THE STARS TWINKLING ABOVE OUR HEADS. AND THE MOONS WHIRLING IN THE PULL OF GRAVITY.
I CAME TO YOU THE SAME WAY. I'M DRAWN TO YOU, CHARLIE. I'M DRAWN TO ANYONE WHO NEEDS HELP. CHILDREN LIKE YOURSELF.
WHERE ARE THEY GOING? THE CREATURES?
NOT CREATURES... NIGHTMARES! I'LL FLY YOU UP TO THAT MOON IF YOU LIVE WITH US. LIKE AN ASTRONAUT! I'LL EVEN MAKE YOU BETTER.
YOU CAN'T MAKE ME BETTER. NO ONE CAN.
WRONG! I CAN SAVE YOU, CHARLIE. FROM BEDTIMES AND PARENTS AND ROTTEN TUMORS GROWING INSIDE YOUR LITTLE SKULL. BUT ONLY IF YOU JOIN ME. ONLY IF YOU HELP MR. BEDTIME.
I NEVER LIE. I'M NOT LIKE MOMMY AND DADDY. LET ME SHOW YOU WHAT I CAN DO.

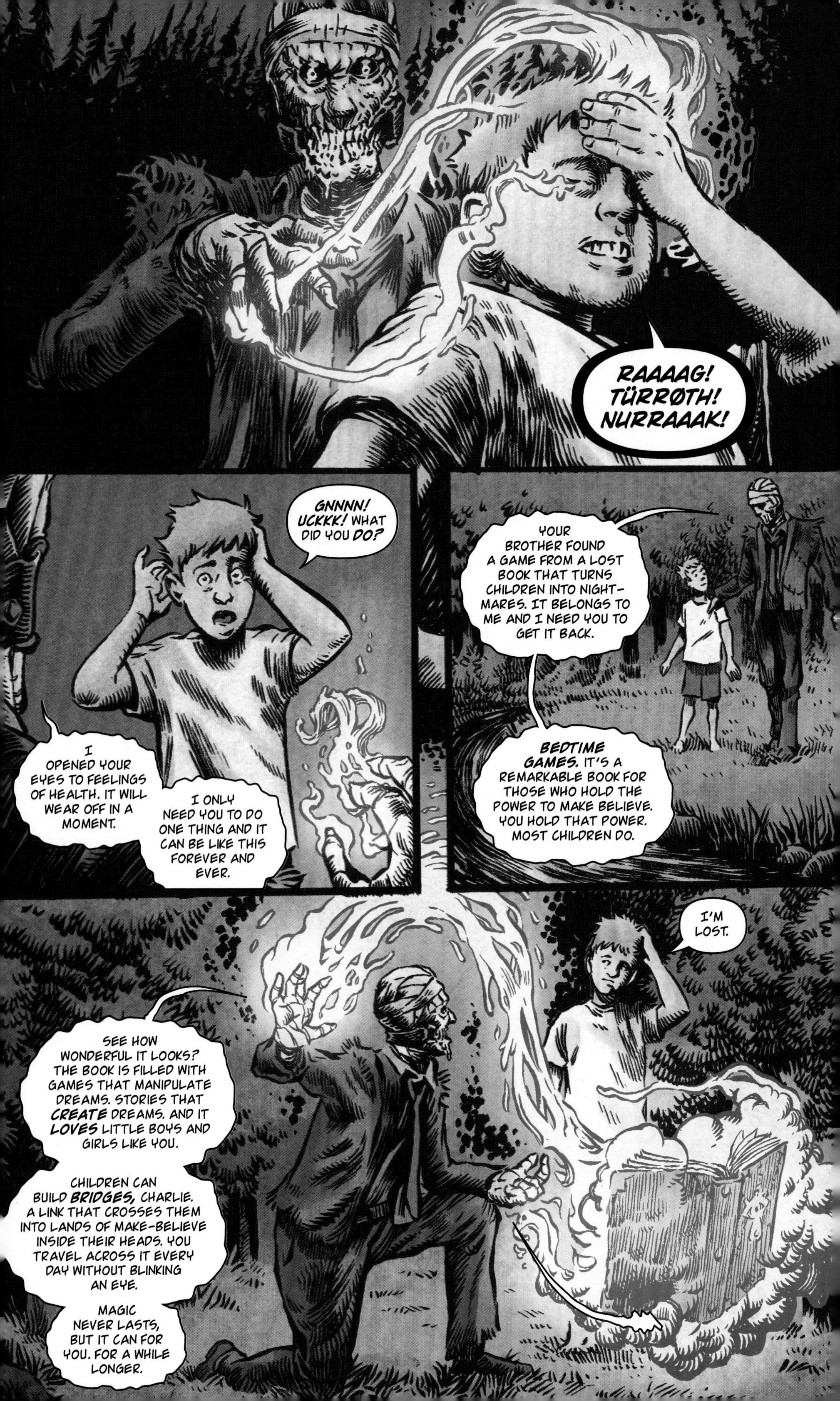
RAAAAG! TÜRRØTH! NURRAAAK!
GNNNN! UCKKK! WHAT DID YOU DO?
I OPENED YOUR EYES TO FEELINGS OF HEALTH. IT WILL WEAR OFF IN A MOMENT.
I ONLY NEED YOU TO DO ONE THING AND IT CAN BE LIKE THIS FOREVER AND EVER.
YOUR BROTHER FOUND A GAME FROM A LOST BOOK THAT TURNS CHILDREN INTO NIGHT-MARES. IT BELONGS TO ME AND I NEED YOU TO GET IT BACK.
BEDTIME GAMES. IT'S A REMARKABLE BOOK FOR THOSE WHO HOLD THE POWER TO MAKE BELIEVE. YOU HOLD THAT POWER. MOST CHILDREN DO.
I'M LOST.
SEE HOW WONDERFUL IT LOOKS? THE BOOK IS FILLED WITH GAMES THAT MANIPULATE DREAMS. STORIES THAT CREATE DREAMS. AND IT LOVES LITTLE BOYS AND GIRLS LIKE YOU.
CHILDREN CAN BUILD BRIDGES, CHARLIE. A LINK THAT CROSSES THEM INTO LANDS OF MAKE-BELIEVE INSIDE THEIR HEADS. YOU TRAVEL ACROSS IT EVERY DAY WITHOUT BLINKING AN EYE.
MAGIC NEVER LASTS, BUT IT CAN FOR YOU. FOR A WHILE LONGER.

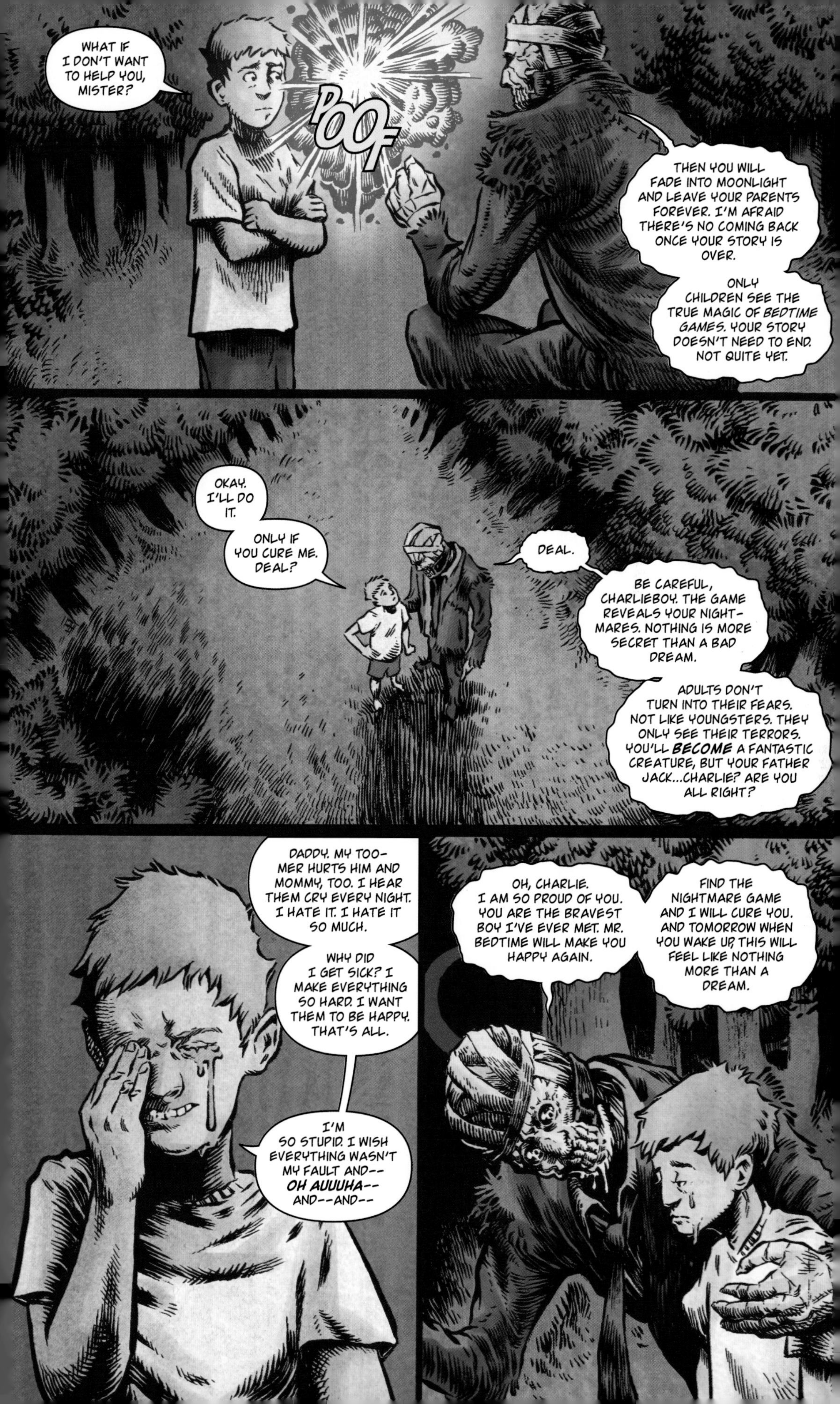
WHAT IF I DON'T WANT TO HELP YOU, MISTER?
POOF
THEN YOU WILL FADE INTO MOONLIGHT AND LEAVE YOUR PARENTS FOREVER. I'M AFRAID THERE'S NO COMING BACK ONCE YOUR STORY IS OVER.
ONLY CHILDREN SEE THE TRUE MAGIC OF *BEDTIME GAMES*. YOUR STORY DOESN'T NEED TO END. NOT QUITE YET.
OKAY. I'LL DO IT.
ONLY IF YOU CURE ME. DEAL?
DEAL.
BE CAREFUL, CHARLIEBOY. THE GAME REVEALS YOUR NIGHT-MARES. NOTHING IS MORE SECRET THAN A BAD DREAM.
ADULTS DON'T TURN INTO THEIR FEARS. NOT LIKE YOUNGSTERS. THEY ONLY SEE THEIR TERRORS. YOU'LL ***BECOME*** A FANTASTIC CREATURE, BUT YOUR FATHER JACK...CHARLIE? ARE YOU ALL RIGHT?
DADDY. MY TOO-MER HURTS HIM AND MOMMY, TOO. I HEAR THEM CRY EVERY NIGHT. I HATE IT. I HATE IT SO MUCH.
WHY DID I GET SICK? I MAKE EVERYTHING SO HARD. I WANT THEM TO BE HAPPY. THAT'S ALL.
I'M SO STUPID. I WISH EVERYTHING WASN'T MY FAULT AND-- ***OH AUUUHA--*** AND--AND--
OH, CHARLIE. I AM SO PROUD OF YOU. YOU ARE THE BRAVEST BOY I'VE EVER MET. MR. BEDTIME WILL MAKE YOU HAPPY AGAIN.
FIND THE NIGHTMARE GAME AND I WILL CURE YOU. AND TOMORROW WHEN YOU WAKE UP, THIS WILL FEEL LIKE NOTHING MORE THAN A DREAM.

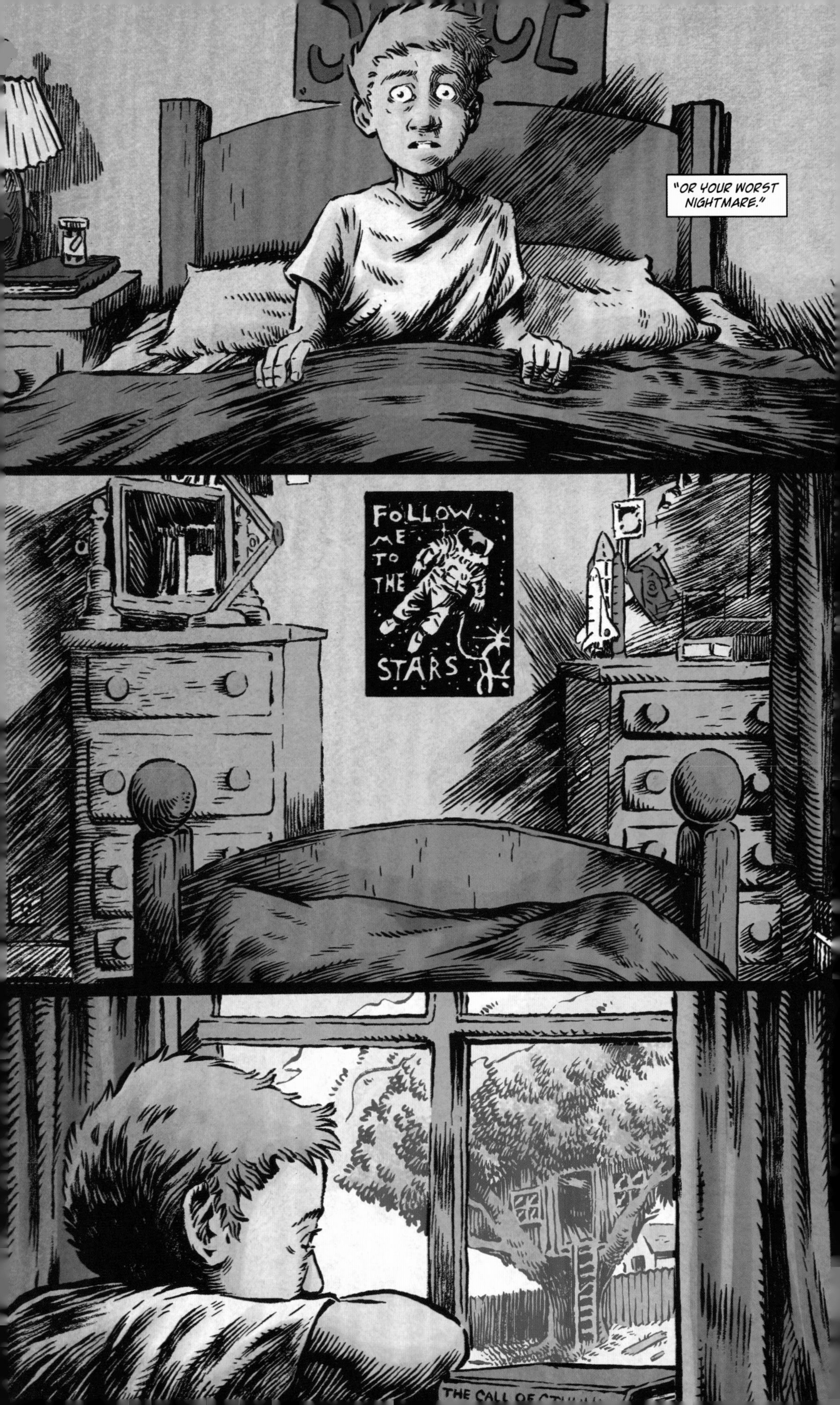
"OR YOUR WORST NIGHTMARE."
FOLLOW ME TO THE STARS
THE CALL OF

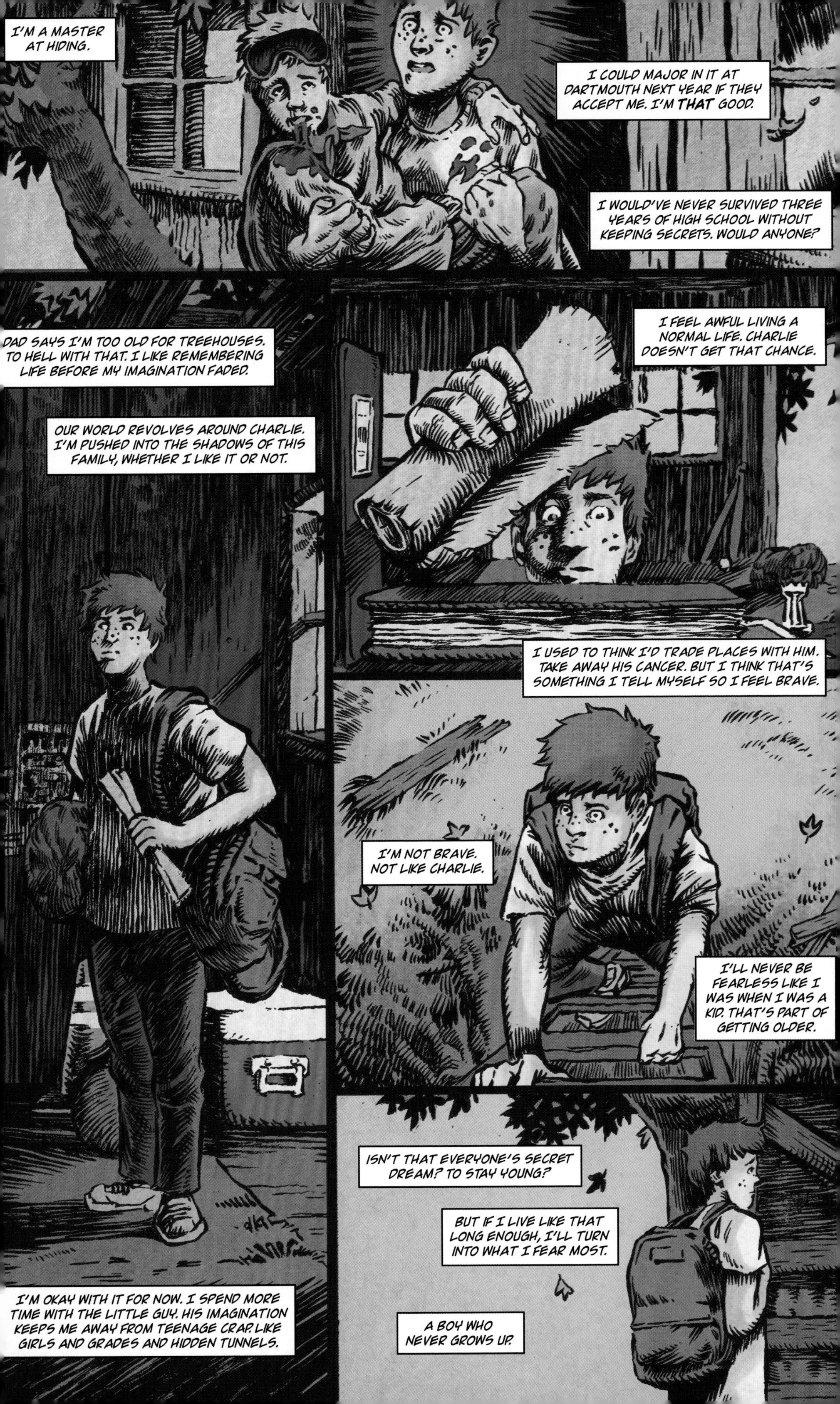
I'M A MASTER AT HIDING.
I COULD MAJOR IN IT AT DARTMOUTH NEXT YEAR IF THEY ACCEPT ME. I'M **THAT** GOOD.
I WOULD'VE NEVER SURVIVED THREE YEARS OF HIGH SCHOOL WITHOUT KEEPING SECRETS. WOULD ANYONE?
DAD SAYS I'M TOO OLD FOR TREEHOUSES. TO HELL WITH THAT. I LIKE REMEMBERING LIFE BEFORE MY IMAGINATION FADED.
OUR WORLD REVOLVES AROUND CHARLIE. I'M PUSHED INTO THE SHADOWS OF THIS FAMILY, WHETHER I LIKE IT OR NOT.
I'M OKAY WITH IT FOR NOW. I SPEND MORE TIME WITH THE LITTLE GUY. HIS IMAGINATION KEEPS ME AWAY FROM TEENAGE CRAP. LIKE GIRLS AND GRADES AND HIDDEN TUNNELS.
I FEEL AWFUL LIVING A NORMAL LIFE. CHARLIE DOESN'T GET THAT CHANCE.
I USED TO THINK I'D TRADE PLACES WITH HIM. TAKE AWAY HIS CANCER. BUT I THINK THAT'S SOMETHING I TELL MYSELF SO I FEEL BRAVE.
I'M NOT BRAVE. NOT LIKE CHARLIE.
I'LL NEVER BE FEARLESS LIKE I WAS WHEN I WAS A KID. THAT'S PART OF GETTING OLDER.
ISN'T THAT EVERYONE'S SECRET DREAM? TO STAY YOUNG?
BUT IF I LIVE LIKE THAT LONG ENOUGH, I'LL TURN INTO WHAT I FEAR MOST.
A BOY WHO NEVER GROWS UP.

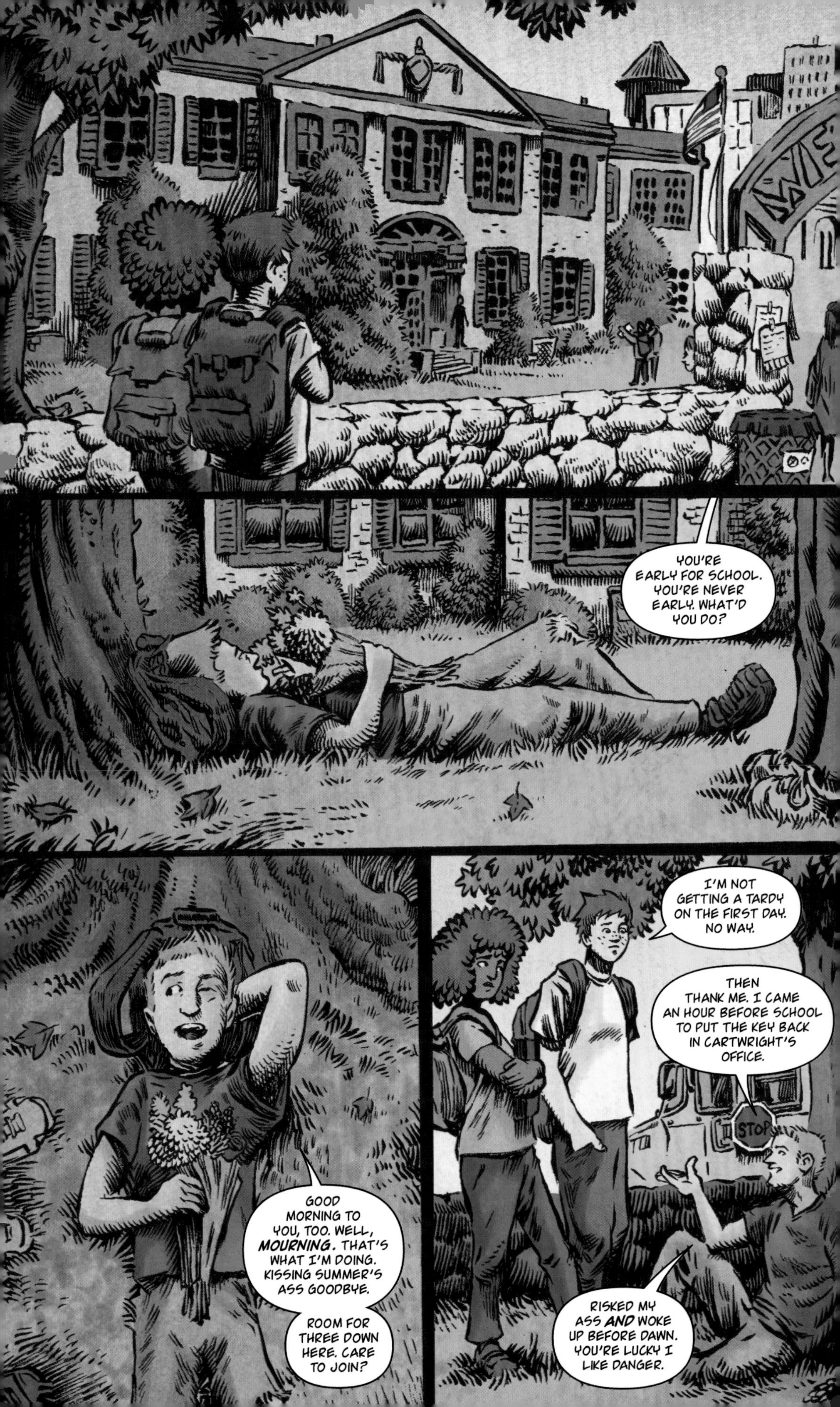

YOU'RE EARLY FOR SCHOOL. YOU'RE NEVER EARLY. WHAT'D YOU DO?
GOOD MORNING TO YOU, TOO. WELL, **MOURNING.** THAT'S WHAT I'M DOING. KISSING SUMMER'S ASS GOODBYE.
ROOM FOR THREE DOWN HERE. CARE TO JOIN?
I'M NOT GETTING A TARDY ON THE FIRST DAY. NO WAY.
THEN THANK ME. I CAME AN HOUR BEFORE SCHOOL TO PUT THE KEY BACK IN CARTWRIGHT'S OFFICE.
STOP
RISKED MY ASS ***AND*** WOKE UP BEFORE DAWN. YOU'RE LUCKY I LIKE DANGER.

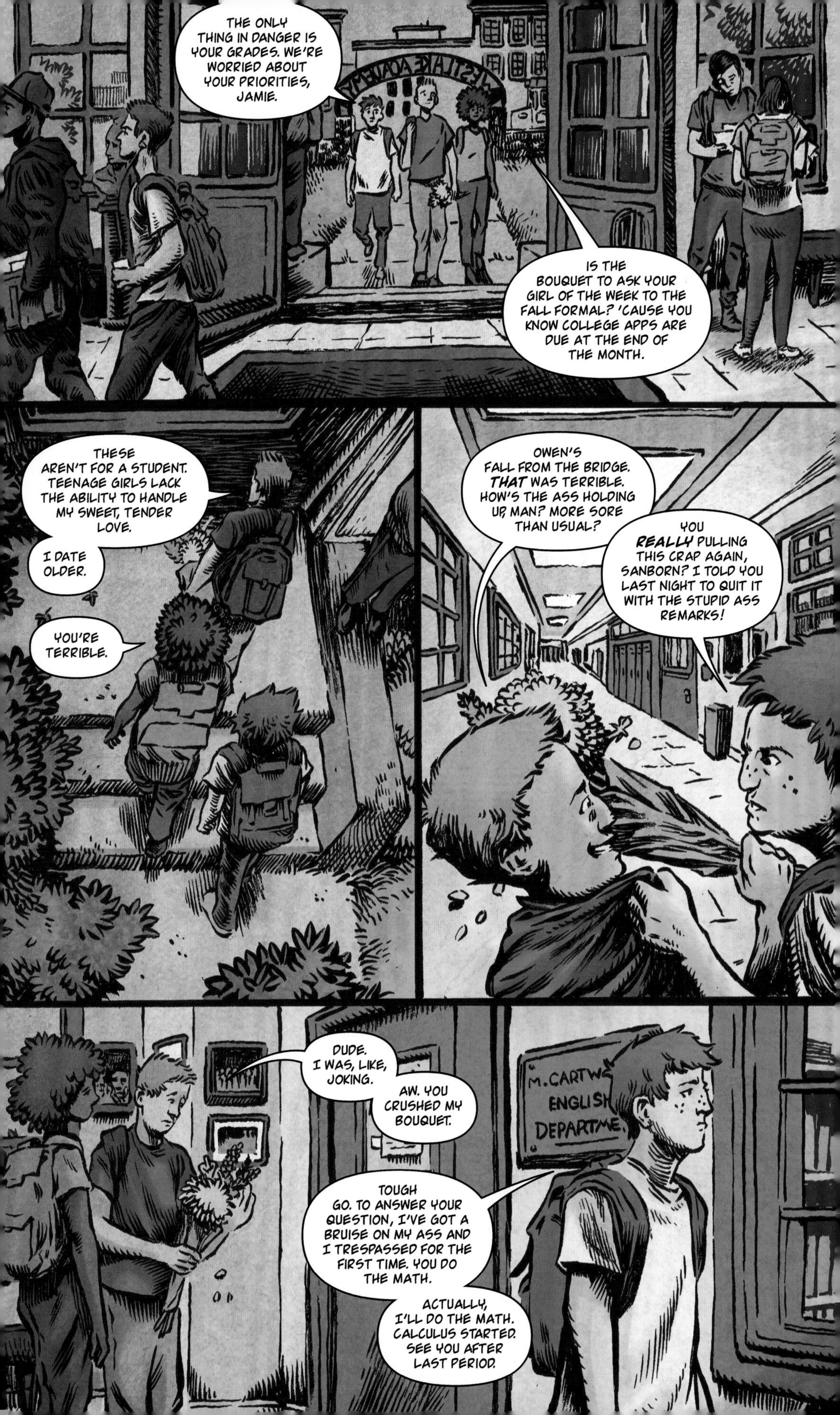
THE ONLY THING IN DANGER IS YOUR GRADES. WE'RE WORRIED ABOUT YOUR PRIORITIES, JAMIE.
IS THE BOUQUET TO ASK YOUR GIRL OF THE WEEK TO THE FALL FORMAL? 'CAUSE YOU KNOW COLLEGE APPS ARE DUE AT THE END OF THE MONTH.
THESE AREN'T FOR A STUDENT. TEENAGE GIRLS LACK THE ABILITY TO HANDLE MY SWEET, TENDER LOVE.
I DATE OLDER.
YOU'RE TERRIBLE.
OWEN'S FALL FROM THE BRIDGE. *THAT* WAS TERRIBLE. HOW'S THE ASS HOLDING UP, MAN? MORE SORE THAN USUAL?
YOU *REALLY* PULLING THIS CRAP AGAIN, SANBORN? I TOLD YOU LAST NIGHT TO QUIT IT WITH THE STUPID ASS REMARKS!
DUDE. I WAS, LIKE, JOKING.
AW. YOU CRUSHED MY BOUQUET.
TOUGH GO. TO ANSWER YOUR QUESTION, I'VE GOT A BRUISE ON MY ASS AND I TRESPASSED FOR THE FIRST TIME. YOU DO THE MATH.
ACTUALLY, I'LL DO THE MATH. CALCULUS STARTED. SEE YOU AFTER LAST PERIOD.

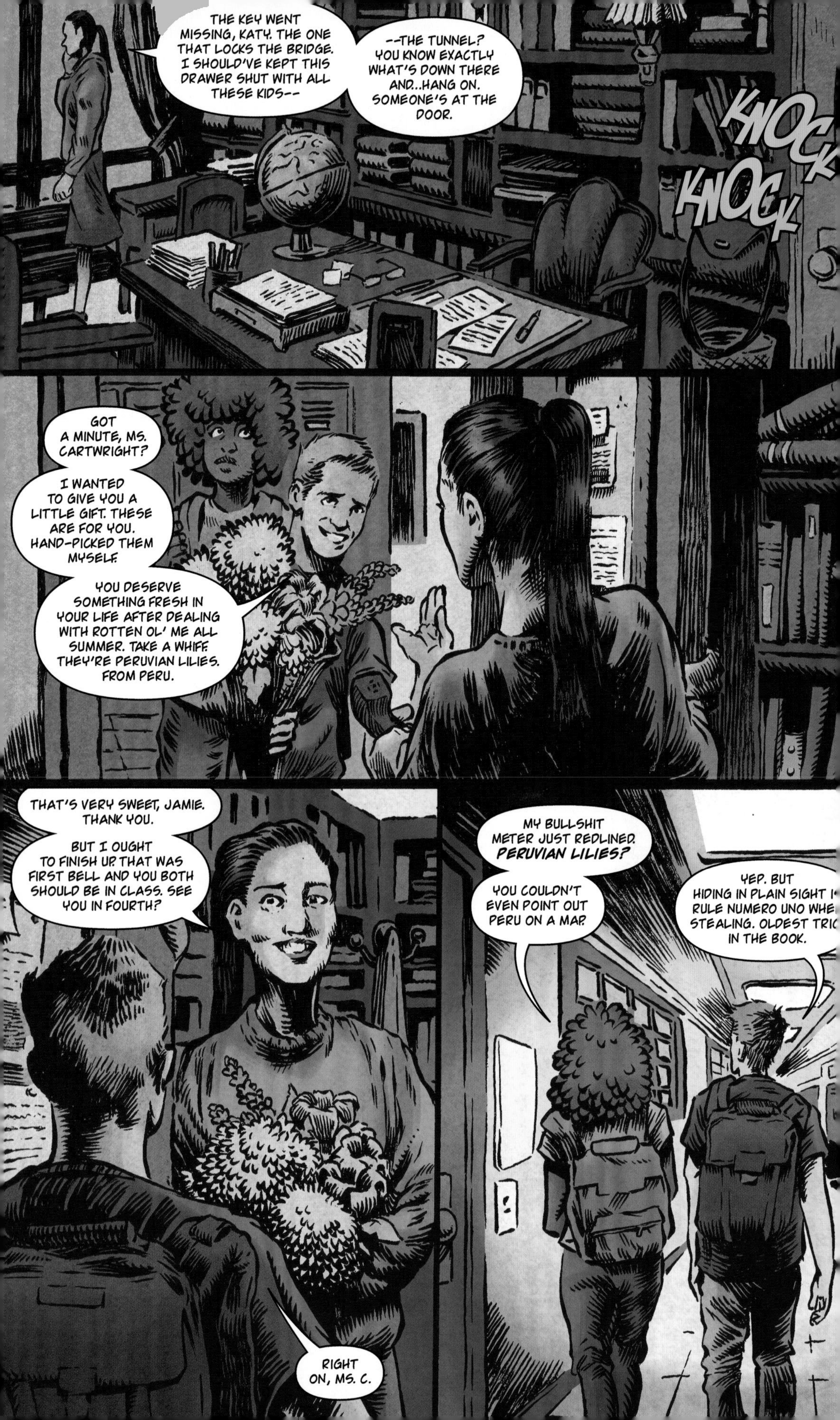
THE KEY WENT MISSING, KATY. THE ONE THAT LOCKS THE BRIDGE. I SHOULD'VE KEPT THIS DRAWER SHUT WITH ALL THESE KIDS--
--THE TUNNEL? YOU KNOW EXACTLY WHAT'S DOWN THERE AND...HANG ON. SOMEONE'S AT THE DOOR.
KNOCK
KNOCK
GOT A MINUTE, MS. CARTWRIGHT?
I WANTED TO GIVE YOU A LITTLE GIFT. THESE ARE FOR YOU. HAND-PICKED THEM MYSELF.
YOU DESERVE SOMETHING FRESH IN YOUR LIFE AFTER DEALING WITH ROTTEN OL' ME ALL SUMMER. TAKE A WHIFF. THEY'RE PERUVIAN LILIES. FROM PERU.
THAT'S VERY SWEET, JAMIE. THANK YOU.
BUT I OUGHT TO FINISH UP. THAT WAS FIRST BELL AND YOU BOTH SHOULD BE IN CLASS. SEE YOU IN FOURTH?
RIGHT ON, MS. C.
MY BULLSHIT METER JUST REDLINED. *PERUVIAN LILIES?*
YOU COULDN'T EVEN POINT OUT PERU ON A MAP.
YEP. BUT HIDING IN PLAIN SIGHT I RULE NUMERO UNO WHE STEALING. OLDEST TRIC IN THE BOOK.

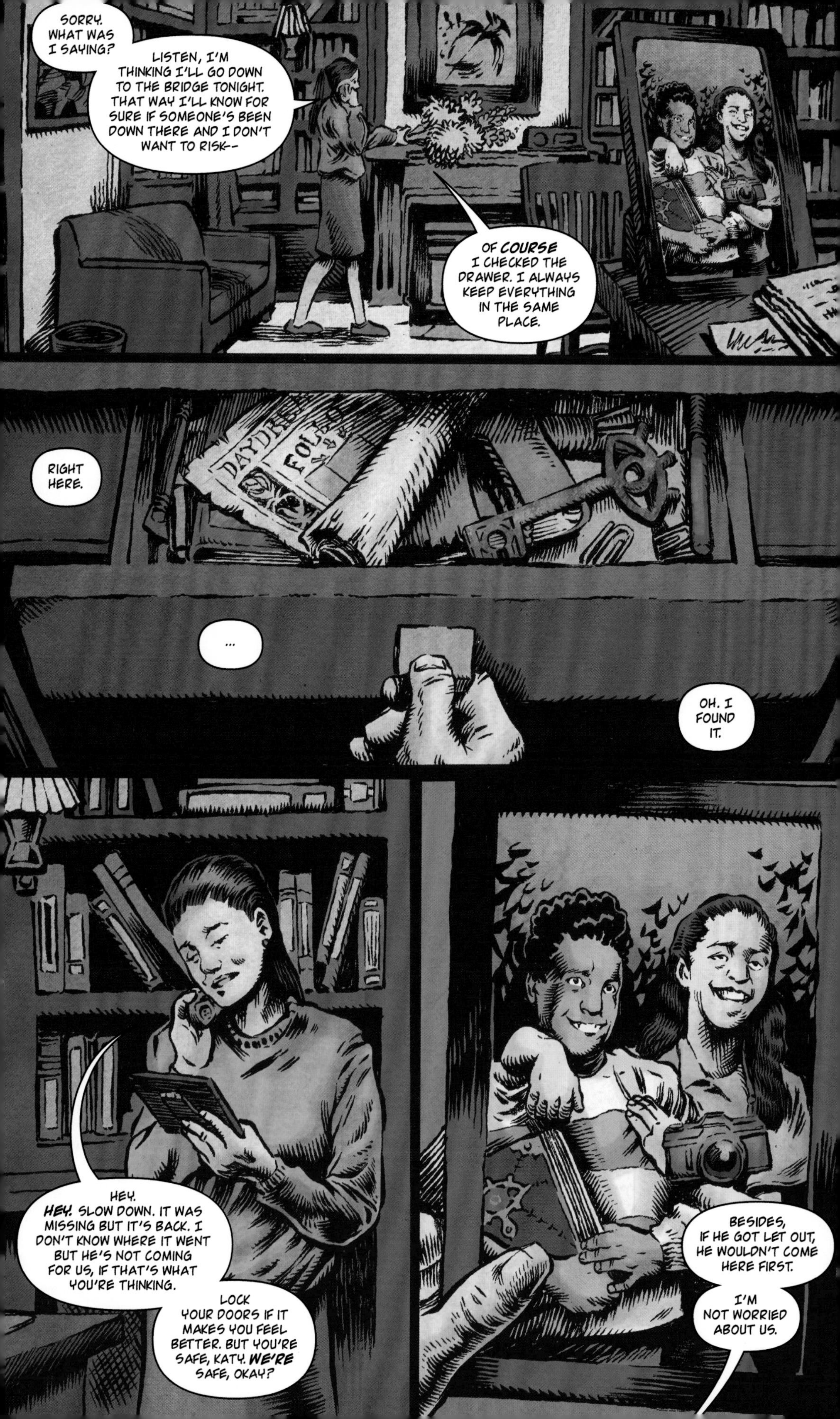
SORRY. WHAT WAS I SAYING?
LISTEN, I'M THINKING I'LL GO DOWN TO THE BRIDGE TONIGHT. THAT WAY I'LL KNOW FOR SURE IF SOMEONE'S BEEN DOWN THERE AND I DON'T WANT TO RISK--
OF COURSE I CHECKED THE DRAWER. I ALWAYS KEEP EVERYTHING IN THE SAME PLACE.
RIGHT HERE.
...
OH. I FOUND IT.
HEY. HEY. SLOW DOWN. IT WAS MISSING BUT IT'S BACK. I DON'T KNOW WHERE IT WENT BUT HE'S NOT COMING FOR US, IF THAT'S WHAT YOU'RE THINKING.
LOCK YOUR DOORS IF IT MAKES YOU FEEL BETTER. BUT YOU'RE SAFE, KATY. WE'RE SAFE, OKAY?
BESIDES, IF HE GOT LET OUT, HE WOULDN'T COME HERE FIRST.
I'M NOT WORRIED ABOUT US.

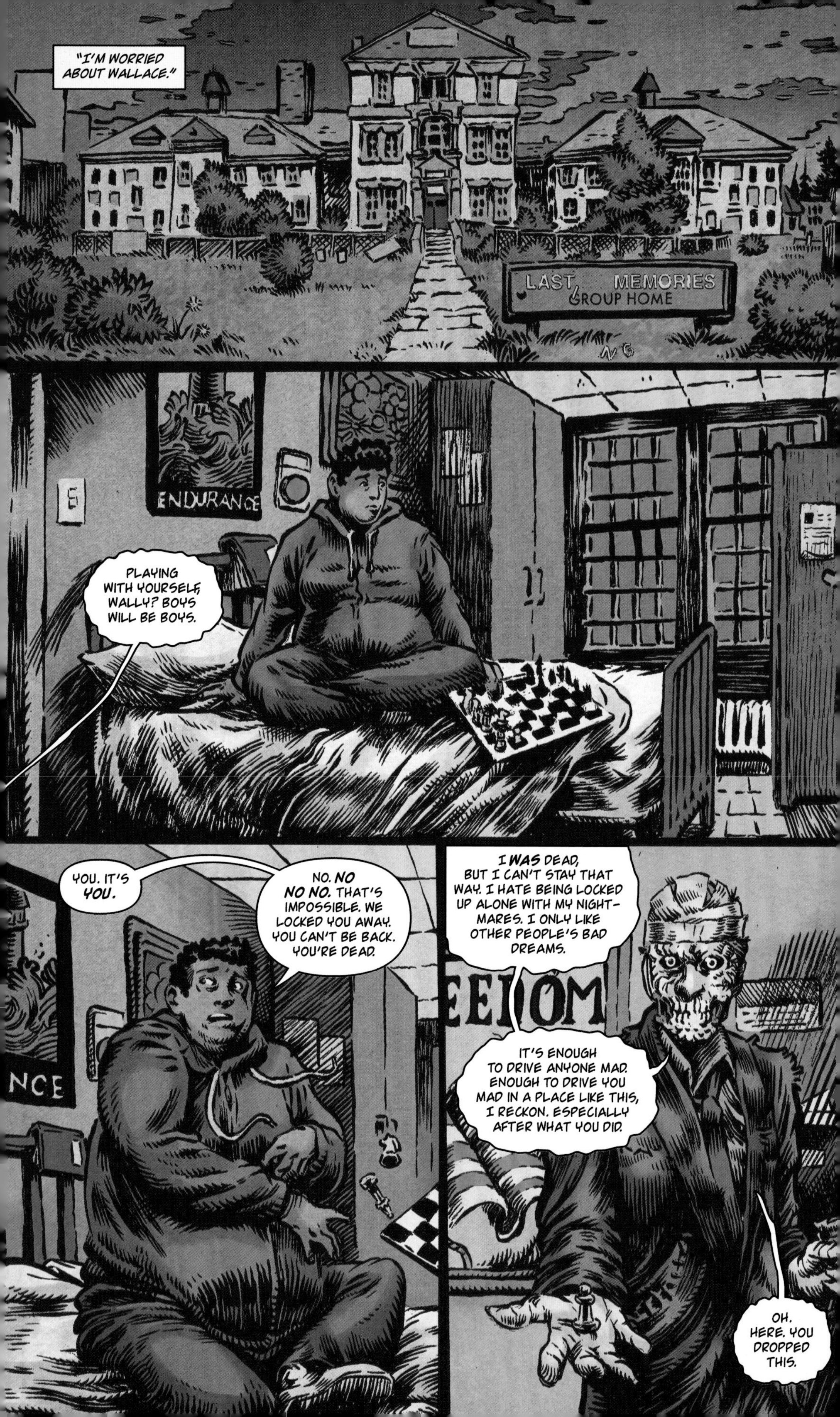
"I'M WORRIED ABOUT WALLACE."
LAST MEMORIES GROUP HOME
ENDURANCE
PLAYING WITH YOURSELF, WALLY? BOYS WILL BE BOYS.
YOU. IT'S *YOU.*
NO. *NO NO NO.* THAT'S IMPOSSIBLE. WE LOCKED YOU AWAY. YOU CAN'T BE BACK. YOU'RE DEAD.
I *WAS* DEAD, BUT I CAN'T STAY THAT WAY. I HATE BEING LOCKED UP ALONE WITH MY NIGHTMARES. I ONLY LIKE OTHER PEOPLE'S BAD DREAMS.
IT'S ENOUGH TO DRIVE ANYONE MAD. ENOUGH TO DRIVE YOU MAD IN A PLACE LIKE THIS, I RECKON. ESPECIALLY AFTER WHAT YOU DID.
OH. HERE. YOU DROPPED THIS.

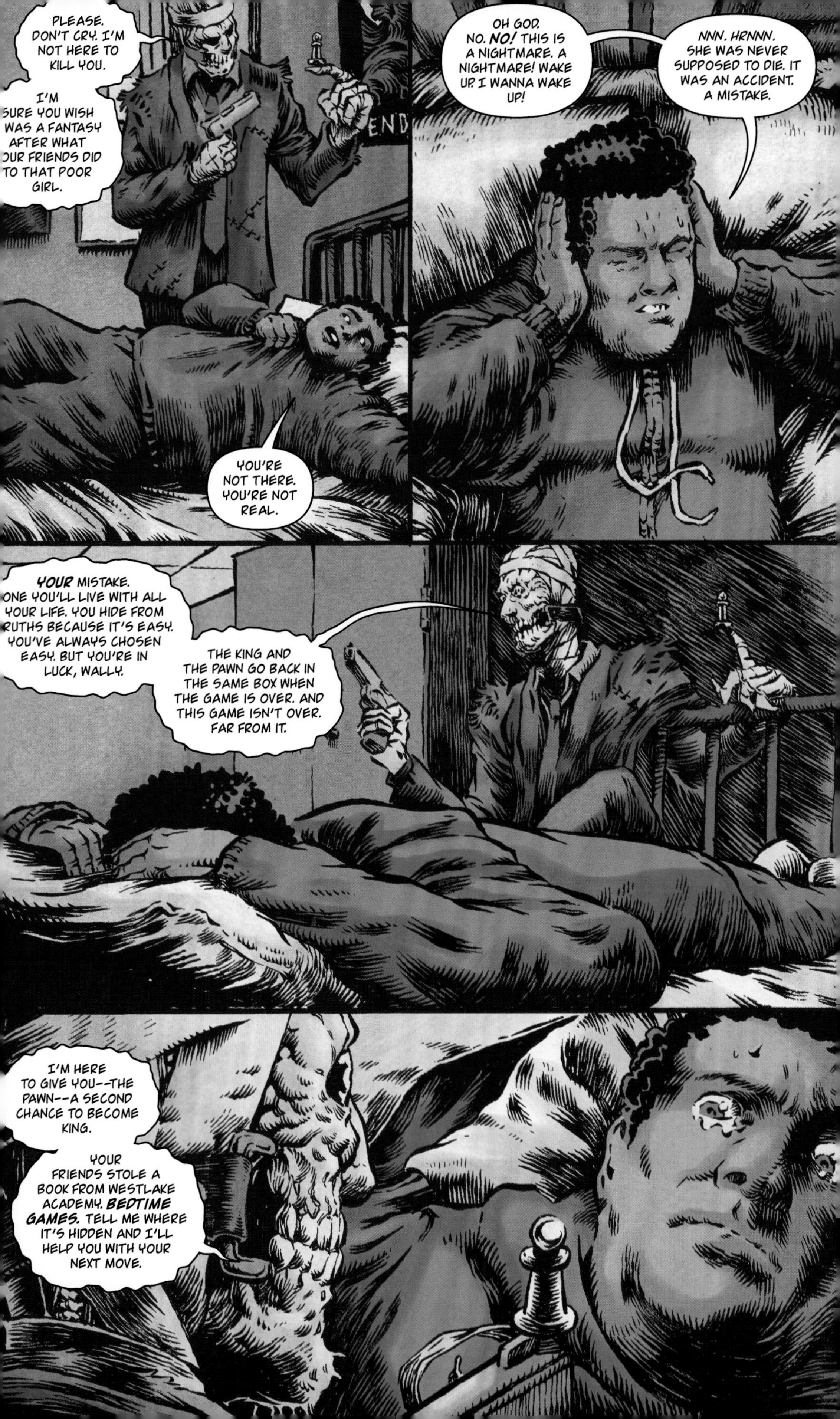
PLEASE. DON'T CRY. I'M NOT HERE TO KILL YOU.
I'M SURE YOU WISH WAS A FANTASY AFTER WHAT OUR FRIENDS DID TO THAT POOR GIRL.
YOU'RE NOT THERE. YOU'RE NOT REAL.
OH GOD. NO. NO! THIS IS A NIGHTMARE. A NIGHTMARE! WAKE UP. I WANNA WAKE UP!
NNN. HRNNN. SHE WAS NEVER SUPPOSED TO DIE. IT WAS AN ACCIDENT. A MISTAKE.
YOUR MISTAKE. ONE YOU'LL LIVE WITH ALL YOUR LIFE. YOU HIDE FROM TRUTHS BECAUSE IT'S EASY. YOU'VE ALWAYS CHOSEN EASY. BUT YOU'RE IN LUCK, WALLY.
THE KING AND THE PAWN GO BACK IN THE SAME BOX WHEN THE GAME IS OVER. AND THIS GAME ISN'T OVER. FAR FROM IT.
I'M HERE TO GIVE YOU--THE PAWN--A SECOND CHANCE TO BECOME KING.
YOUR FRIENDS STOLE A BOOK FROM WESTLAKE ACADEMY. BEDTIME GAMES. TELL ME WHERE IT'S HIDDEN AND I'LL HELP YOU WITH YOUR NEXT MOVE.

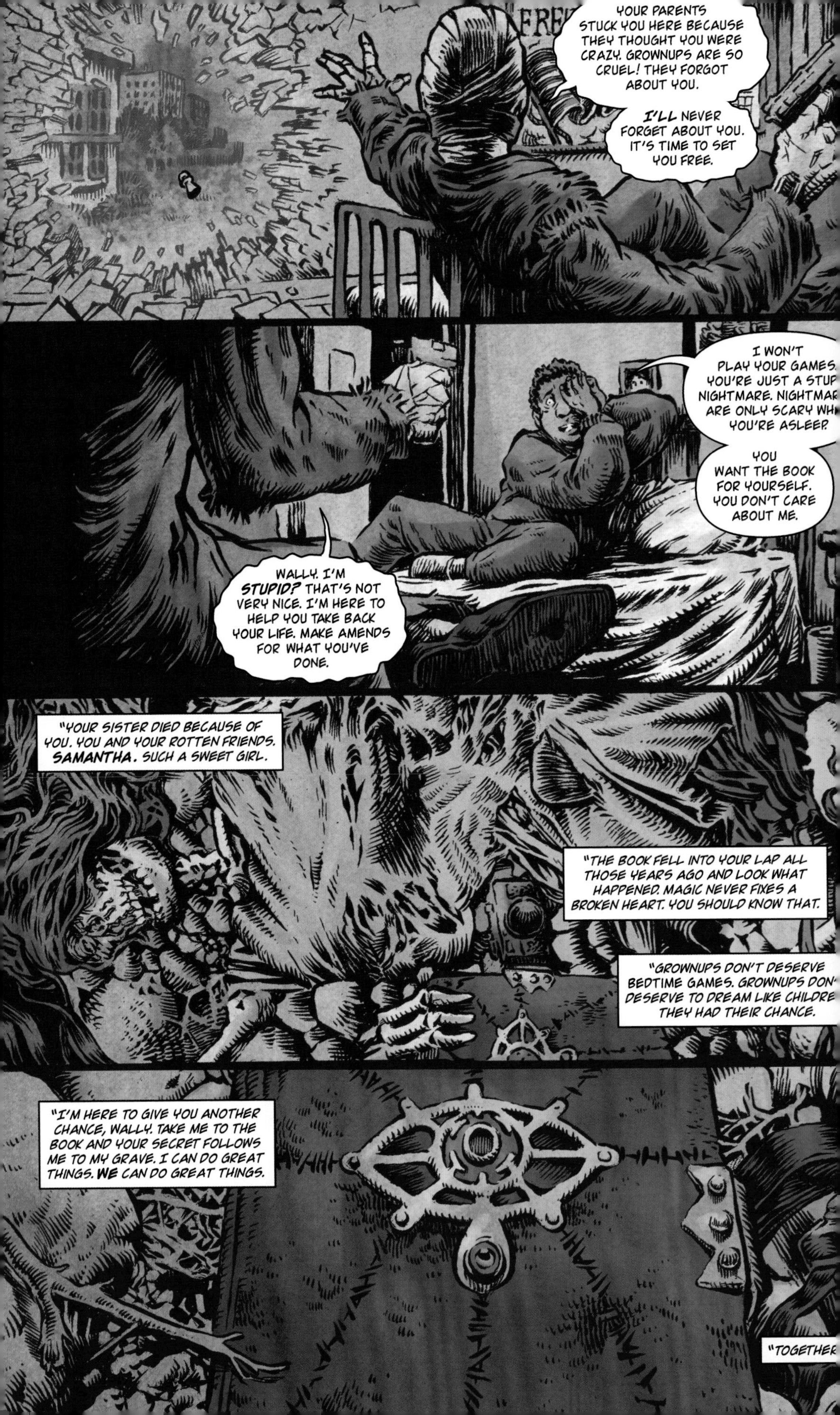
YOUR PARENTS STUCK YOU HERE BECAUSE THEY THOUGHT YOU WERE CRAZY. GROWNUPS ARE SO CRUEL! THEY FORGOT ABOUT YOU.
I'LL NEVER FORGET ABOUT YOU. IT'S TIME TO SET YOU FREE.
I WON'T PLAY YOUR GAMES. YOU'RE JUST A STUP NIGHTMARE. NIGHTMAR ARE ONLY SCARY WH YOU'RE ASLEEP.
YOU WANT THE BOOK FOR YOURSELF. YOU DON'T CARE ABOUT ME.
WALLY. I'M STUPID? THAT'S NOT VERY NICE. I'M HERE TO HELP YOU TAKE BACK YOUR LIFE. MAKE AMENDS FOR WHAT YOU'VE DONE.
"YOUR SISTER DIED BECAUSE OF YOU. YOU AND YOUR ROTTEN FRIENDS. SAMANTHA. SUCH A SWEET GIRL.
"THE BOOK FELL INTO YOUR LAP ALL THOSE YEARS AGO AND LOOK WHAT HAPPENED. MAGIC NEVER FIXES A BROKEN HEART. YOU SHOULD KNOW THAT.
"GROWNUPS DON'T DESERVE BEDTIME GAMES. GROWNUPS DON' DESERVE TO DREAM LIKE CHILDRE THEY HAD THEIR CHANCE.
"I'M HERE TO GIVE YOU ANOTHER CHANCE, WALLY. TAKE ME TO THE BOOK AND YOUR SECRET FOLLOWS ME TO MY GRAVE. I CAN DO GREAT THINGS. WE CAN DO GREAT THINGS.
"TOGETHER

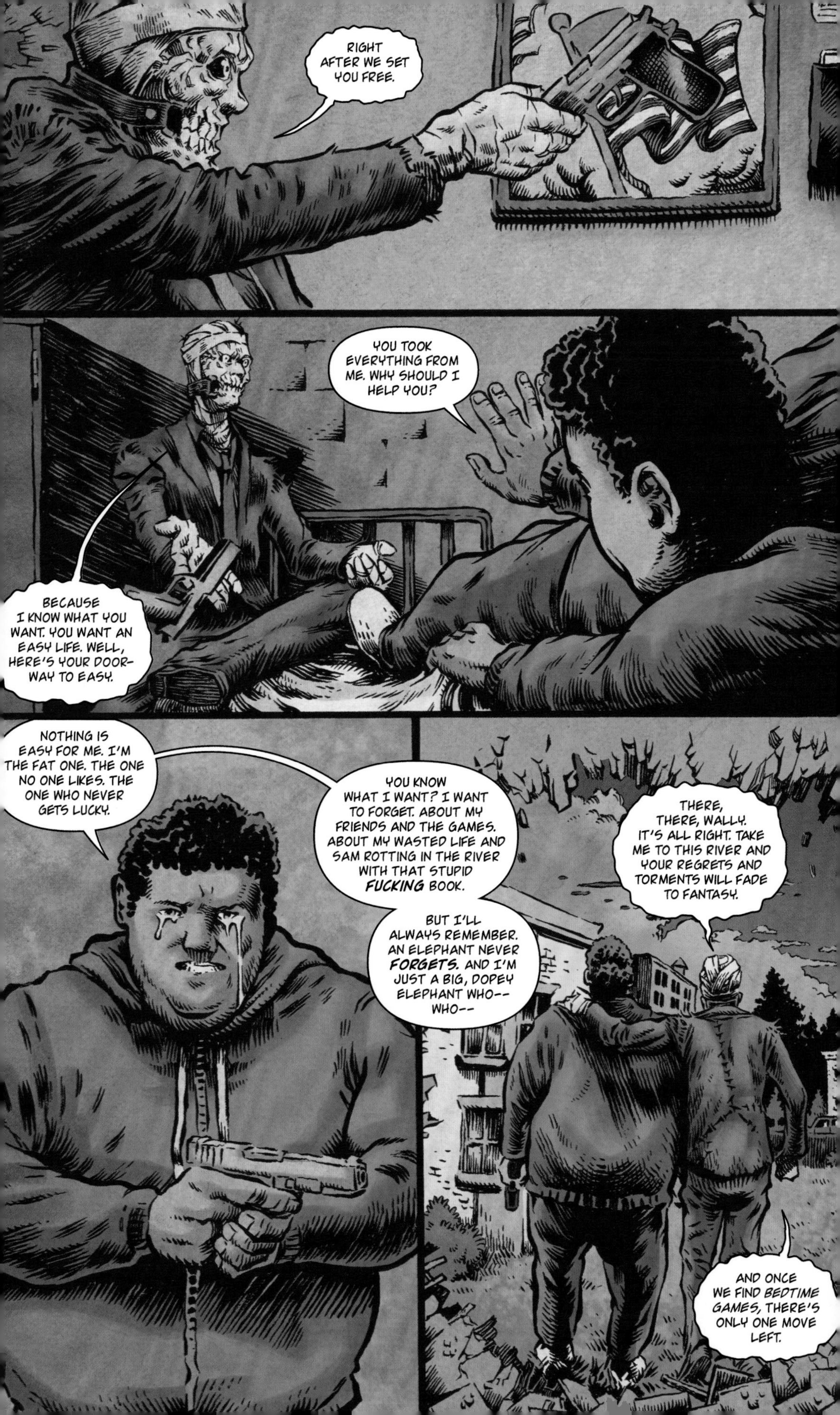
RIGHT AFTER WE SET YOU FREE.
YOU TOOK EVERYTHING FROM ME. WHY SHOULD I HELP YOU?
BECAUSE I KNOW WHAT YOU WANT. YOU WANT AN EASY LIFE. WELL, HERE'S YOUR DOOR-WAY TO EASY.
NOTHING IS EASY FOR ME. I'M THE FAT ONE. THE ONE NO ONE LIKES. THE ONE WHO NEVER GETS LUCKY.
YOU KNOW WHAT I WANT? I WANT TO FORGET. ABOUT MY FRIENDS AND THE GAMES. ABOUT MY WASTED LIFE AND SAM ROTTING IN THE RIVER WITH THAT STUPID **FUCKING** BOOK.
BUT I'LL ALWAYS REMEMBER. AN ELEPHANT NEVER **FORGETS.** AND I'M JUST A BIG, DOPEY ELEPHANT WHO-- WHO--
THERE, THERE, WALLY. IT'S ALL RIGHT. TAKE ME TO THIS RIVER AND YOUR REGRETS AND TORMENTS WILL FADE TO FANTASY.
AND ONCE WE FIND *BEDTIME GAMES*, THERE'S ONLY ONE MOVE LEFT.

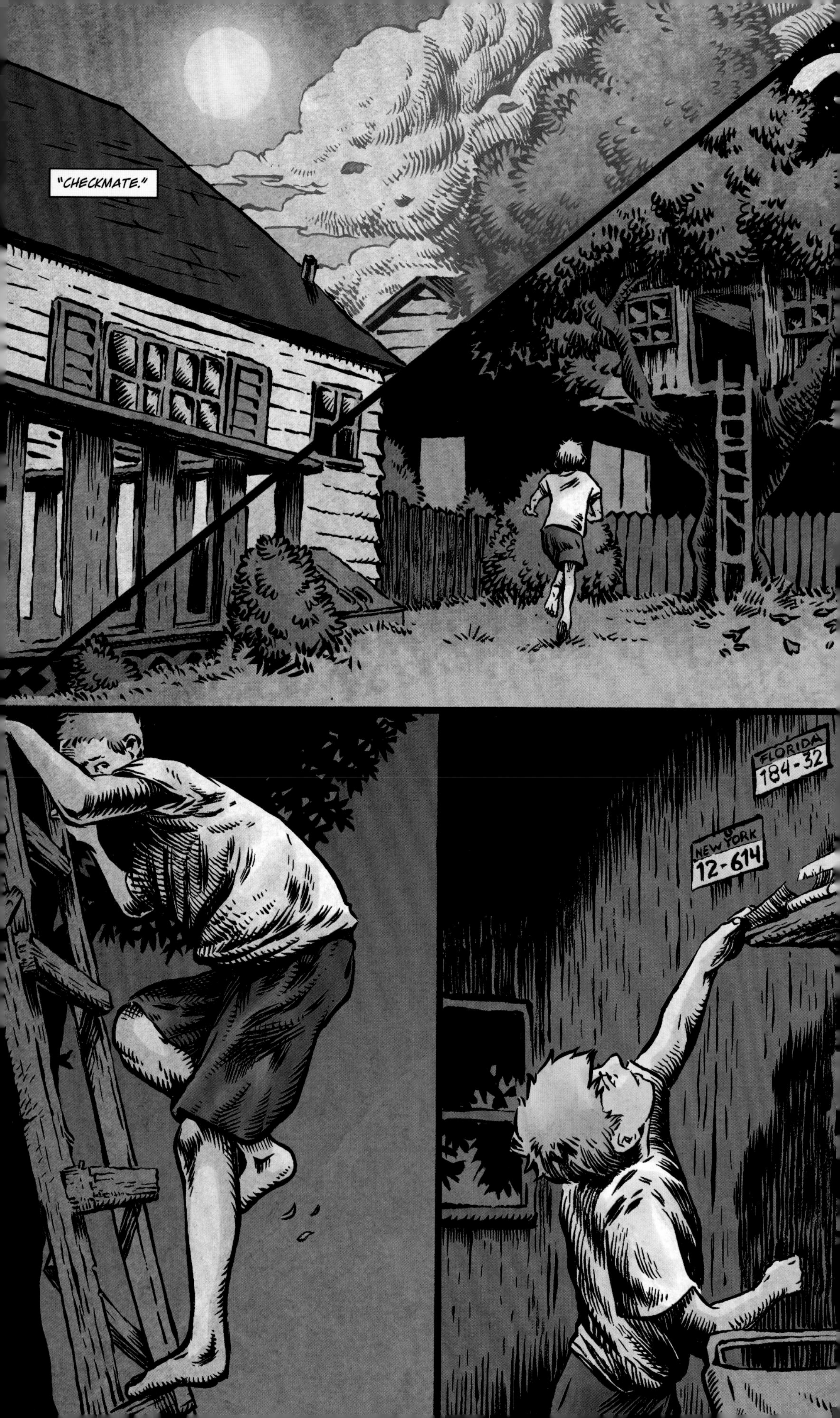
"CHECKMATE."
FLORIDA
184-32
NEW YORK
12-614

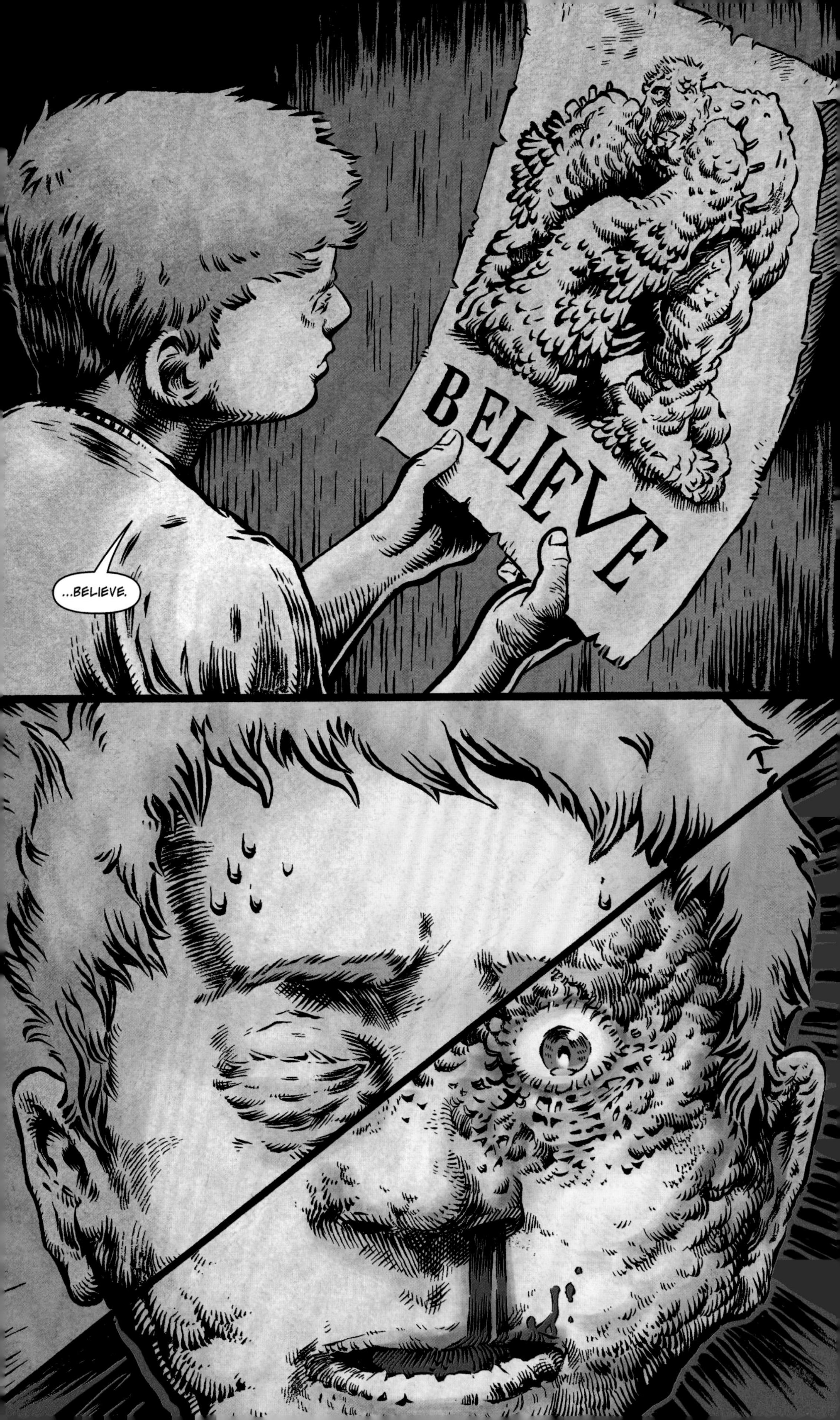
BELIEVE
...BELIEVE.

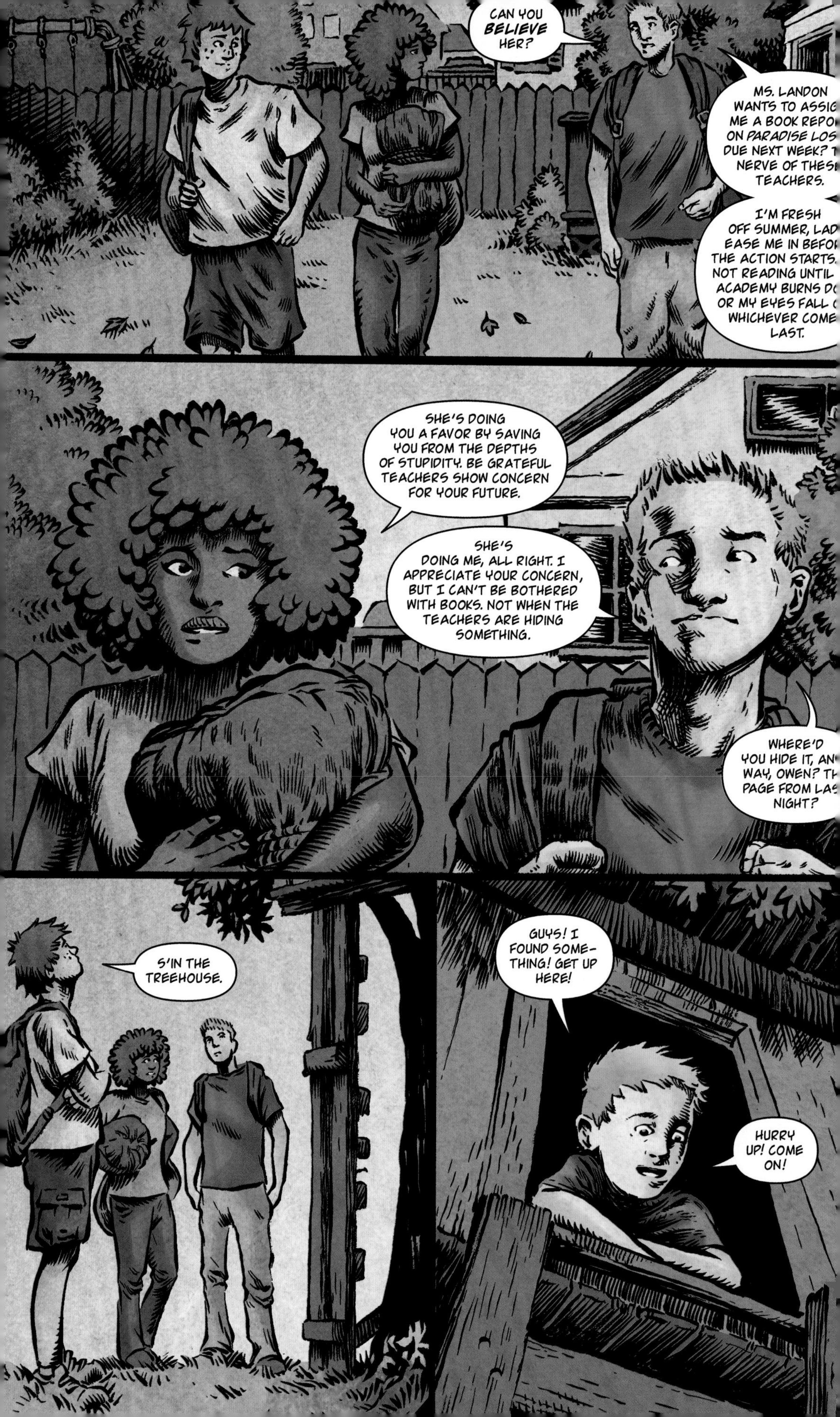
CAN YOU *BELIEVE* HER?
MS. LANDON WANTS TO ASSIG ME A BOOK REPO ON *PARADISE LOS* DUE NEXT WEEK? T NERVE OF THES TEACHERS.
I'M FRESH OFF SUMMER, LAD EASE ME IN BEFO THE ACTION STARTS. NOT READING UNTIL ACADEMY BURNS D OR MY EYES FALL WHICHEVER COME LAST.
SHE'S DOING YOU A FAVOR BY SAVING YOU FROM THE DEPTHS OF STUPIDITY. BE GRATEFUL TEACHERS SHOW CONCERN FOR YOUR FUTURE.
SHE'S DOING ME, ALL RIGHT. I APPRECIATE YOUR CONCERN, BUT I CAN'T BE BOTHERED WITH BOOKS. NOT WHEN THE TEACHERS ARE HIDING SOMETHING.
WHERE'D YOU HIDE IT, AN WAY, OWEN? TH PAGE FROM LAS NIGHT?
S'IN THE TREEHOUSE.
GUYS! I FOUND SOME-THING! GET UP HERE!
HURRY UP! COME ON!

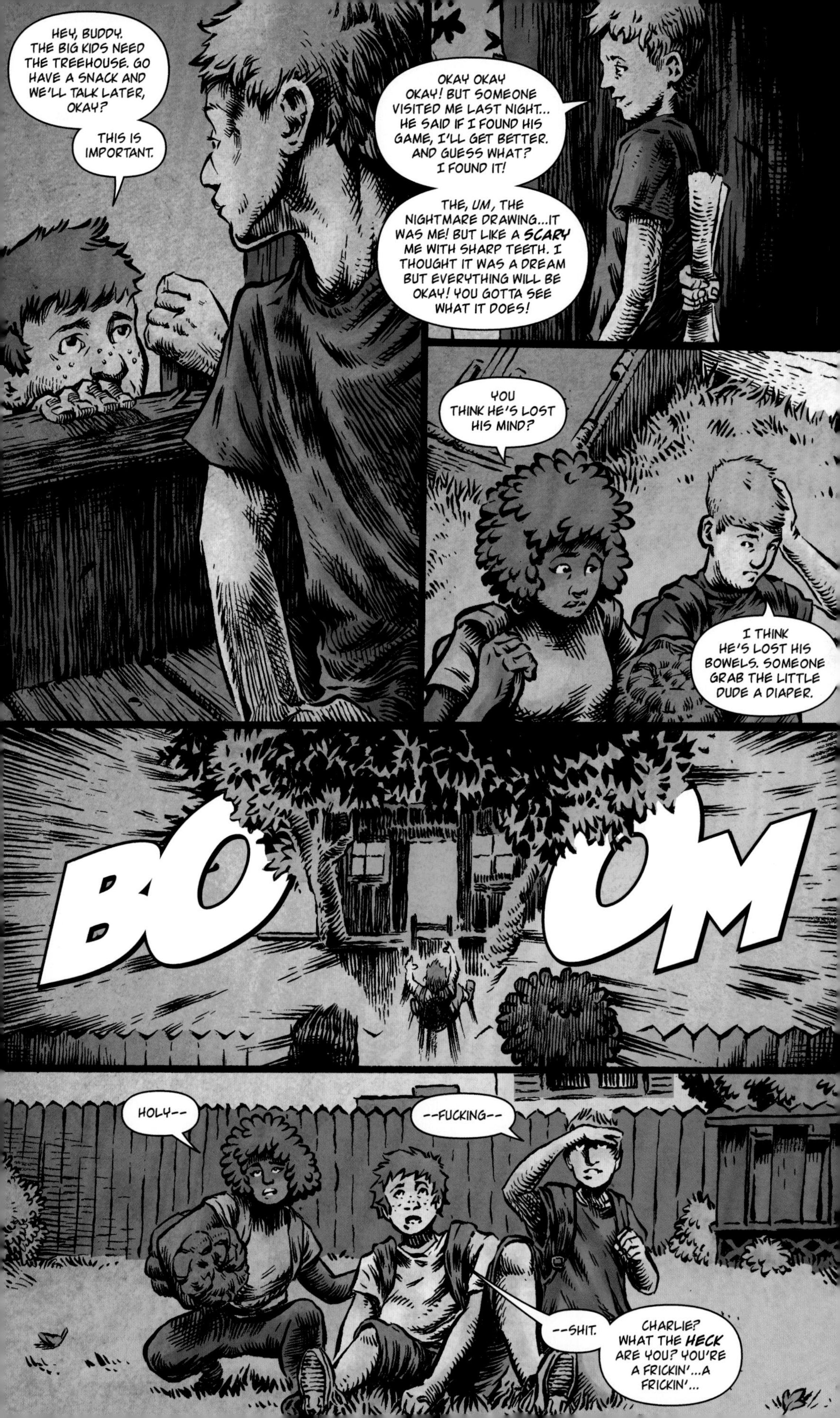
HEY, BUDDY. THE BIG KIDS NEED THE TREEHOUSE. GO HAVE A SNACK AND WE'LL TALK LATER, OKAY?
THIS IS IMPORTANT.
OKAY OKAY OKAY! BUT SOMEONE VISITED ME LAST NIGHT... HE SAID IF I FOUND HIS GAME, I'LL GET BETTER. AND GUESS WHAT? I FOUND IT!
THE, UM, THE NIGHTMARE DRAWING...IT WAS ME! BUT LIKE A SCARY ME WITH SHARP TEETH. I THOUGHT IT WAS A DREAM BUT EVERYTHING WILL BE OKAY! YOU GOTTA SEE WHAT IT DOES!
YOU THINK HE'S LOST HIS MIND?
I THINK HE'S LOST HIS BOWELS. SOMEONE GRAB THE LITTLE DUDE A DIAPER.
BOOM
HOLY--
--FUCKING--
--SHIT.
CHARLIE? WHAT THE HECK ARE YOU? YOU'RE A FRICKIN'...A FRICKIN'...

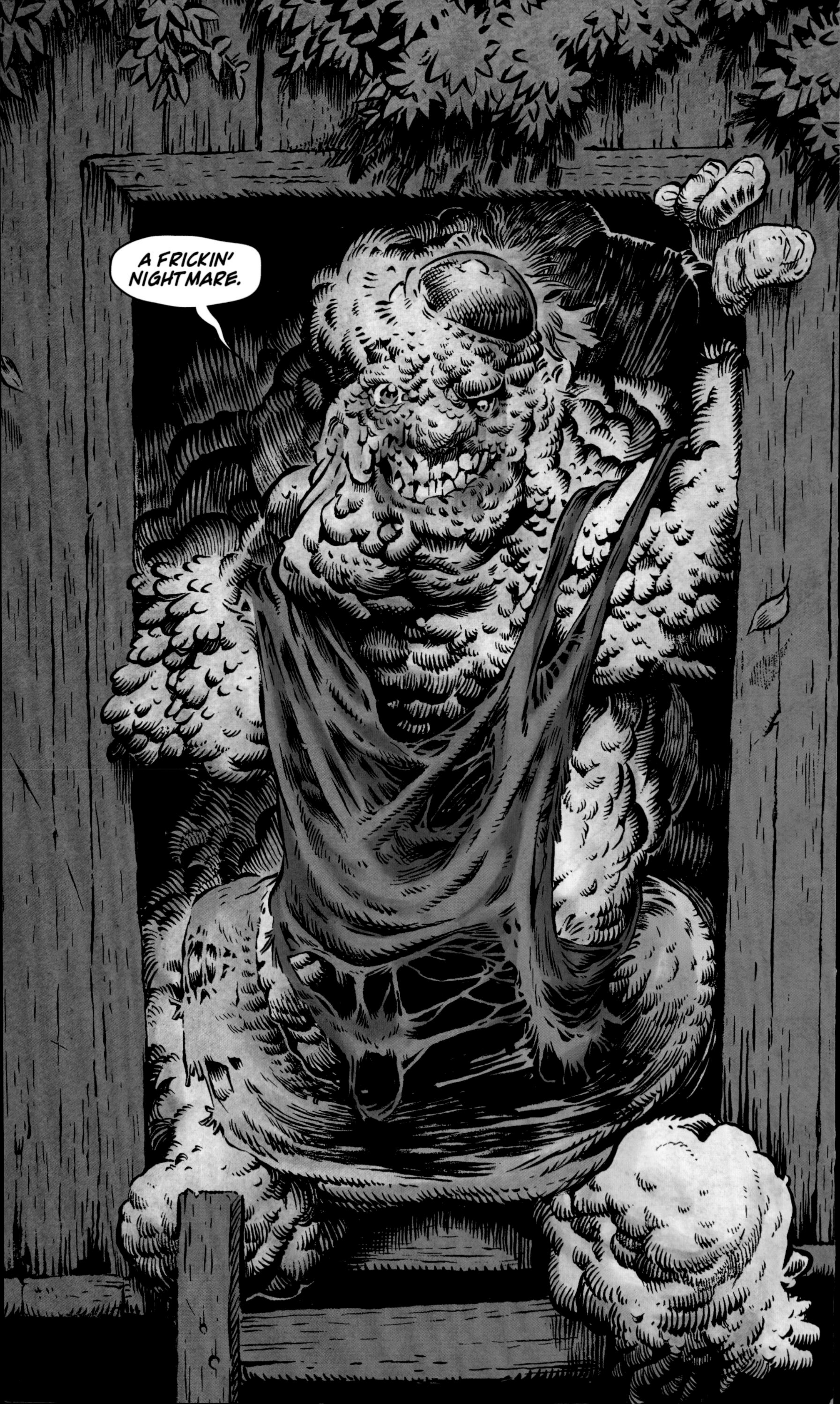
A FRICKIN' NIGHTMARE.

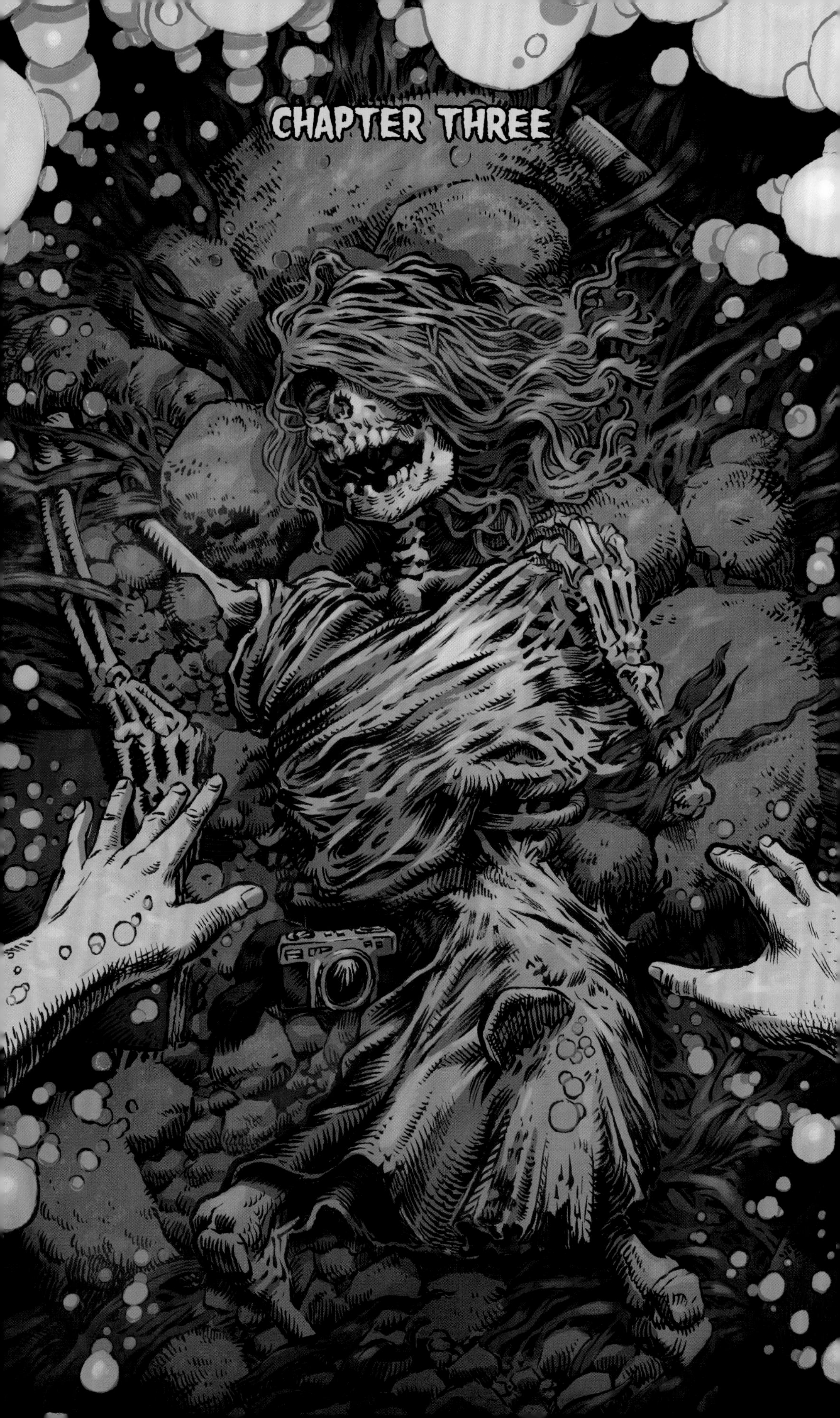
CHAPTER THREE

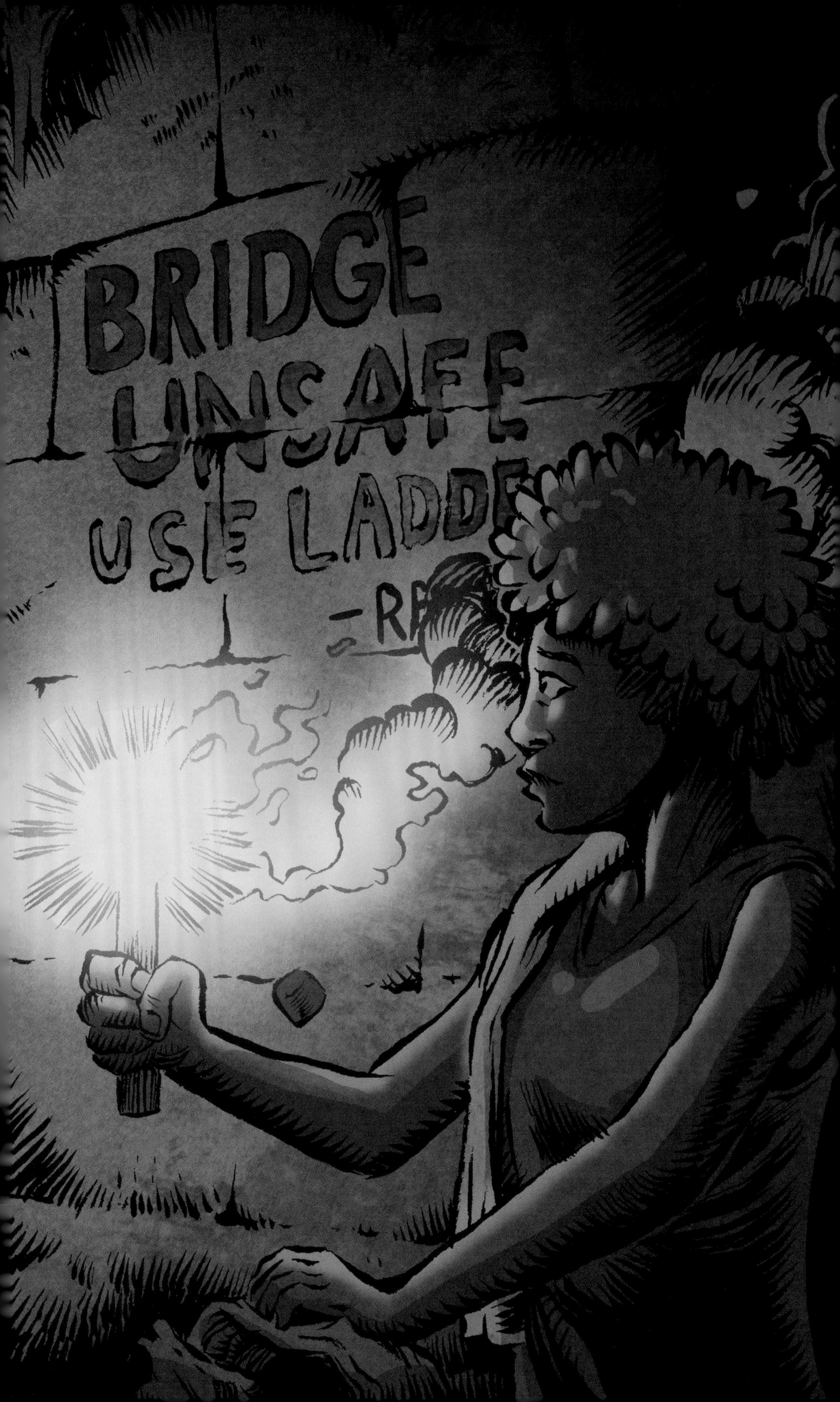
BRIDGE
UNSAFE
USE LADDE
-R

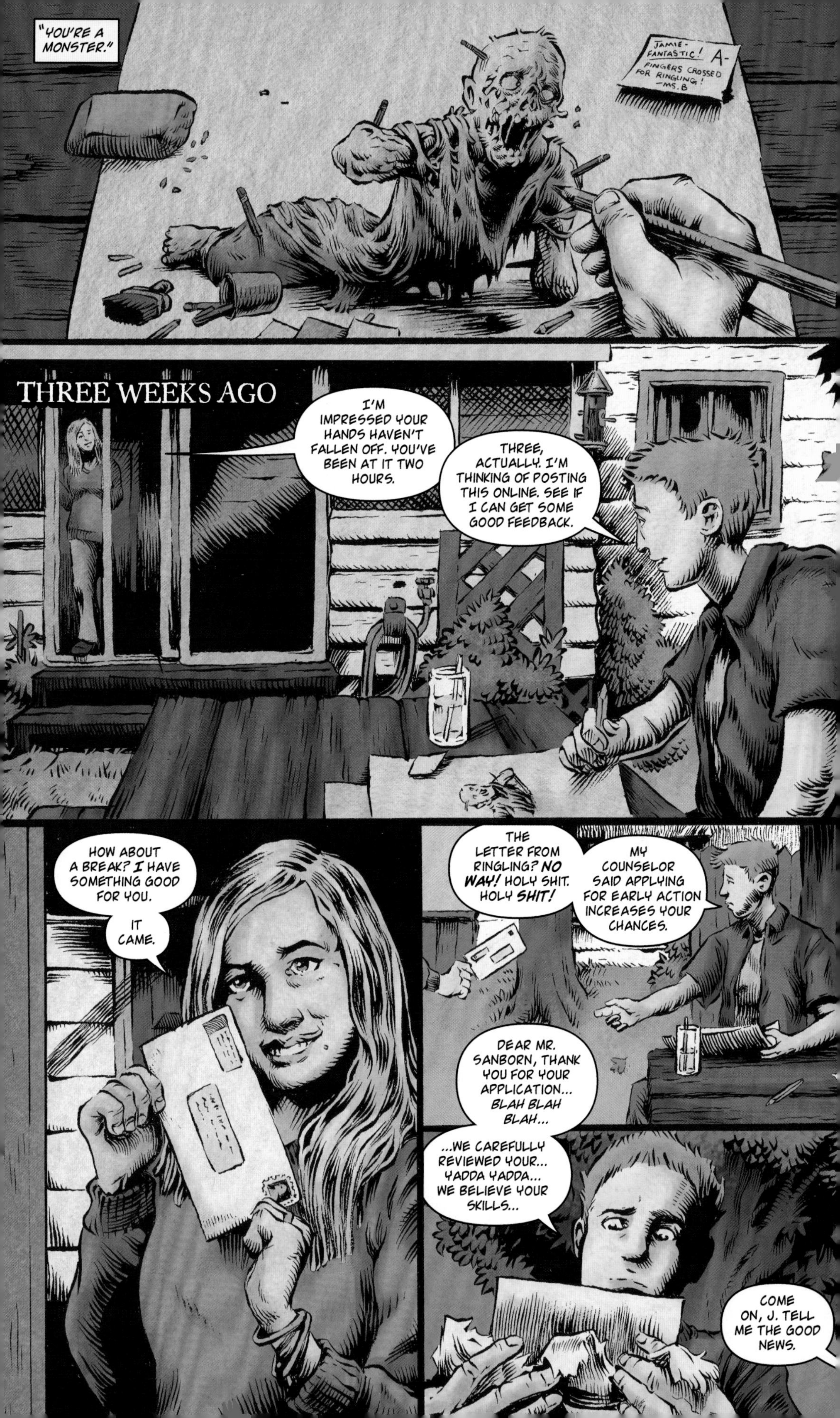

"YOU'RE A MONSTER."
JAMIE- FANTASTIC! A- FINGERS CROSSED FOR RINGLING! -MS. B
THREE WEEKS AGO
I'M IMPRESSED YOUR HANDS HAVEN'T FALLEN OFF. YOU'VE BEEN AT IT TWO HOURS.
THREE, ACTUALLY. I'M THINKING OF POSTING THIS ONLINE. SEE IF I CAN GET SOME GOOD FEEDBACK.
HOW ABOUT A BREAK? I HAVE SOMETHING GOOD FOR YOU.
IT CAME.
THE LETTER FROM RINGLING? NO WAY! HOLY SHIT. HOLY SHIT!
MY COUNSELOR SAID APPLYING FOR EARLY ACTION INCREASES YOUR CHANCES.
DEAR MR. SANBORN, THANK YOU FOR YOUR APPLICATION... BLAH BLAH BLAH...
...WE CAREFULLY REVIEWED YOUR... YADDA YADDA... WE BELIEVE YOUR SKILLS...
COME ON, J. TELL ME THE GOOD NEWS.

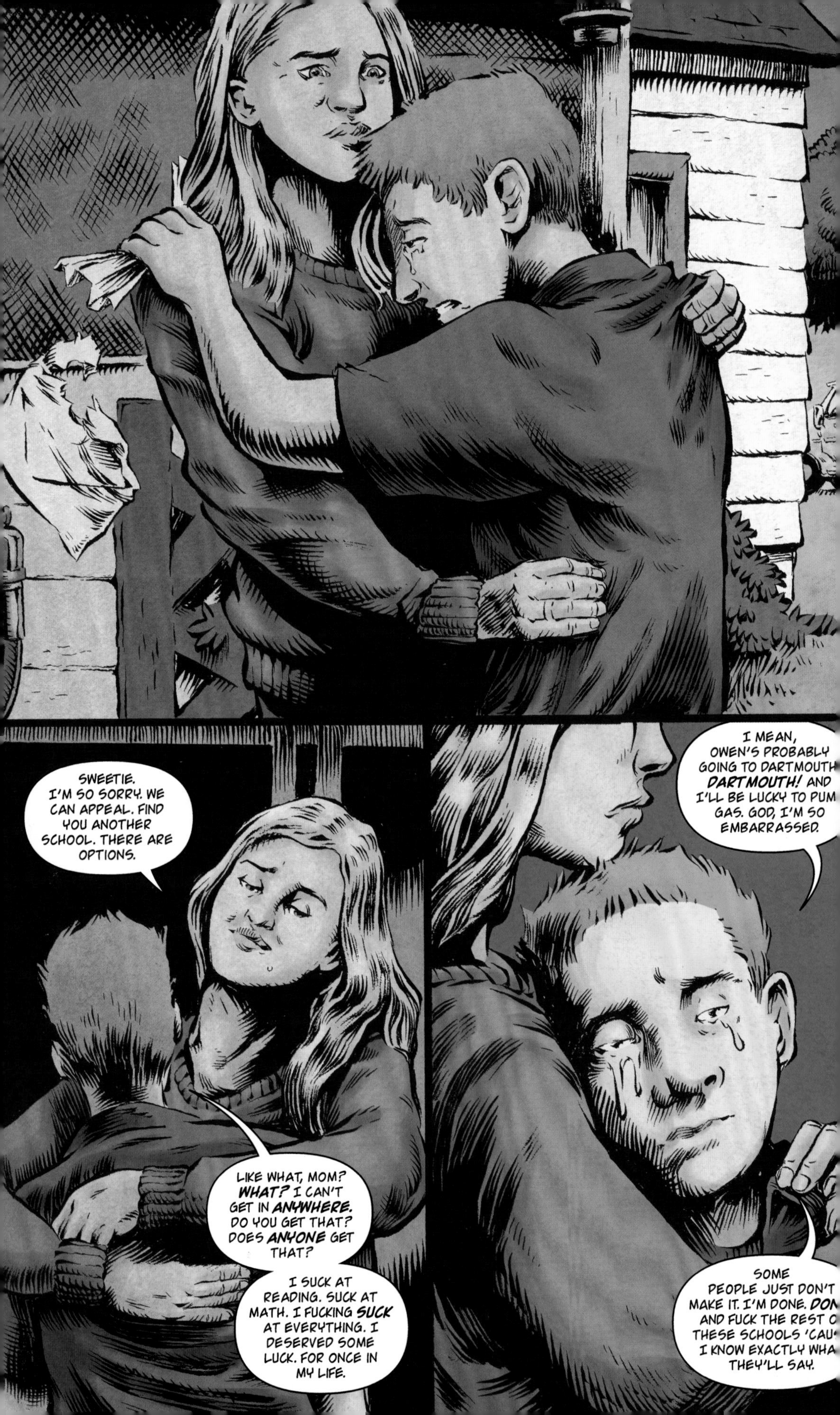
SWEETIE. I'M SO SORRY. WE CAN APPEAL. FIND YOU ANOTHER SCHOOL. THERE ARE OPTIONS.
LIKE WHAT, MOM? WHAT? I CAN'T GET IN ANYWHERE. DO YOU GET THAT? DOES ANYONE GET THAT?
I SUCK AT READING. SUCK AT MATH. I FUCKING SUCK AT EVERYTHING. I DESERVED SOME LUCK. FOR ONCE IN MY LIFE.
I MEAN, OWEN'S PROBABLY GOING TO DARTMOUTH. DARTMOUTH! AND I'LL BE LUCKY TO PUM GAS. GOD, I'M SO EMBARRASSED.
SOME PEOPLE JUST DON'T MAKE IT. I'M DONE. DON AND FUCK THE REST C THESE SCHOOLS 'CAU I KNOW EXACTLY WHA THEY'LL SAY.

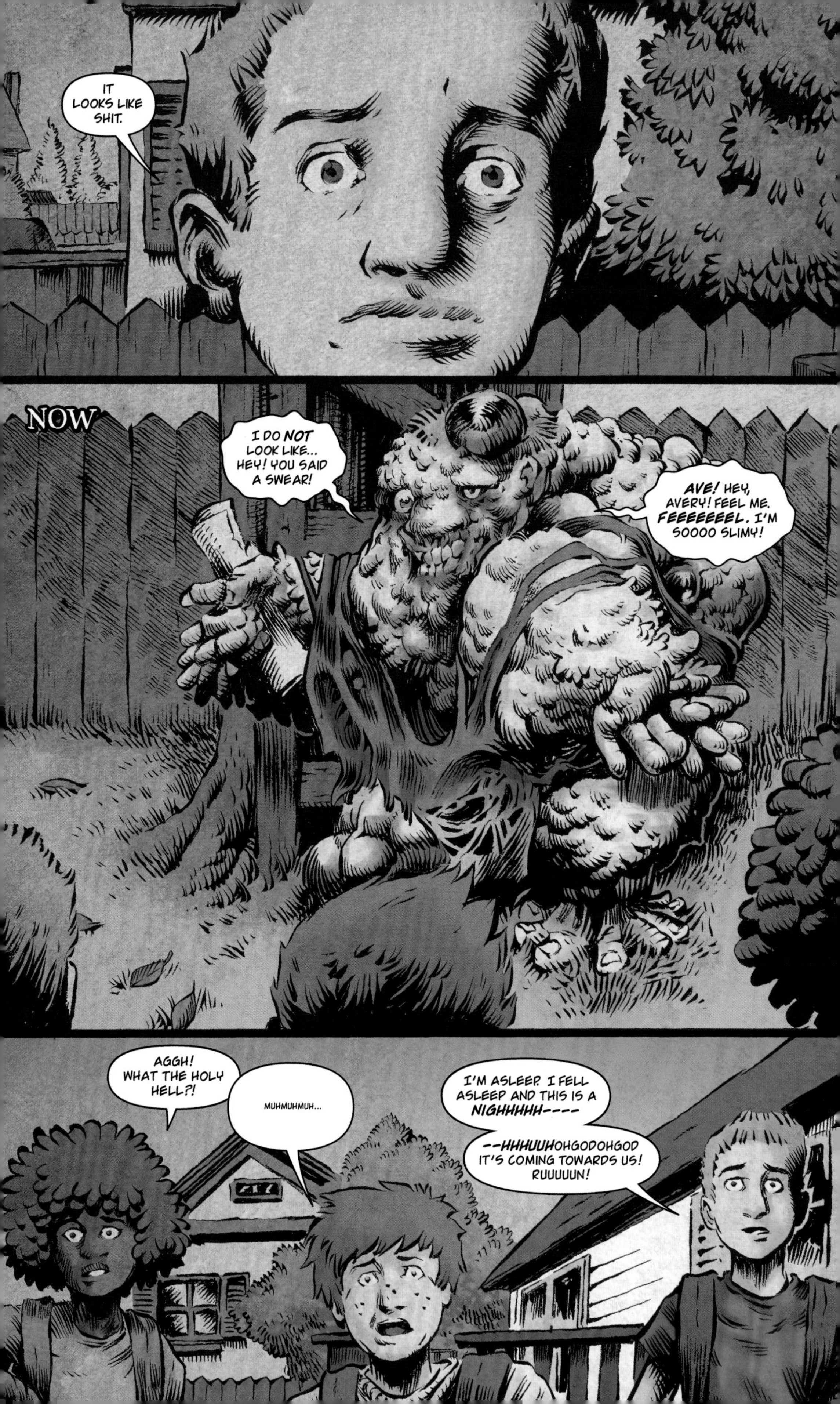
IT LOOKS LIKE SHIT.
NOW
I DO **NOT** LOOK LIKE... HEY! YOU SAID A SWEAR!
AVE! HEY, AVERY! FEEL ME. ***FEEEEEEEL.*** I'M SOOOO SLIMY!
AGGH! WHAT THE HOLY HELL?!
MUHMUHMUH...
I'M ASLEEP. I FELL ASLEEP AND THIS IS A ***NIGHHHHH----***
--HHHUUHOHGODOHGOD IT'S COMING TOWARDS US! RUUUUUN!

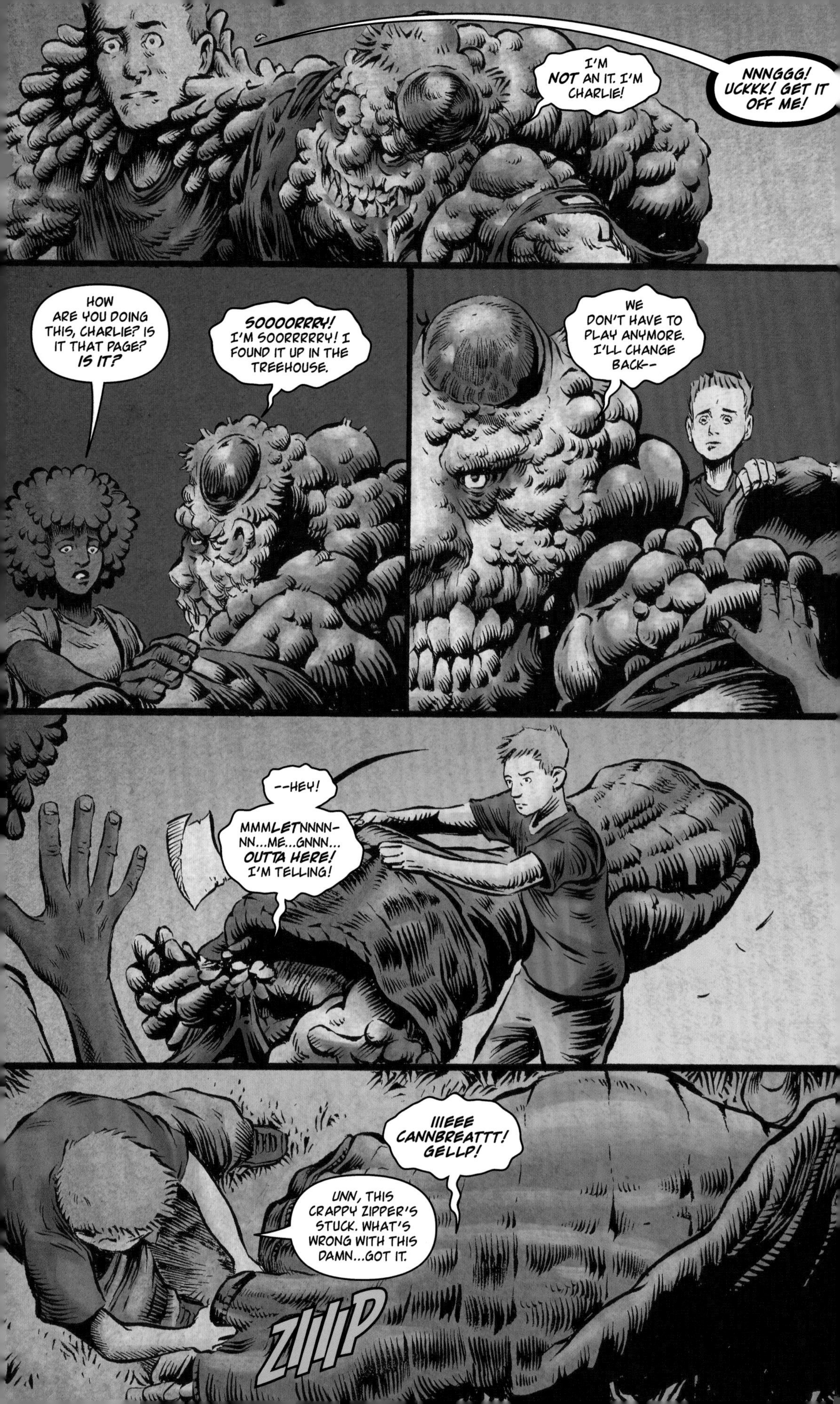
I'M NOT AN IT. I'M CHARLIE!
NNNGGG! UCKKK! GET IT OFF ME!
HOW ARE YOU DOING THIS, CHARLIE? IS IT THAT PAGE? IS IT?
SOOOORRRY! I'M SOORRRRRY! I FOUND IT UP IN THE TREEHOUSE.
WE DON'T HAVE TO PLAY ANYMORE. I'LL CHANGE BACK--
--HEY!
MMMLETNNNN-NN...ME...GNNN... OUTTA HERE! I'M TELLING!
IIIEEE CANNBREATTT! GELLP!
UNN, THIS CRAPPY ZIPPER'S STUCK. WHAT'S WRONG WITH THIS DAMN...GOT IT.
ZIIIP

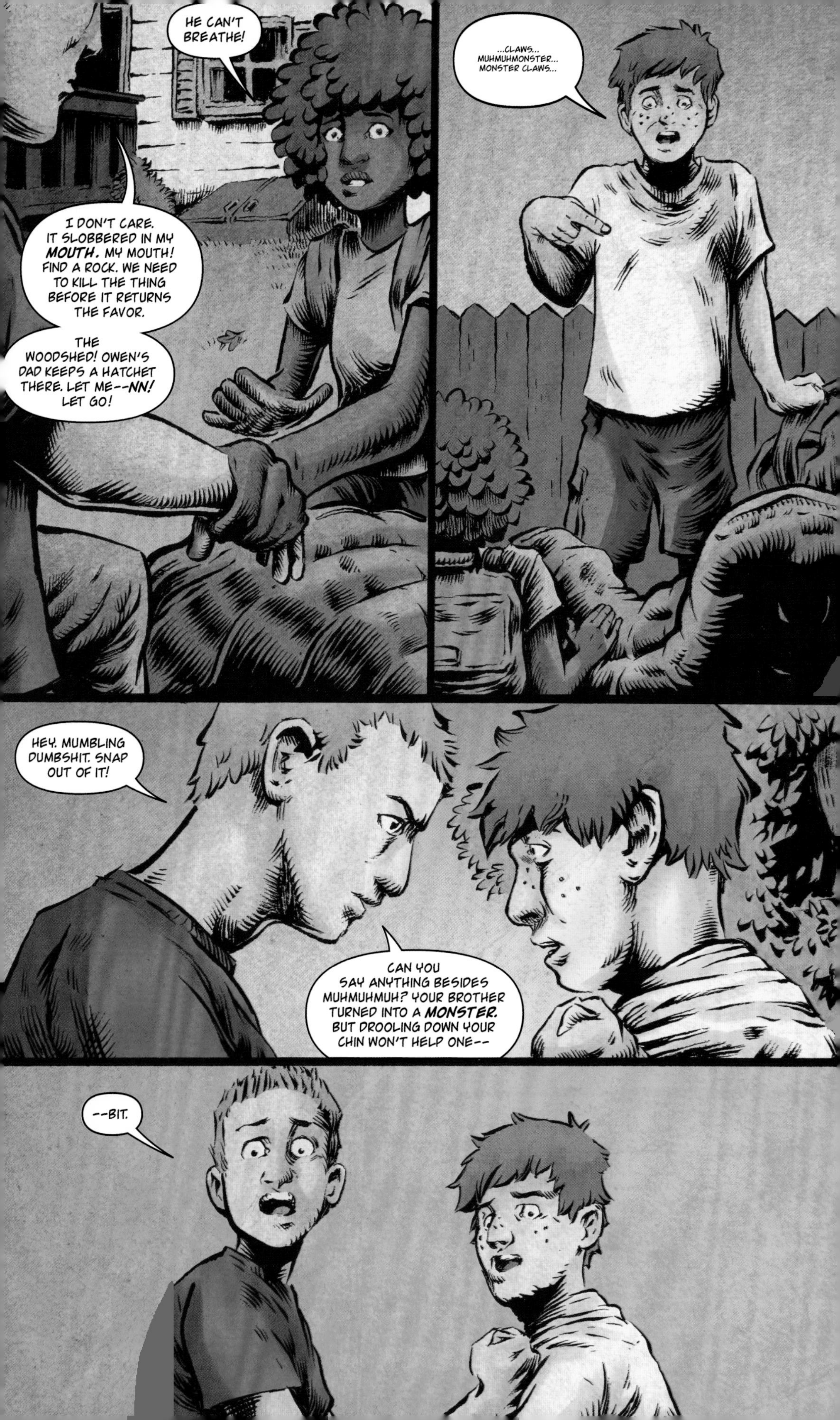
HE CAN'T BREATHE!
I DON'T CARE. IT SLOBBERED IN MY MOUTH. MY MOUTH! FIND A ROCK. WE NEED TO KILL THE THING BEFORE IT RETURNS THE FAVOR.
THE WOODSHED! OWEN'S DAD KEEPS A HATCHET THERE. LET ME--NN! LET GO!
...CLAWS... MUHMUHMONSTER... MONSTER CLAWS...
HEY. MUMBLING DUMBSHIT. SNAP OUT OF IT!
CAN YOU SAY ANYTHING BESIDES MUHMUHMUH? YOUR BROTHER TURNED INTO A MONSTER. BUT DROOLING DOWN YOUR CHIN WON'T HELP ONE--
--BIT.

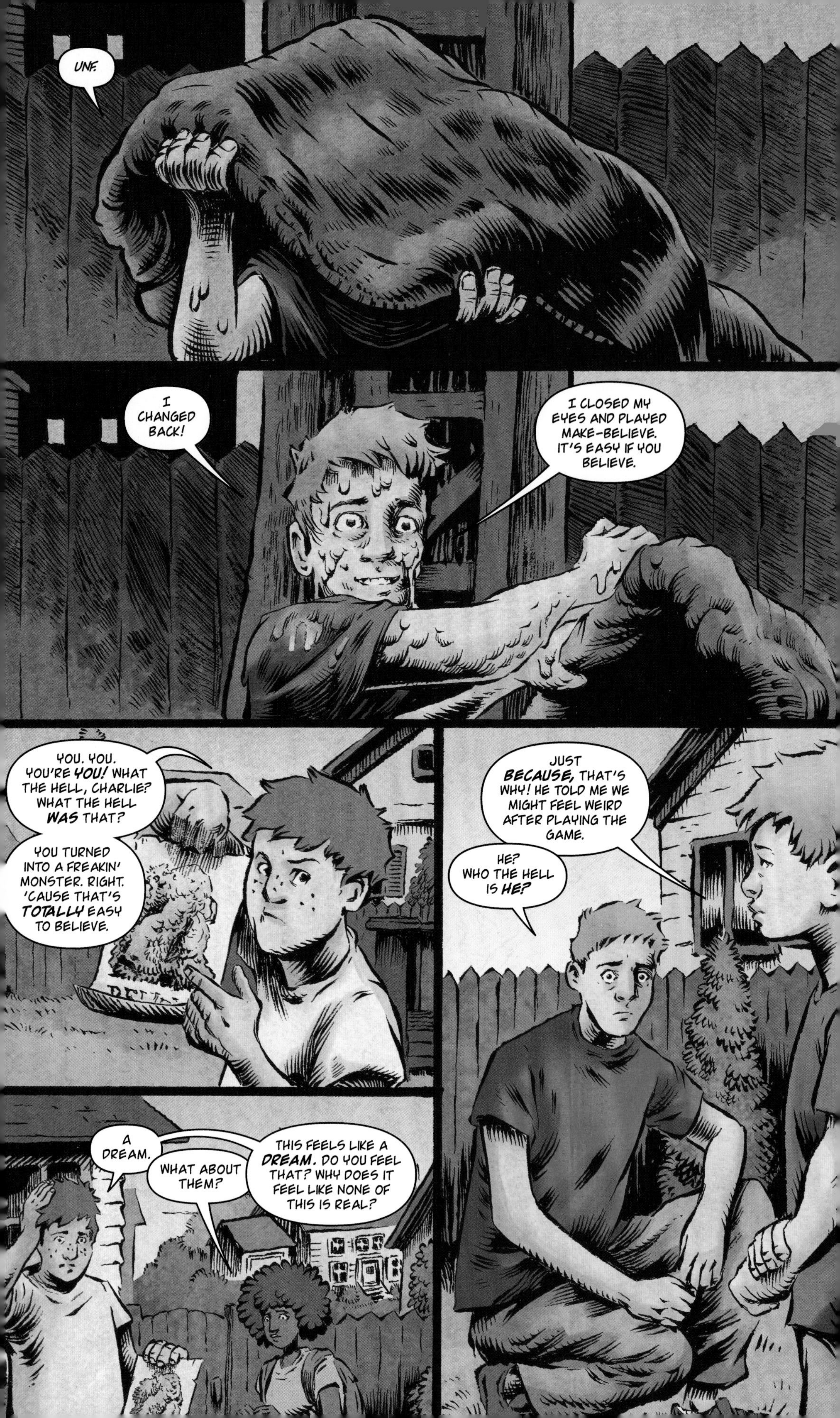
UNF.
I CHANGED BACK!
I CLOSED MY EYES AND PLAYED MAKE-BELIEVE. IT'S EASY IF YOU BELIEVE.
YOU. YOU. YOU'RE YOU! WHAT THE HELL, CHARLIE? WHAT THE HELL WAS THAT?
YOU TURNED INTO A FREAKIN' MONSTER. RIGHT. 'CAUSE THAT'S TOTALLY EASY TO BELIEVE.
JUST BECAUSE, THAT'S WHY! HE TOLD ME WE MIGHT FEEL WEIRD AFTER PLAYING THE GAME.
HE? WHO THE HELL IS HE?
A DREAM.
WHAT ABOUT THEM?
THIS FEELS LIKE A DREAM. DO YOU FEEL THAT? WHY DOES IT FEEL LIKE NONE OF THIS IS REAL?

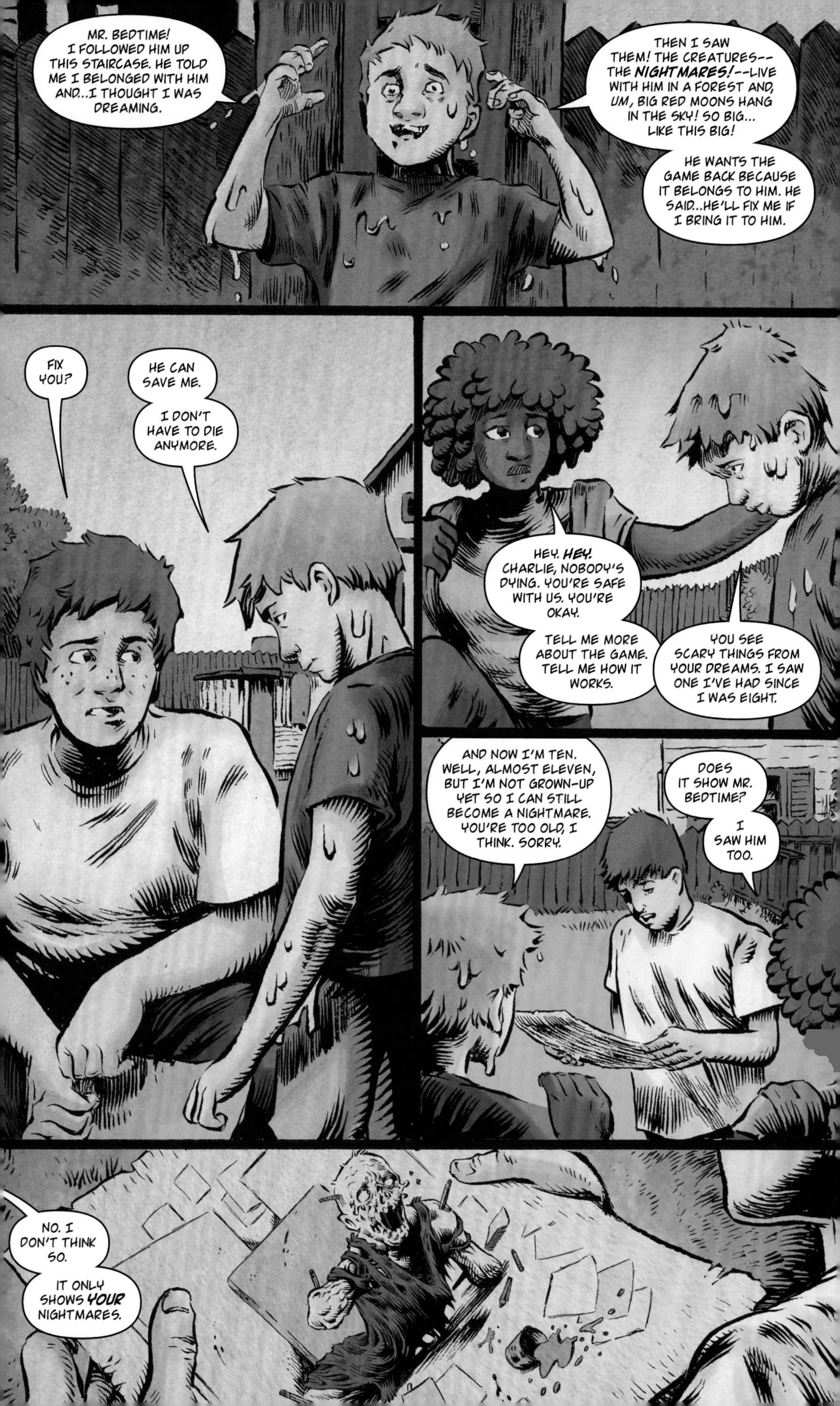
MR. BEDTIME! I FOLLOWED HIM UP THIS STAIRCASE. HE TOLD ME I BELONGED WITH HIM AND...I THOUGHT I WAS DREAMING.
THEN I SAW THEM! THE CREATURES-- THE ***NIGHTMARES!***--LIVE WITH HIM IN A FOREST AND, *UM*, BIG RED MOONS HANG IN THE SKY! SO BIG... LIKE THIS BIG!
HE WANTS THE GAME BACK BECAUSE IT BELONGS TO HIM. HE SAID...HE'LL FIX ME IF I BRING IT TO HIM.
FIX YOU?
HE CAN SAVE ME.
I DON'T HAVE TO DIE ANYMORE.
HEY. ***HEY.*** CHARLIE, NOBODY'S DYING. YOU'RE SAFE WITH US. YOU'RE OKAY.
TELL ME MORE ABOUT THE GAME. TELL ME HOW IT WORKS.
YOU SEE SCARY THINGS FROM YOUR DREAMS. I SAW ONE I'VE HAD SINCE I WAS EIGHT.
AND NOW I'M TEN. WELL, ALMOST ELEVEN, BUT I'M NOT GROWN-UP YET SO I CAN STILL BECOME A NIGHTMARE. YOU'RE TOO OLD, I THINK. SORRY.
DOES IT SHOW MR. BEDTIME?
I SAW HIM TOO.
NO. I DON'T THINK SO.
IT ONLY SHOWS ***YOUR*** NIGHTMARES.

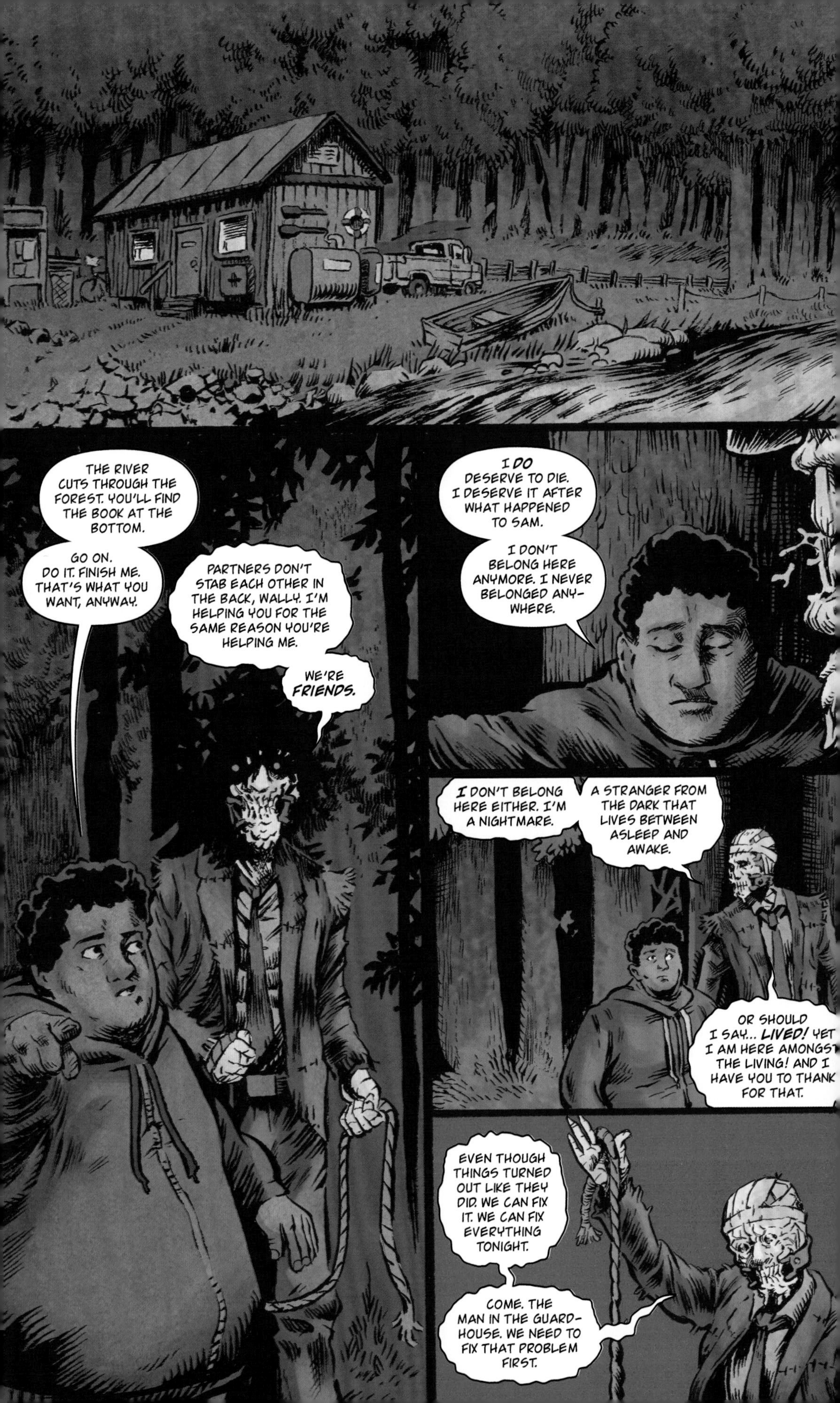
THE RIVER CUTS THROUGH THE FOREST. YOU'LL FIND THE BOOK AT THE BOTTOM.
GO ON. DO IT. FINISH ME. THAT'S WHAT YOU WANT, ANYWAY.
PARTNERS DON'T STAB EACH OTHER IN THE BACK, WALLY. I'M HELPING YOU FOR THE SAME REASON YOU'RE HELPING ME.
WE'RE FRIENDS.
I DO DESERVE TO DIE. I DESERVE IT AFTER WHAT HAPPENED TO SAM.
I DON'T BELONG HERE ANYMORE. I NEVER BELONGED ANY-WHERE.
I DON'T BELONG HERE EITHER. I'M A NIGHTMARE.
A STRANGER FROM THE DARK THAT LIVES BETWEEN ASLEEP AND AWAKE.
OR SHOULD I SAY... LIVED! YET I AM HERE AMONGST THE LIVING! AND I HAVE YOU TO THANK FOR THAT.
EVEN THOUGH THINGS TURNED OUT LIKE THEY DID, WE CAN FIX IT. WE CAN FIX EVERYTHING TONIGHT.
COME. THE MAN IN THE GUARD-HOUSE. WE NEED TO FIX THAT PROBLEM FIRST.

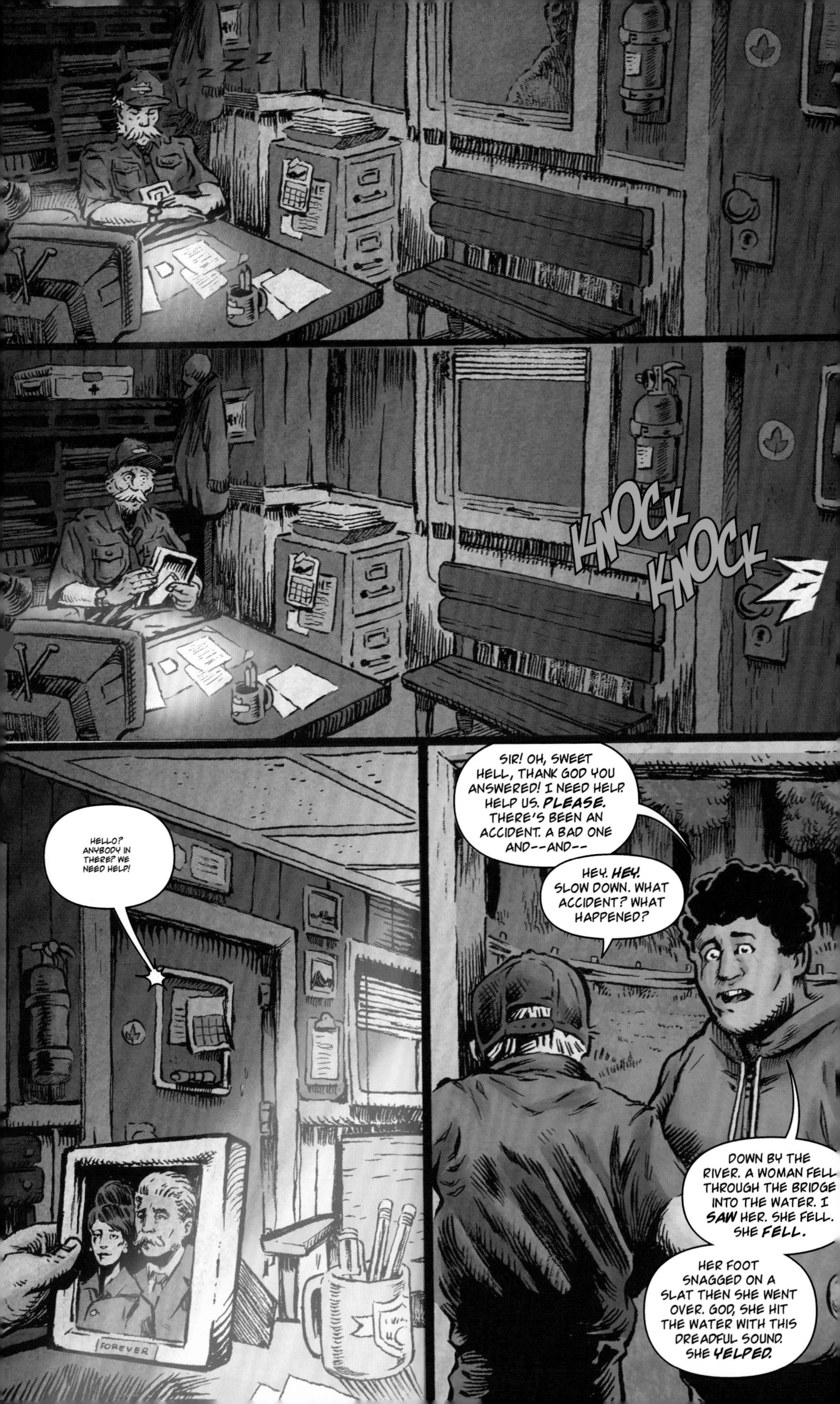

ZZZZ
KNOCK KNOCK
HELLO? ANYBODY IN THERE? WE NEED HELP!
SIR! OH, SWEET HELL, THANK GOD YOU ANSWERED! I NEED HELP. HELP US. PLEASE. THERE'S BEEN AN ACCIDENT. A BAD ONE AND--AND--
HEY. HEY. SLOW DOWN. WHAT ACCIDENT? WHAT HAPPENED?
DOWN BY THE RIVER. A WOMAN FELL THROUGH THE BRIDGE INTO THE WATER. I SAW HER. SHE FELL. SHE FELL.
HER FOOT SNAGGED ON A SLAT THEN SHE WENT OVER. GOD, SHE HIT THE WATER WITH THIS DREADFUL SOUND. SHE YELPED.
FOREVER

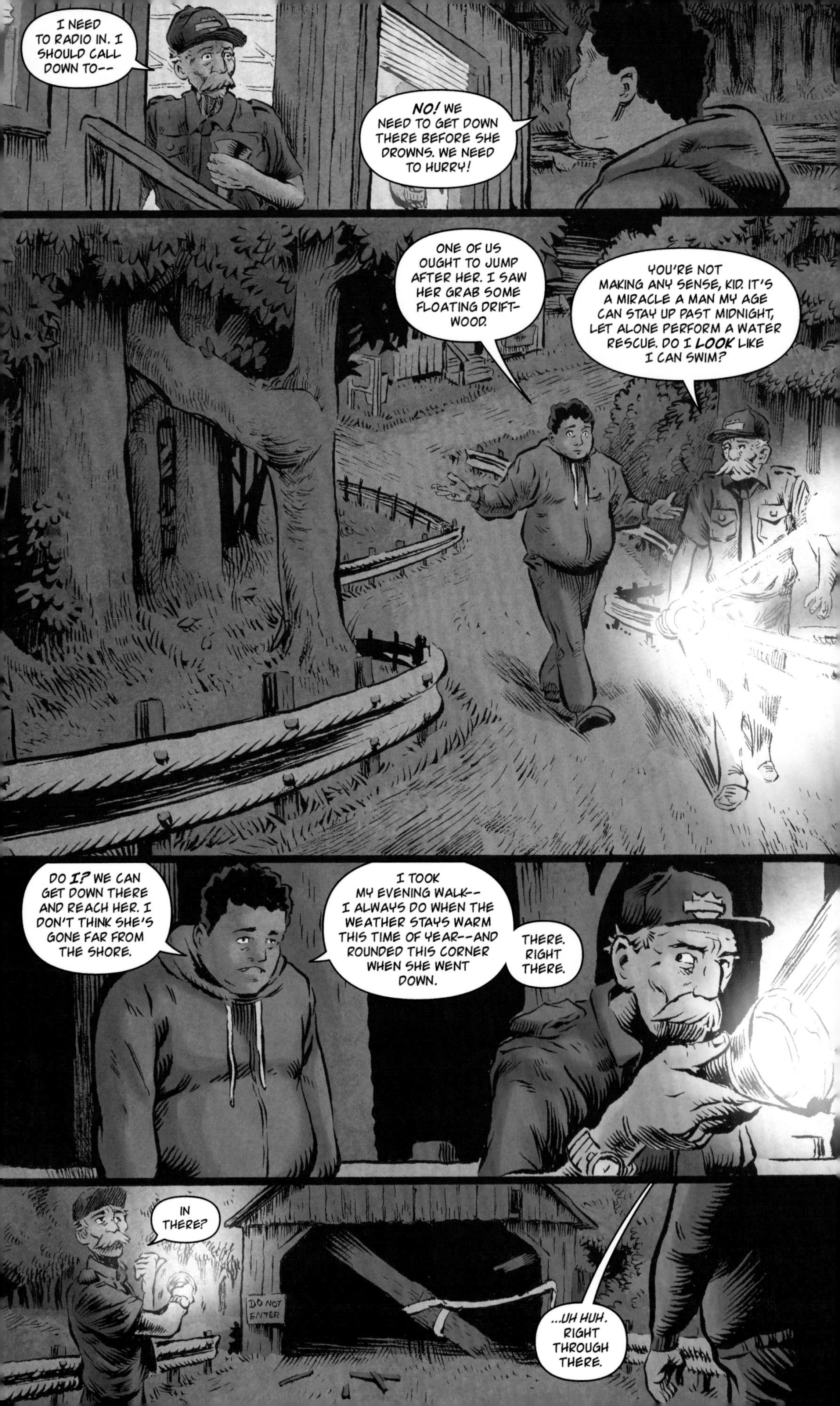
I NEED TO RADIO IN. I SHOULD CALL DOWN TO--
NO! WE NEED TO GET DOWN THERE BEFORE SHE DROWNS. WE NEED TO HURRY!
ONE OF US OUGHT TO JUMP AFTER HER. I SAW HER GRAB SOME FLOATING DRIFT-WOOD.
YOU'RE NOT MAKING ANY SENSE, KID. IT'S A MIRACLE A MAN MY AGE CAN STAY UP PAST MIDNIGHT, LET ALONE PERFORM A WATER RESCUE. DO I LOOK LIKE I CAN SWIM?
DO I? WE CAN GET DOWN THERE AND REACH HER. I DON'T THINK SHE'S GONE FAR FROM THE SHORE.
I TOOK MY EVENING WALK-- I ALWAYS DO WHEN THE WEATHER STAYS WARM THIS TIME OF YEAR--AND ROUNDED THIS CORNER WHEN SHE WENT DOWN.
THERE. RIGHT THERE.
IN THERE?
DO NOT ENTER
...UH HUH. RIGHT THROUGH THERE.

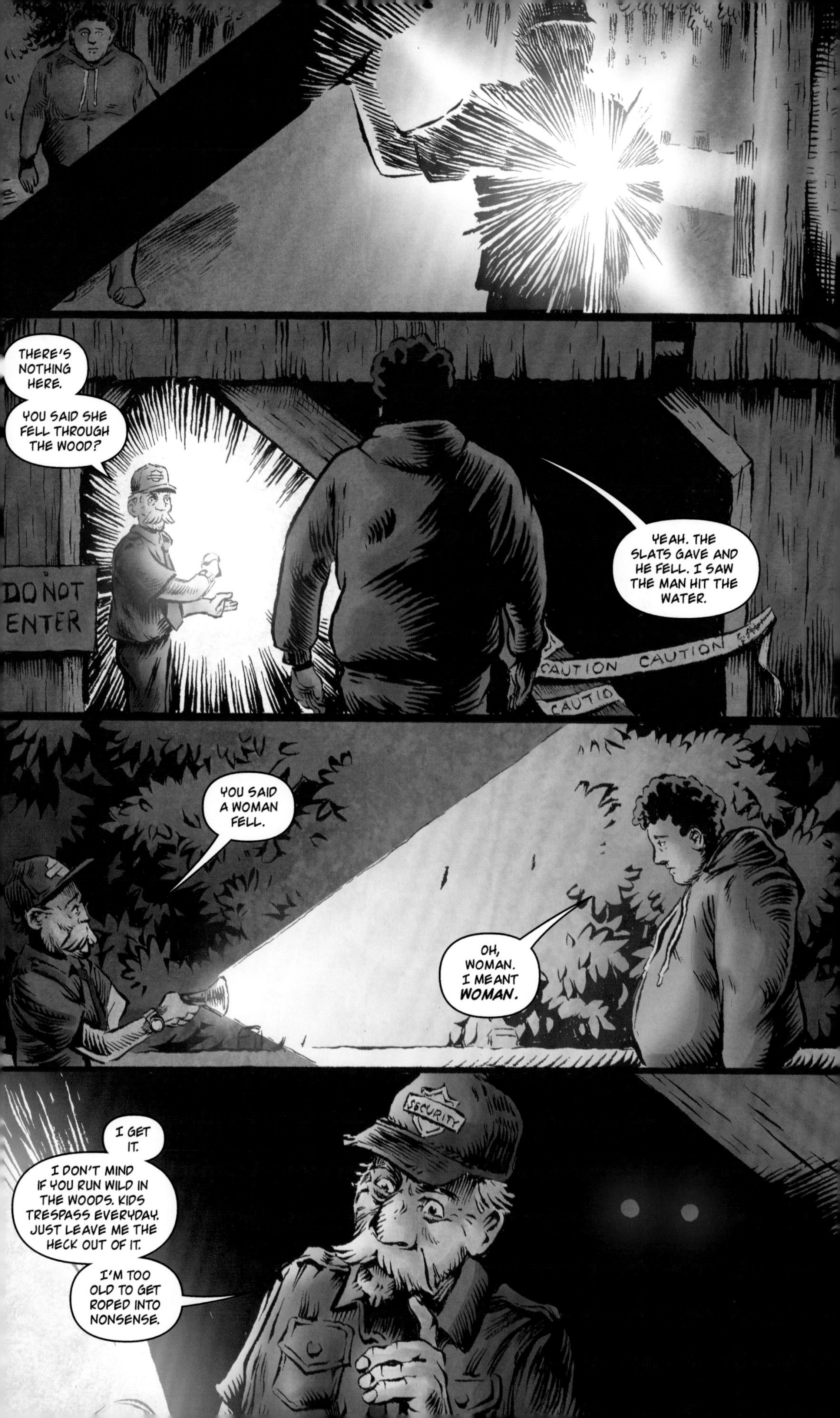
THERE'S NOTHING HERE.
YOU SAID SHE FELL THROUGH THE WOOD?
DO NOT ENTER
YEAH. THE SLATS GAVE AND HE FELL. I SAW THE MAN HIT THE WATER.
CAUTION CAUTION
YOU SAID A WOMAN FELL.
OH, WOMAN. I MEANT WOMAN.
SECURITY
I GET IT.
I DON'T MIND IF YOU RUN WILD IN THE WOODS. KIDS TRESPASS EVERYDAY. JUST LEAVE ME THE HECK OUT OF IT.
I'M TOO OLD TO GET ROPED INTO NONSENSE.

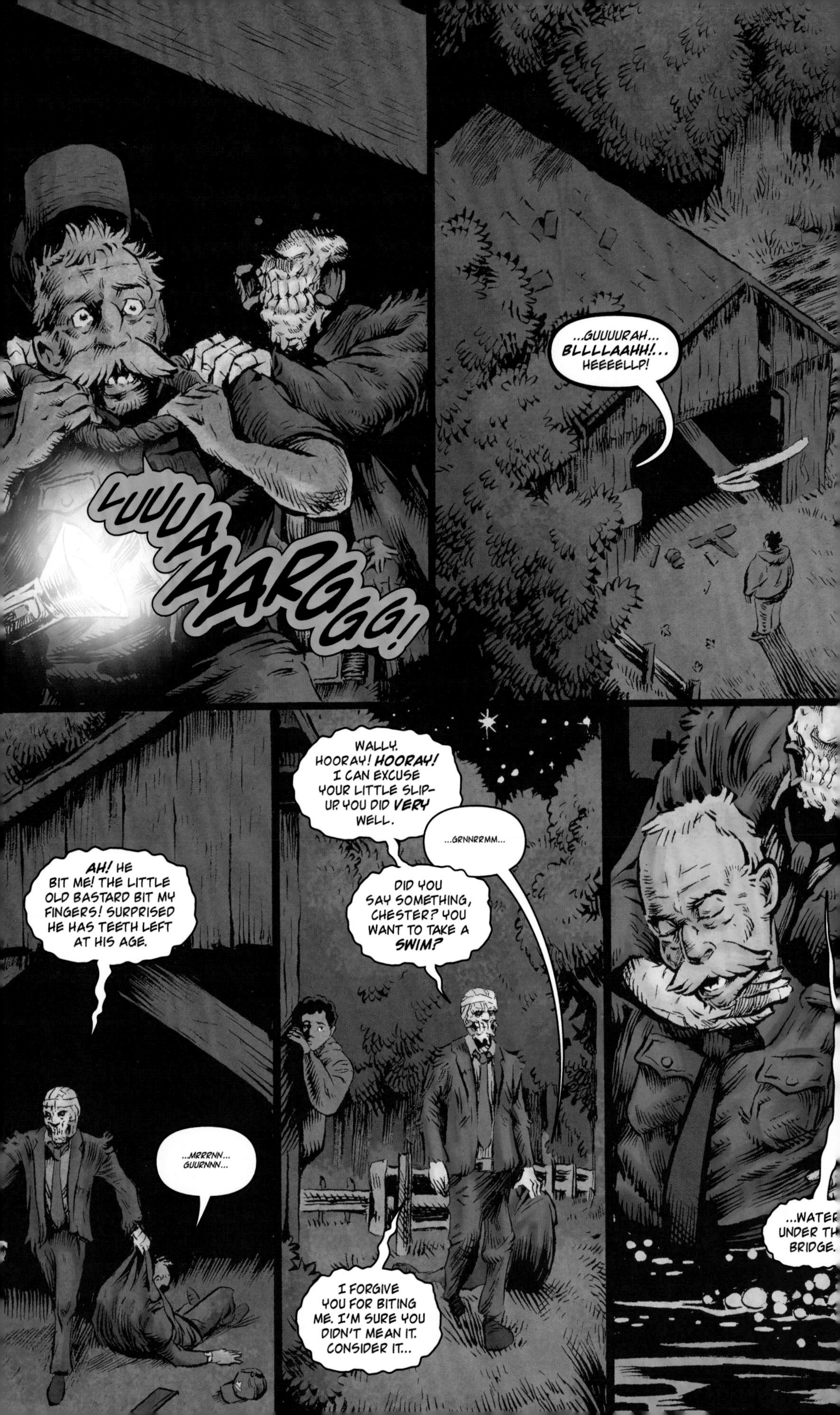
LUUUAAARGGG!
...GUUUURAH... BLLLLAAHH!... HEEEEELLP!
AH! HE BIT ME! THE LITTLE OLD BASTARD BIT MY FINGERS! SURPRISED HE HAS TEETH LEFT AT HIS AGE.
...MRRRNN... GUURNNN...
WALLY. HOORAY! HOORAY! I CAN EXCUSE YOUR LITTLE SLIP-UP. YOU DID VERY WELL.
...GRNNRRMM...
DID YOU SAY SOMETHING, CHESTER? YOU WANT TO TAKE A SWIM?
I FORGIVE YOU FOR BITING ME. I'M SURE YOU DIDN'T MEAN IT. CONSIDER IT...
...WATER UNDER THE BRIDGE.

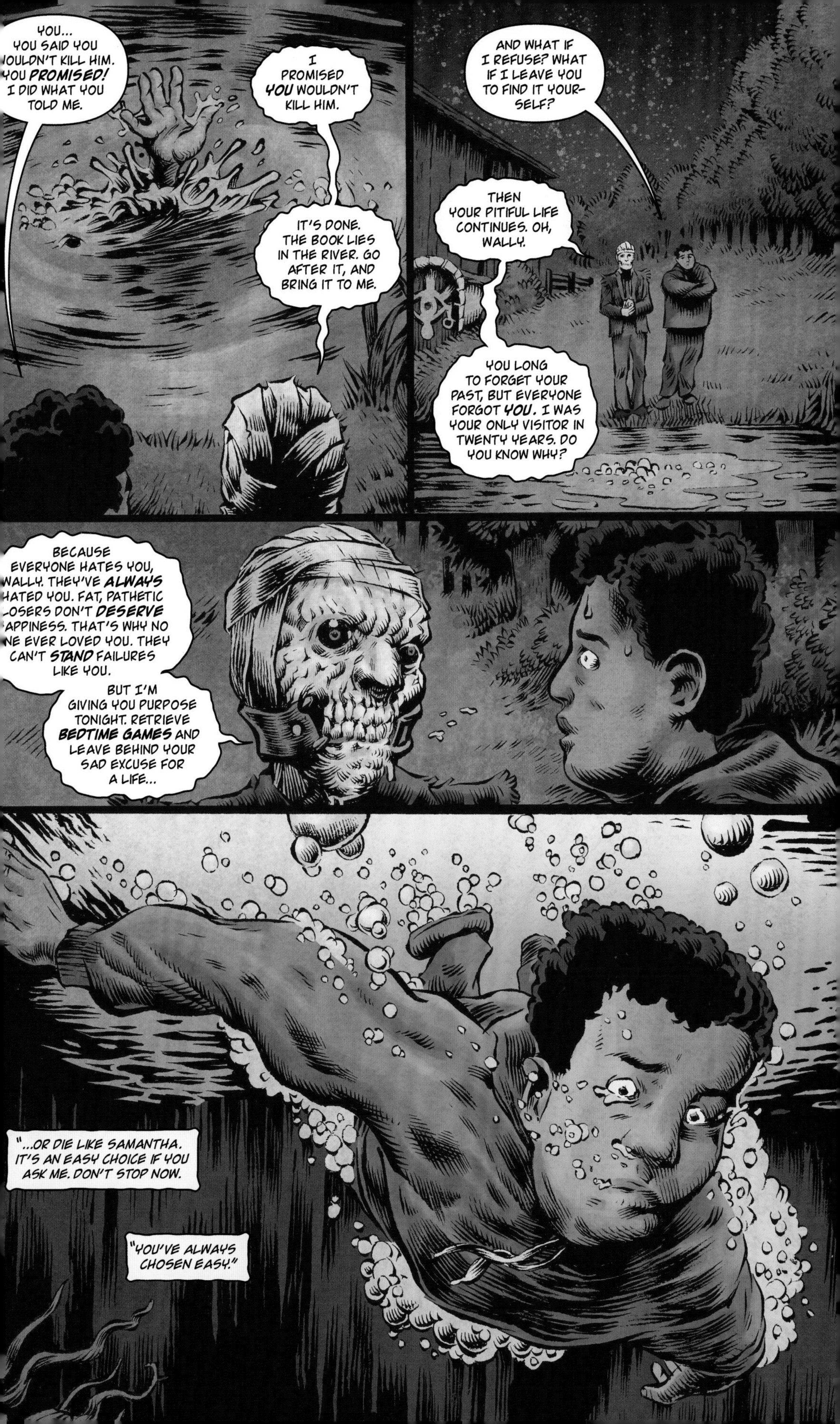
YOU... YOU SAID YOU OULDN'T KILL HIM. OU PROMISED! I DID WHAT YOU TOLD ME.
I PROMISED YOU WOULDN'T KILL HIM.
IT'S DONE. THE BOOK LIES IN THE RIVER. GO AFTER IT, AND BRING IT TO ME.
AND WHAT IF I REFUSE? WHAT IF I LEAVE YOU TO FIND IT YOUR-SELF?
THEN YOUR PITIFUL LIFE CONTINUES. OH, WALLY.
YOU LONG TO FORGET YOUR PAST, BUT EVERYONE FORGOT YOU. I WAS YOUR ONLY VISITOR IN TWENTY YEARS. DO YOU KNOW WHY?
BECAUSE EVERYONE HATES YOU, ALLY. THEY'VE ALWAYS HATED YOU. FAT, PATHETIC OSERS DON'T DESERVE APPINESS. THAT'S WHY NO NE EVER LOVED YOU. THEY CAN'T STAND FAILURES LIKE YOU.
BUT I'M GIVING YOU PURPOSE TONIGHT. RETRIEVE BEDTIME GAMES AND LEAVE BEHIND YOUR SAD EXCUSE FOR A LIFE...
"...OR DIE LIKE SAMANTHA. IT'S AN EASY CHOICE IF YOU ASK ME. DON'T STOP NOW.
"YOU'VE ALWAYS CHOSEN EASY."

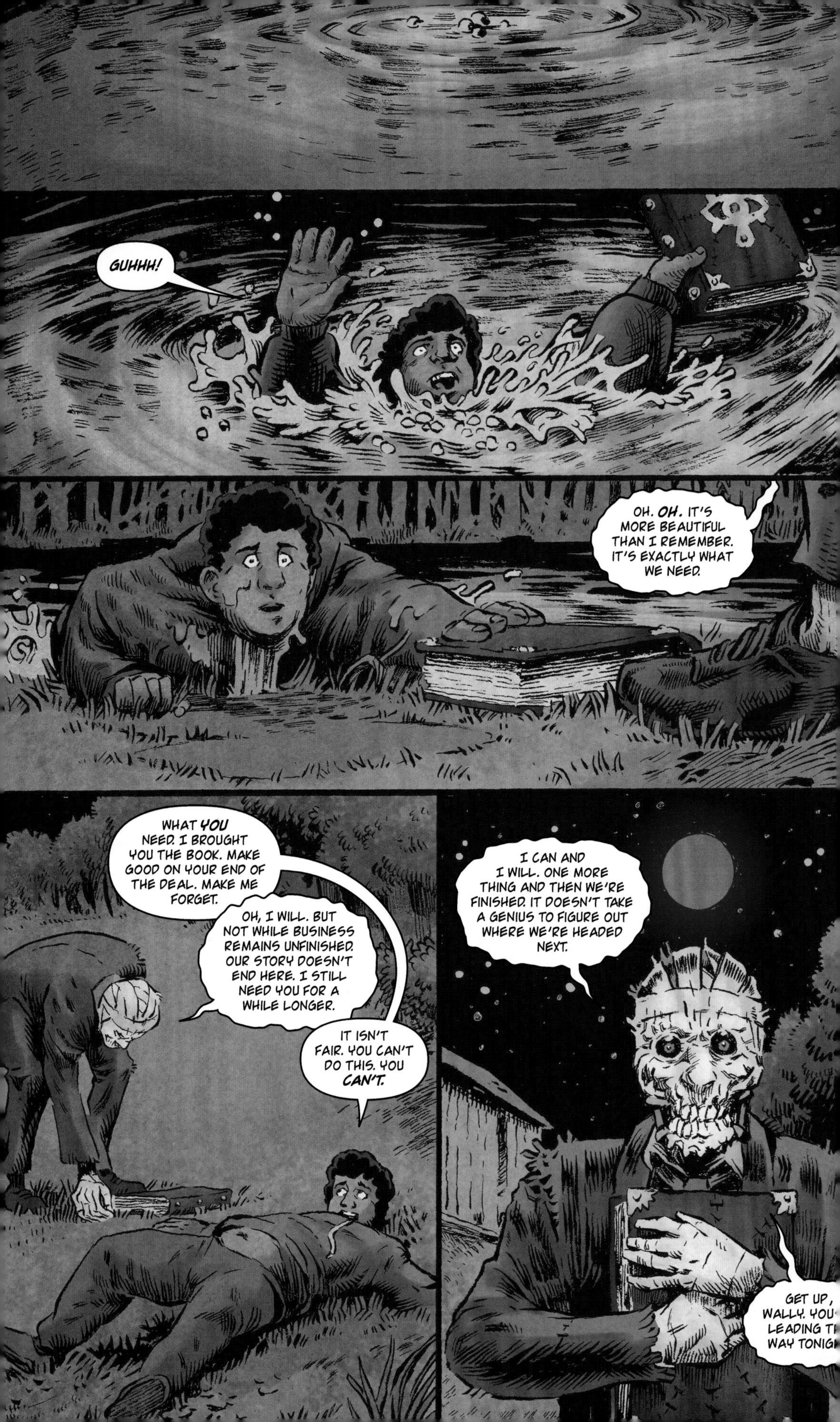
GUHHH!
OH. OH. IT'S MORE BEAUTIFUL THAN I REMEMBER. IT'S EXACTLY WHAT WE NEED.
WHAT YOU NEED. I BROUGHT YOU THE BOOK. MAKE GOOD ON YOUR END OF THE DEAL. MAKE ME FORGET.
OH, I WILL. BUT NOT WHILE BUSINESS REMAINS UNFINISHED. OUR STORY DOESN'T END HERE. I STILL NEED YOU FOR A WHILE LONGER.
IT ISN'T FAIR. YOU CAN'T DO THIS. YOU CAN'T.
I CAN AND I WILL. ONE MORE THING AND THEN WE'RE FINISHED. IT DOESN'T TAKE A GENIUS TO FIGURE OUT WHERE WE'RE HEADED NEXT.

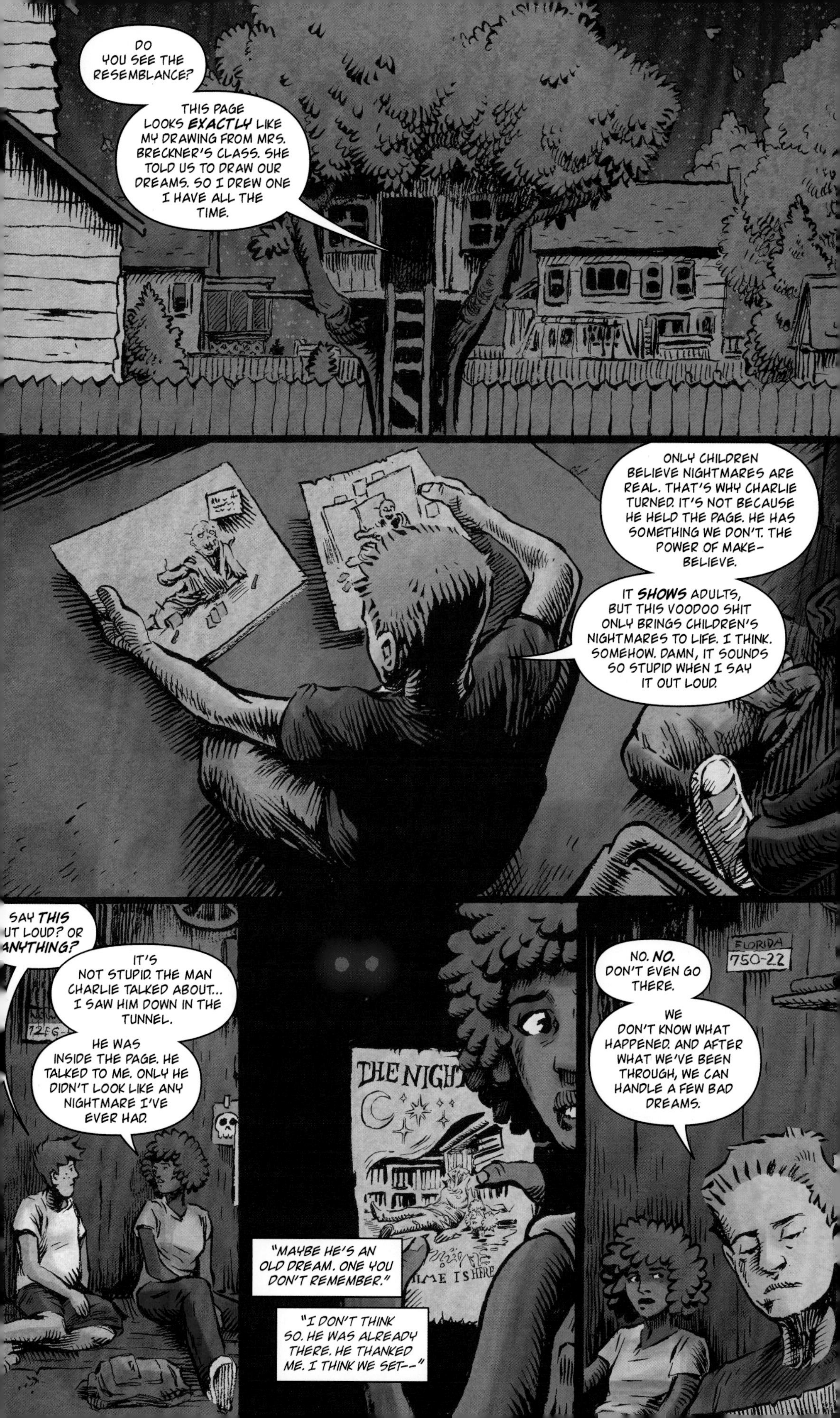
DO YOU SEE THE RESEMBLANCE?
THIS PAGE LOOKS **EXACTLY** LIKE MY DRAWING FROM MRS. BRECKNER'S CLASS. SHE TOLD US TO DRAW OUR DREAMS. SO I DREW ONE I HAVE ALL THE TIME.
ONLY CHILDREN BELIEVE NIGHTMARES ARE REAL. THAT'S WHY CHARLIE TURNED. IT'S NOT BECAUSE HE HELD THE PAGE. HE HAS SOMETHING WE DON'T. THE POWER OF MAKE-BELIEVE.
IT **SHOWS** ADULTS, BUT THIS VOODOO SHIT ONLY BRINGS CHILDREN'S NIGHTMARES TO LIFE. I THINK. SOMEHOW. DAMN, IT SOUNDS SO STUPID WHEN I SAY IT OUT LOUD.
SAY **THIS** UT LOUD? OR ANYTHING?
IT'S NOT STUPID. THE MAN CHARLIE TALKED ABOUT... I SAW HIM DOWN IN THE TUNNEL.
HE WAS INSIDE THE PAGE. HE TALKED TO ME. ONLY HE DIDN'T LOOK LIKE ANY NIGHTMARE I'VE EVER HAD.
THE NIGHT
"MAYBE HE'S AN OLD DREAM. ONE YOU DON'T REMEMBER."
"I DON'T THINK SO. HE WAS ALREADY THERE. HE THANKED ME. I THINK WE SET--"
FLORIDA
750-22
NO. **NO.** DON'T EVEN GO THERE.
WE DON'T KNOW WHAT HAPPENED. AND AFTER WHAT WE'VE BEEN THROUGH, WE CAN HANDLE A FEW BAD DREAMS.

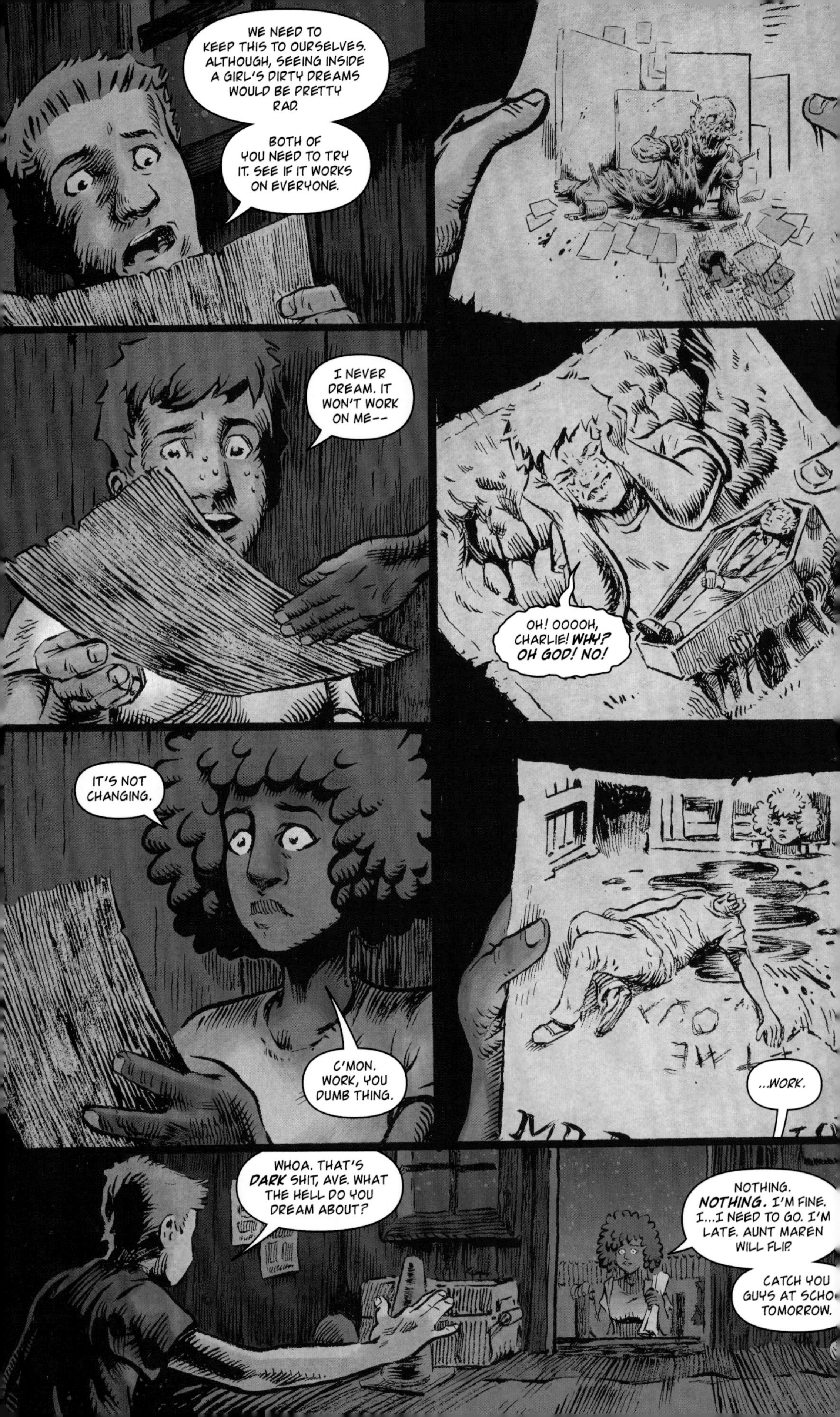
WE NEED TO KEEP THIS TO OURSELVES. ALTHOUGH, SEEING INSIDE A GIRL'S DIRTY DREAMS WOULD BE PRETTY RAD.
BOTH OF YOU NEED TO TRY IT. SEE IF IT WORKS ON EVERYONE.
I NEVER DREAM. IT WON'T WORK ON ME--
OH! OOOOH, CHARLIE! WHY? OH GOD! NO!
IT'S NOT CHANGING.
C'MON. WORK, YOU DUMB THING.
...WORK.
WHOA. THAT'S DARK SHIT, AVE. WHAT THE HELL DO YOU DREAM ABOUT?
NOTHING. NOTHING. I'M FINE. I...I NEED TO GO. I'M LATE. AUNT MAREN WILL FLIP.
CATCH YOU GUYS AT SCHO TOMORROW.

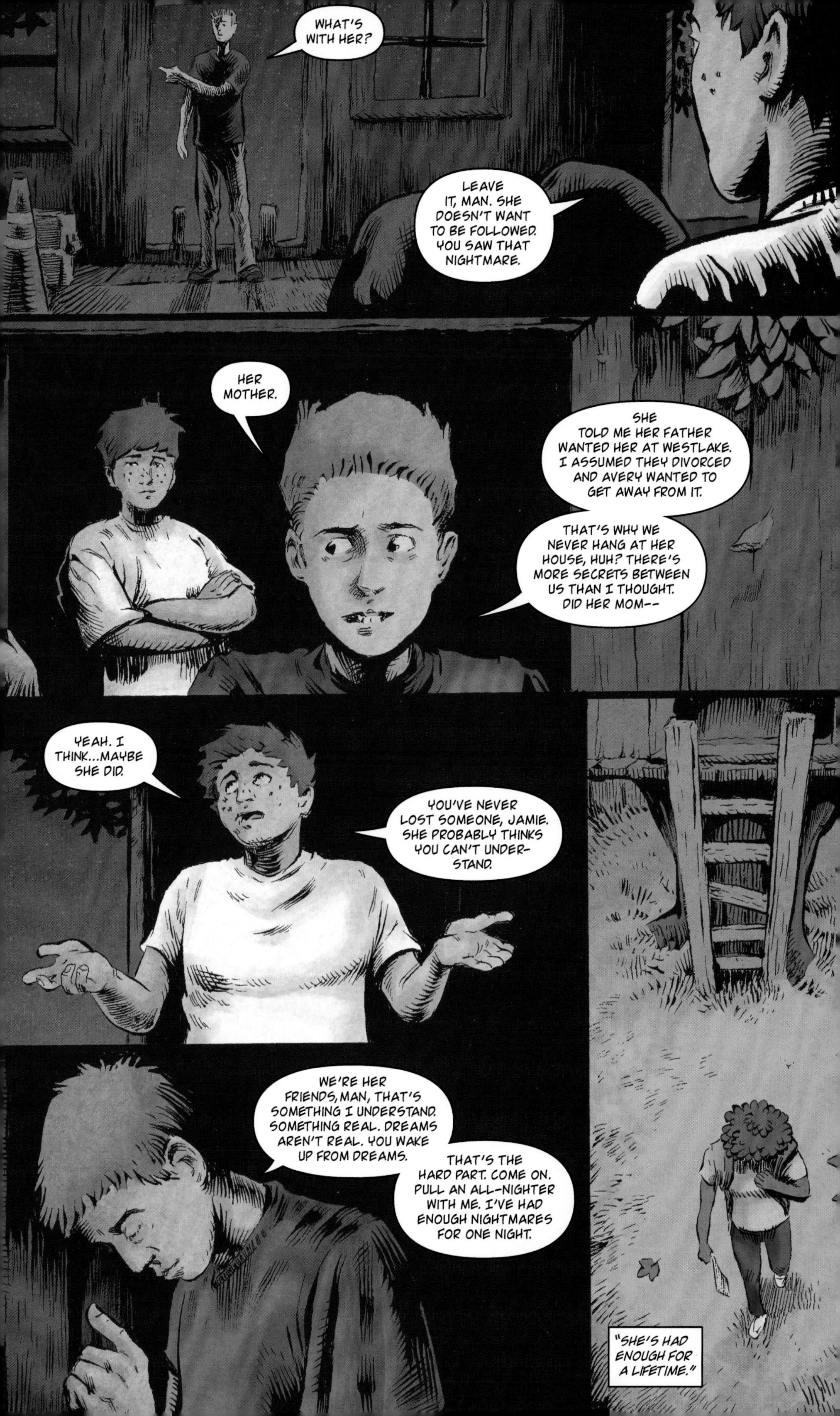
WHAT'S WITH HER?
LEAVE IT, MAN. SHE DOESN'T WANT TO BE FOLLOWED. YOU SAW THAT NIGHTMARE.
HER MOTHER.
SHE TOLD ME HER FATHER WANTED HER AT WESTLAKE. I ASSUMED THEY DIVORCED AND AVERY WANTED TO GET AWAY FROM IT.
THAT'S WHY WE NEVER HANG AT HER HOUSE, HUH? THERE'S MORE SECRETS BETWEEN US THAN I THOUGHT. DID HER MOM--
YEAH. I THINK...MAYBE SHE DID.
YOU'VE NEVER LOST SOMEONE, JAMIE. SHE PROBABLY THINKS YOU CAN'T UNDER-STAND.
WE'RE HER FRIENDS, MAN, THAT'S SOMETHING I UNDERSTAND. SOMETHING REAL. DREAMS AREN'T REAL. YOU WAKE UP FROM DREAMS.
THAT'S THE HARD PART. COME ON. PULL AN ALL-NIGHTER WITH ME. I'VE HAD ENOUGH NIGHTMARES FOR ONE NIGHT.
"SHE'S HAD ENOUGH FOR A LIFETIME."

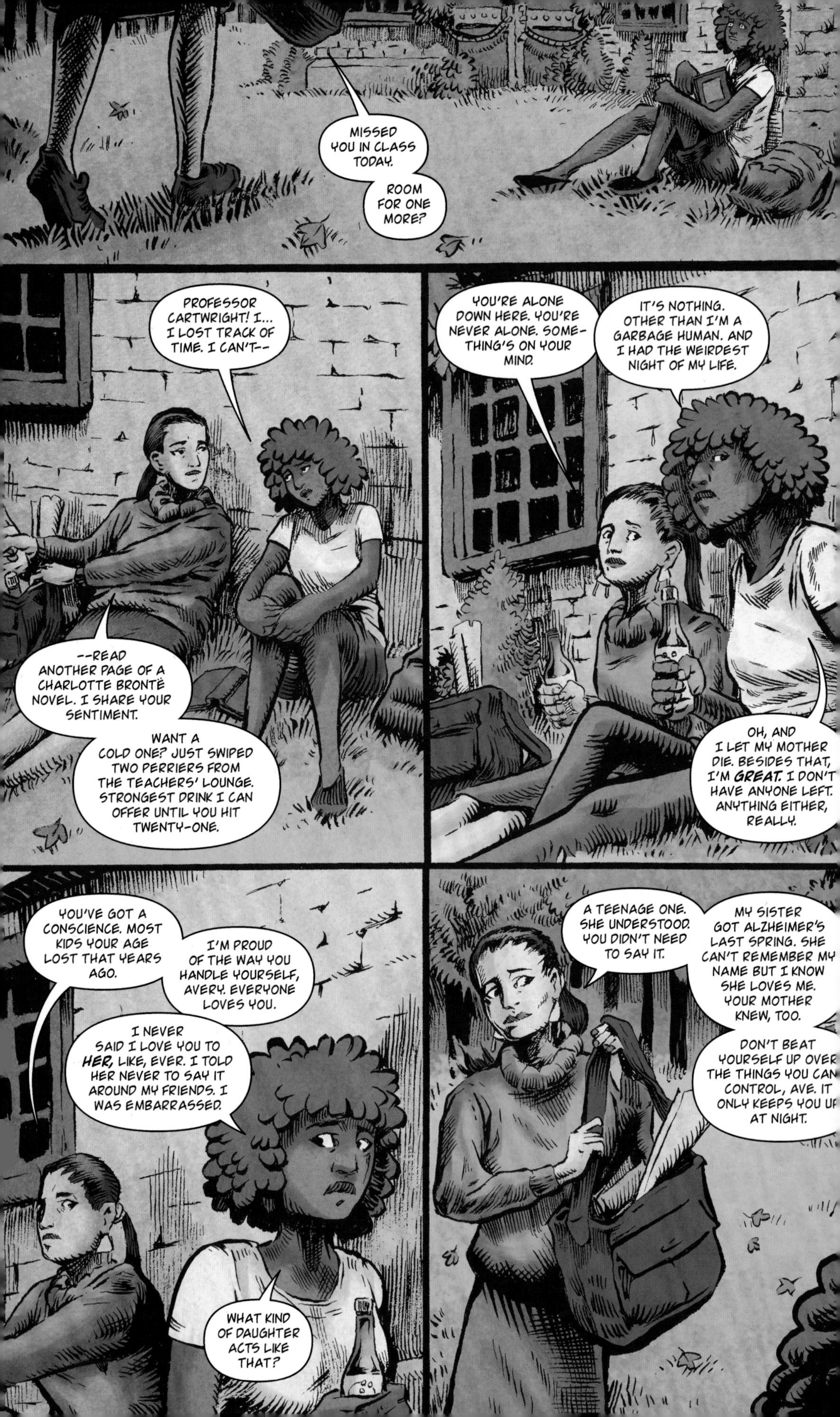
MISSED YOU IN CLASS TODAY.
ROOM FOR ONE MORE?
PROFESSOR CARTWRIGHT! I... I LOST TRACK OF TIME. I CAN'T--
--READ ANOTHER PAGE OF A CHARLOTTE BRONTË NOVEL. I SHARE YOUR SENTIMENT.
WANT A COLD ONE? JUST SWIPED TWO PERRIERS FROM THE TEACHERS' LOUNGE. STRONGEST DRINK I CAN OFFER UNTIL YOU HIT TWENTY-ONE.
YOU'RE ALONE DOWN HERE. YOU'RE NEVER ALONE. SOMETHING'S ON YOUR MIND.
IT'S NOTHING. OTHER THAN I'M A GARBAGE HUMAN. AND I HAD THE WEIRDEST NIGHT OF MY LIFE.
OH, AND I LET MY MOTHER DIE. BESIDES THAT, I'M ***GREAT.*** I DON'T HAVE ANYONE LEFT. ANYTHING EITHER, REALLY.
YOU'VE GOT A CONSCIENCE. MOST KIDS YOUR AGE LOST THAT YEARS AGO.
I'M PROUD OF THE WAY YOU HANDLE YOURSELF, AVERY. EVERYONE LOVES YOU.
I NEVER SAID I LOVE YOU TO ***HER,*** LIKE, EVER. I TOLD HER NEVER TO SAY IT AROUND MY FRIENDS. I WAS EMBARRASSED.
WHAT KIND OF DAUGHTER ACTS LIKE THAT?
A TEENAGE ONE. SHE UNDERSTOOD. YOU DIDN'T NEED TO SAY IT.
MY SISTER GOT ALZHEIMER'S LAST SPRING. SHE CAN'T REMEMBER MY NAME BUT I KNOW SHE LOVES ME. YOUR MOTHER KNEW, TOO.
DON'T BEAT YOURSELF UP OVER THE THINGS YOU CAN CONTROL, AVE. IT ONLY KEEPS YOU UP AT NIGHT.

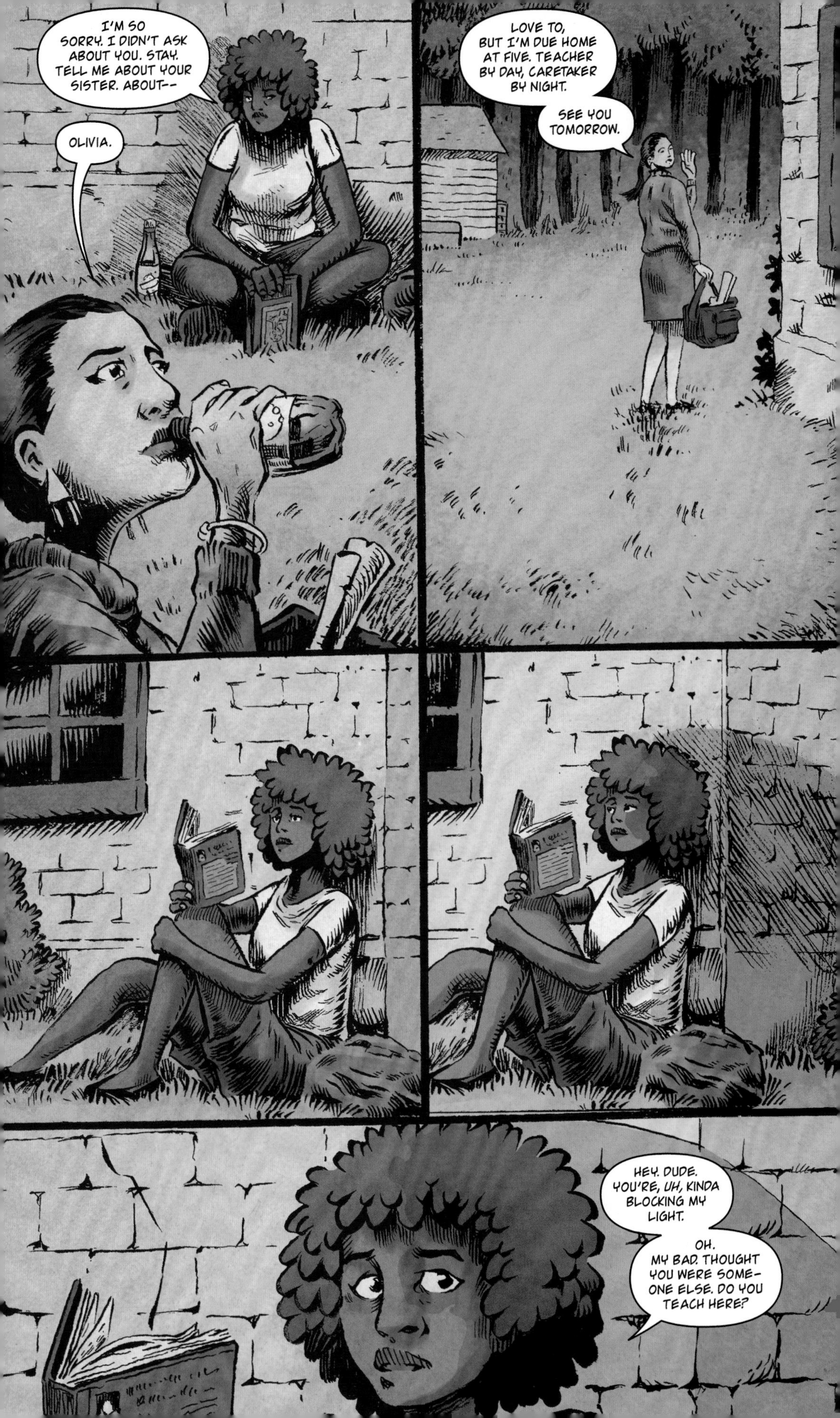
I'M SO SORRY. I DIDN'T ASK ABOUT YOU. STAY. TELL ME ABOUT YOUR SISTER. ABOUT--
OLIVIA.
LOVE TO, BUT I'M DUE HOME AT FIVE. TEACHER BY DAY, CARETAKER BY NIGHT.
SEE YOU TOMORROW.
HEY. DUDE. YOU'RE, UH, KINDA BLOCKING MY LIGHT.
OH. MY BAD. THOUGHT YOU WERE SOME-ONE ELSE. DO YOU TEACH HERE?

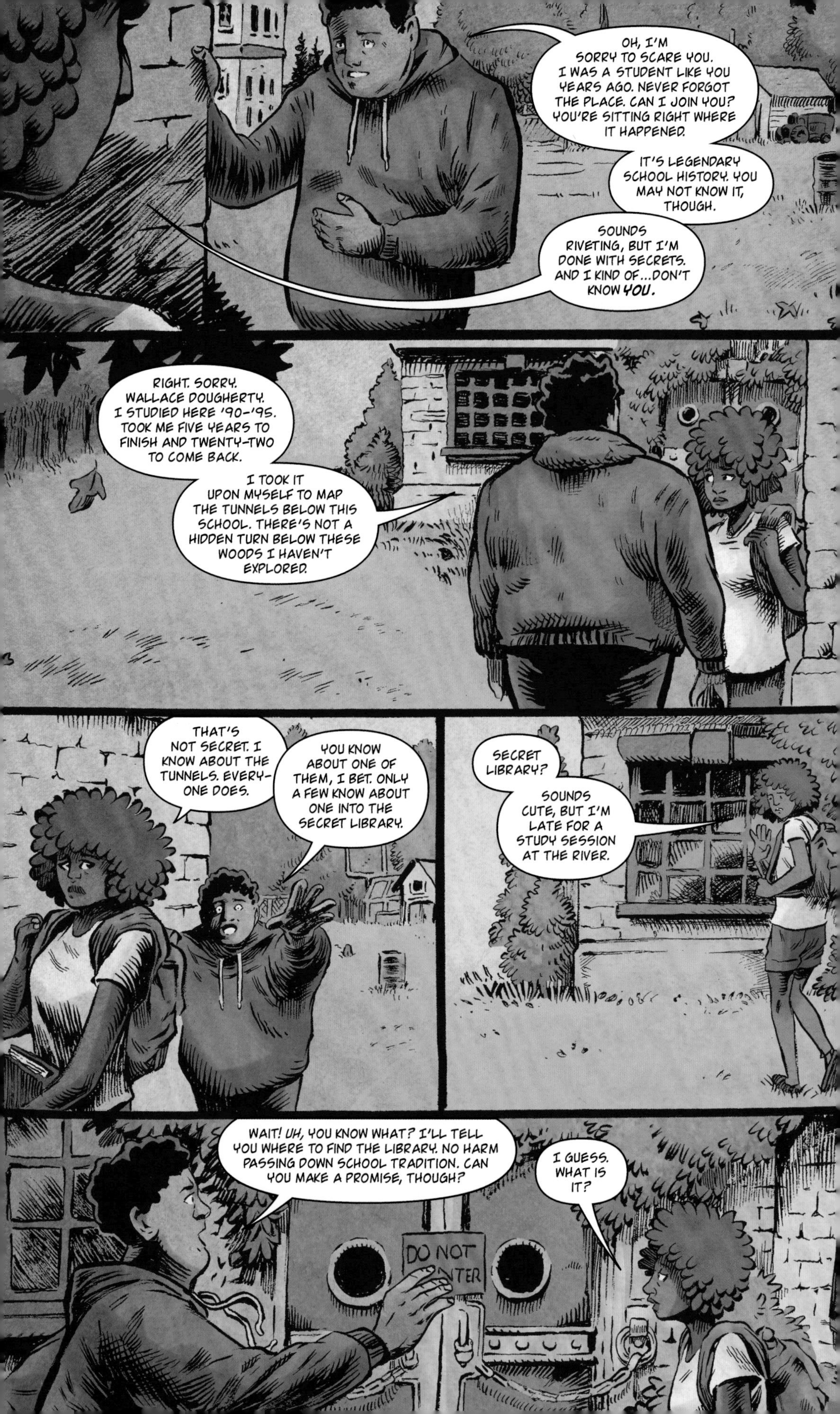
OH, I'M SORRY TO SCARE YOU. I WAS A STUDENT LIKE YOU YEARS AGO. NEVER FORGOT THE PLACE. CAN I JOIN YOU? YOU'RE SITTING RIGHT WHERE IT HAPPENED.
IT'S LEGENDARY SCHOOL HISTORY. YOU MAY NOT KNOW IT, THOUGH.
SOUNDS RIVETING, BUT I'M DONE WITH SECRETS. AND I KIND OF...DON'T KNOW *YOU*.
RIGHT. SORRY. WALLACE DOUGHERTY. I STUDIED HERE '90–'95. TOOK ME FIVE YEARS TO FINISH AND TWENTY-TWO TO COME BACK.
I TOOK IT UPON MYSELF TO MAP THE TUNNELS BELOW THIS SCHOOL. THERE'S NOT A HIDDEN TURN BELOW THESE WOODS I HAVEN'T EXPLORED.
THAT'S NOT SECRET. I KNOW ABOUT THE TUNNELS. EVERY-ONE DOES.
YOU KNOW ABOUT ONE OF THEM, I BET. ONLY A FEW KNOW ABOUT ONE INTO THE SECRET LIBRARY.
SECRET LIBRARY?
SOUNDS CUTE, BUT I'M LATE FOR A STUDY SESSION AT THE RIVER.
WAIT! *UH*, YOU KNOW WHAT? I'LL TELL YOU WHERE TO FIND THE LIBRARY. NO HARM PASSING DOWN SCHOOL TRADITION. CAN YOU MAKE A PROMISE, THOUGH?
I GUESS. WHAT IS IT?
DO NOT ENTER

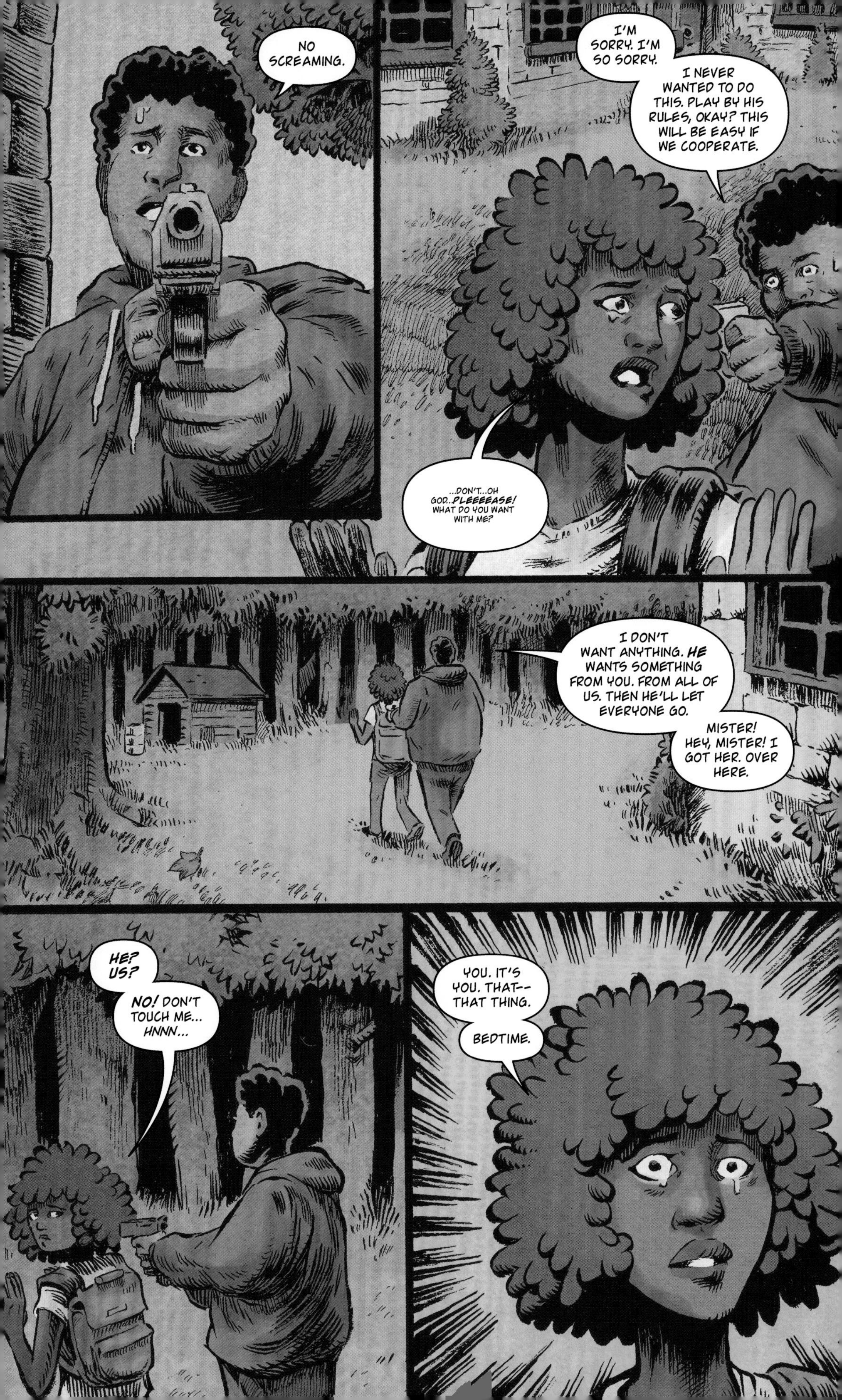
NO SCREAMING.
I'M SORRY. I'M SO SORRY.
I NEVER WANTED TO DO THIS. PLAY BY HIS RULES, OKAY? THIS WILL BE EASY IF WE COOPERATE.
...DON'T...OH GOD...PLEEEEASE! WHAT DO YOU WANT WITH ME?
I DON'T WANT ANYTHING. HE WANTS SOMETHING FROM YOU. FROM ALL OF US. THEN HE'LL LET EVERYONE GO.
MISTER! HEY, MISTER! I GOT HER. OVER HERE.
HE? US?
NO! DON'T TOUCH ME... HNNN...
YOU. IT'S YOU. THAT--THAT THING.
BEDTIME.

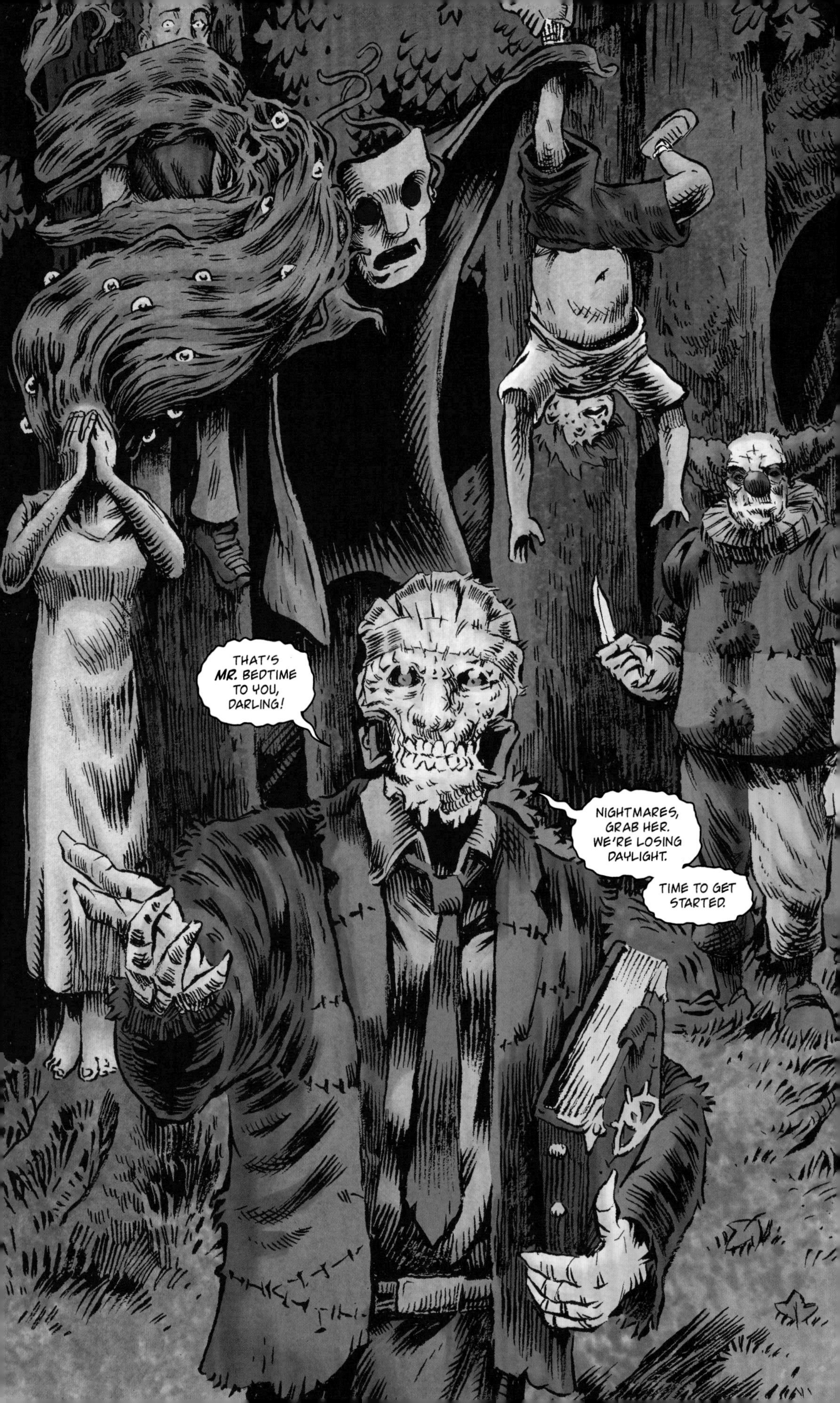
THAT'S MR. BEDTIME TO YOU, DARLING!
NIGHTMARES, GRAB HER. WE'RE LOSING DAYLIGHT.
TIME TO GET STARTED.

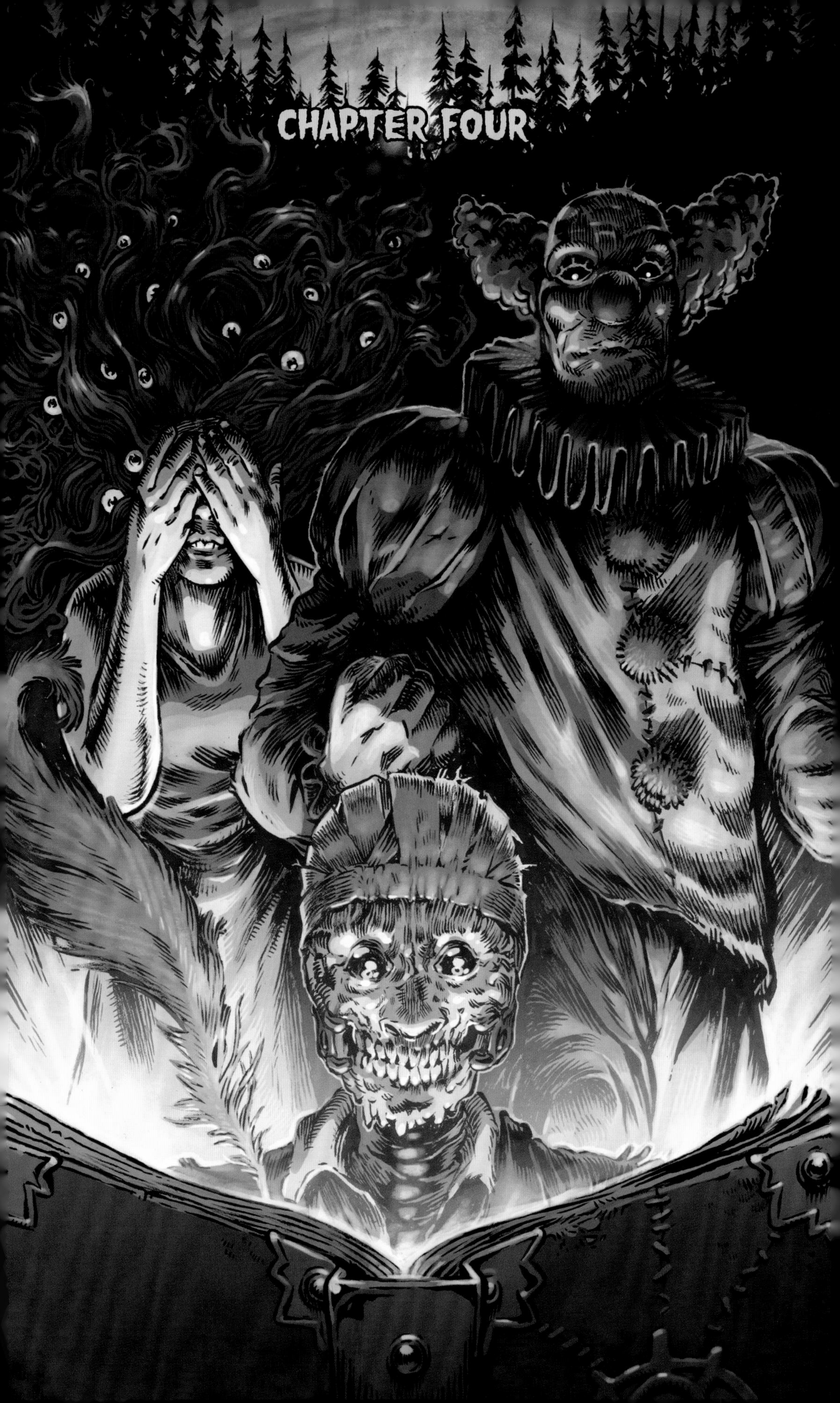
CHAPTER FOUR

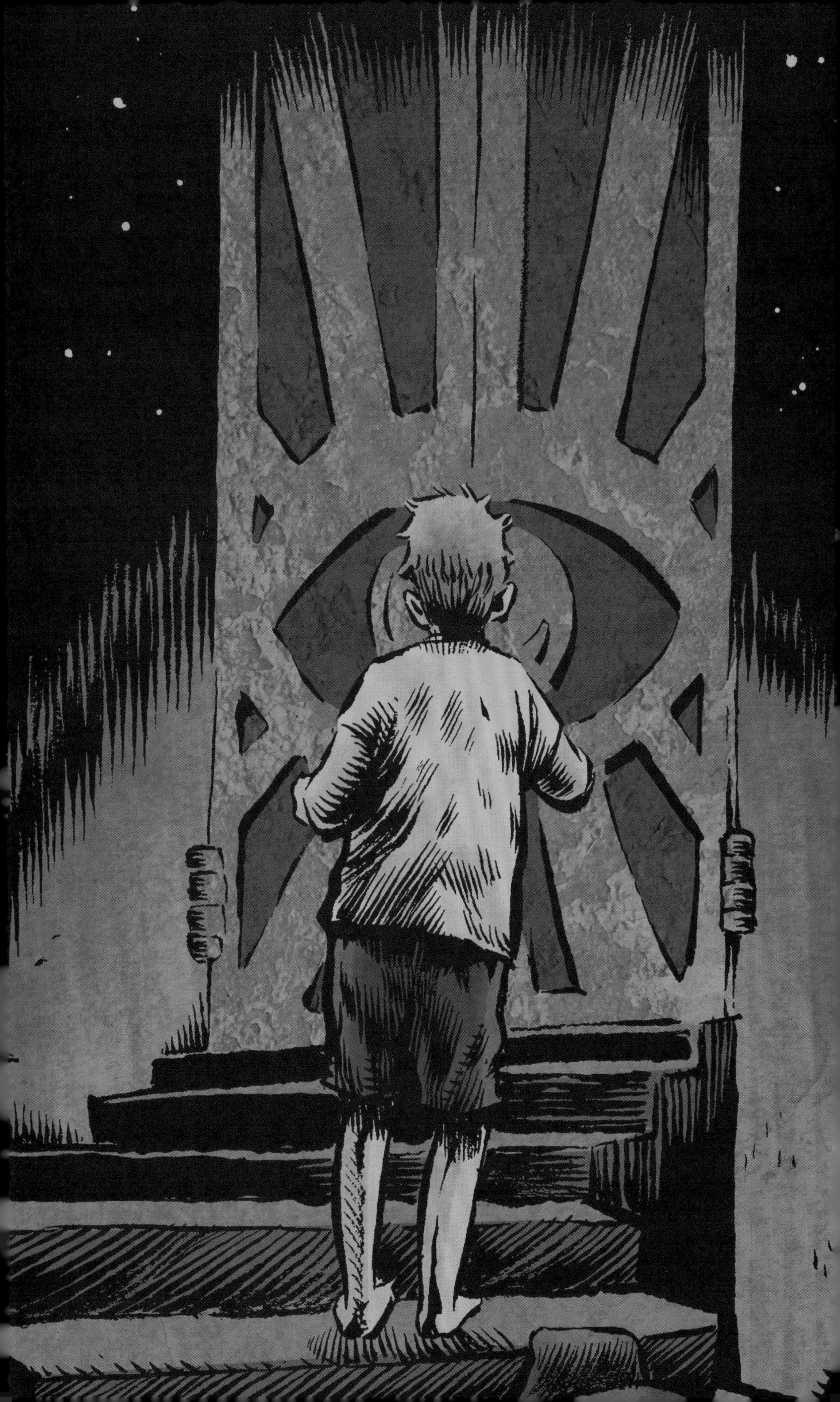

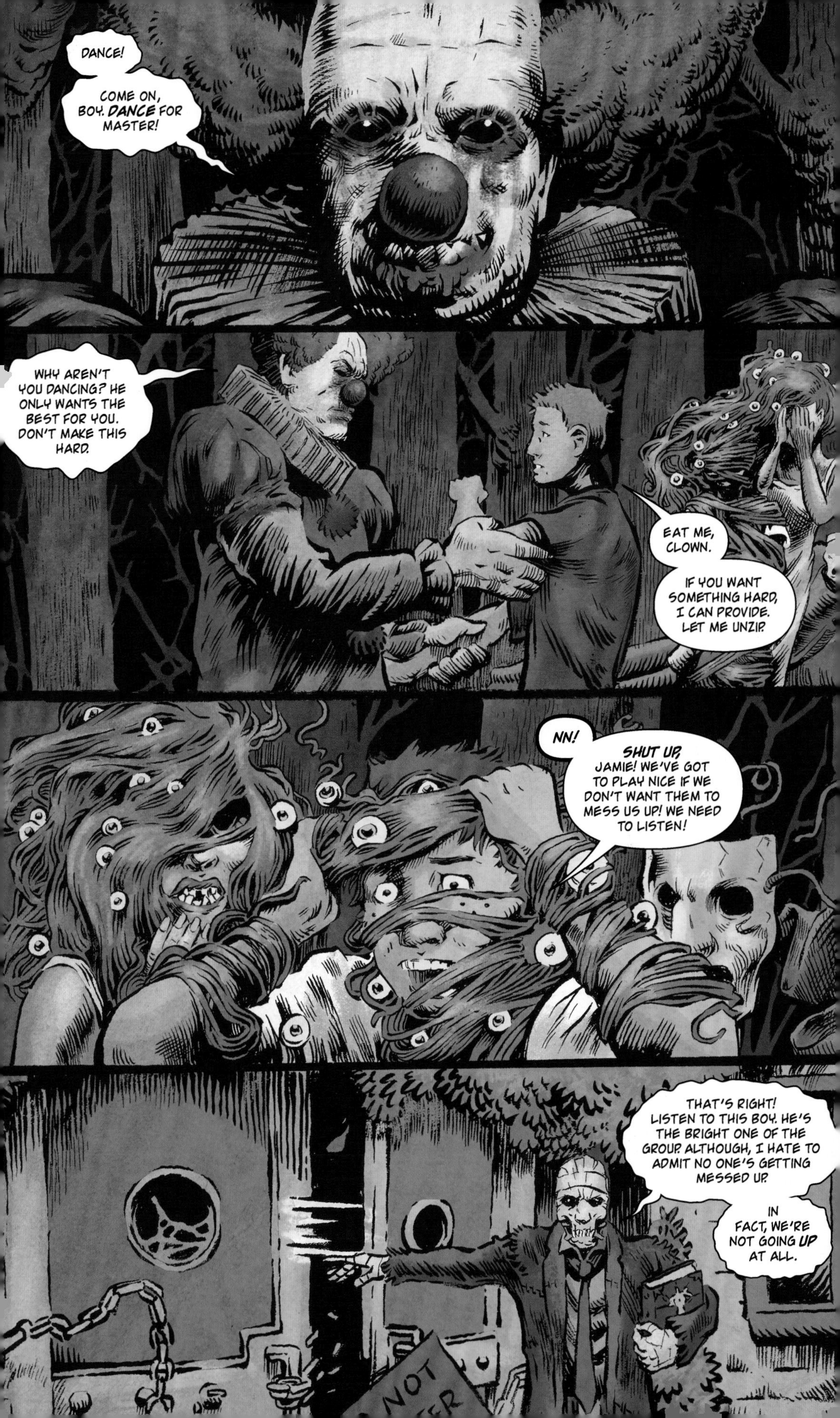
DANCE!
COME ON, BOY. DANCE FOR MASTER!
WHY AREN'T YOU DANCING? HE ONLY WANTS THE BEST FOR YOU. DON'T MAKE THIS HARD.
EAT ME, CLOWN.
IF YOU WANT SOMETHING HARD, I CAN PROVIDE. LET ME UNZIP.
NN!
SHUT UP, JAMIE! WE'VE GOT TO PLAY NICE IF WE DON'T WANT THEM TO MESS US UP! WE NEED TO LISTEN!
THAT'S RIGHT! LISTEN TO THIS BOY. HE'S THE BRIGHT ONE OF THE GROUP. ALTHOUGH, I HATE TO ADMIT NO ONE'S GETTING MESSED UP.
IN FACT, WE'RE NOT GOING UP AT ALL.

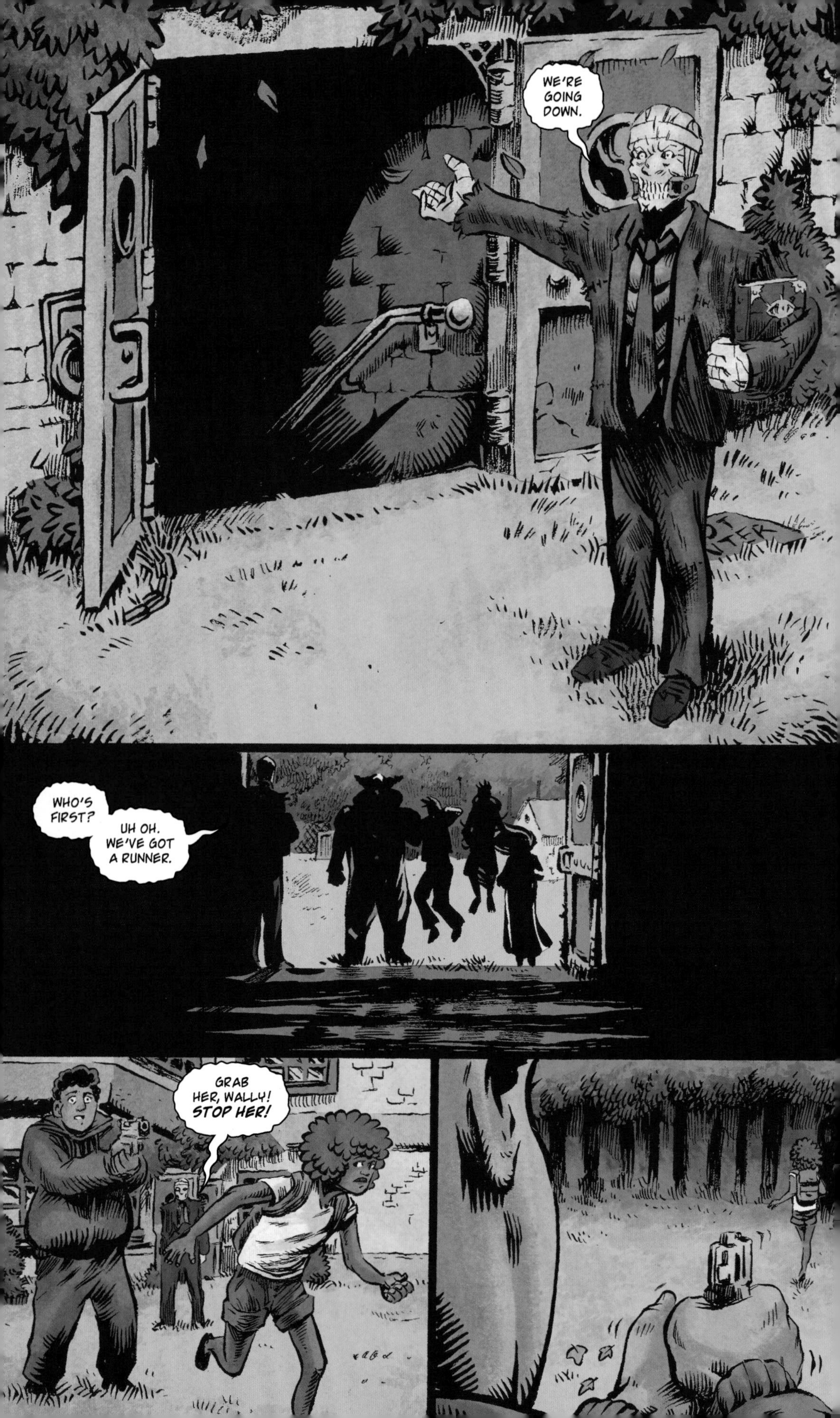
WE'RE GOING DOWN.
WHO'S FIRST?
UH OH. WE'VE GOT A RUNNER.
GRAB HER, WALLY! **STOP HER!**

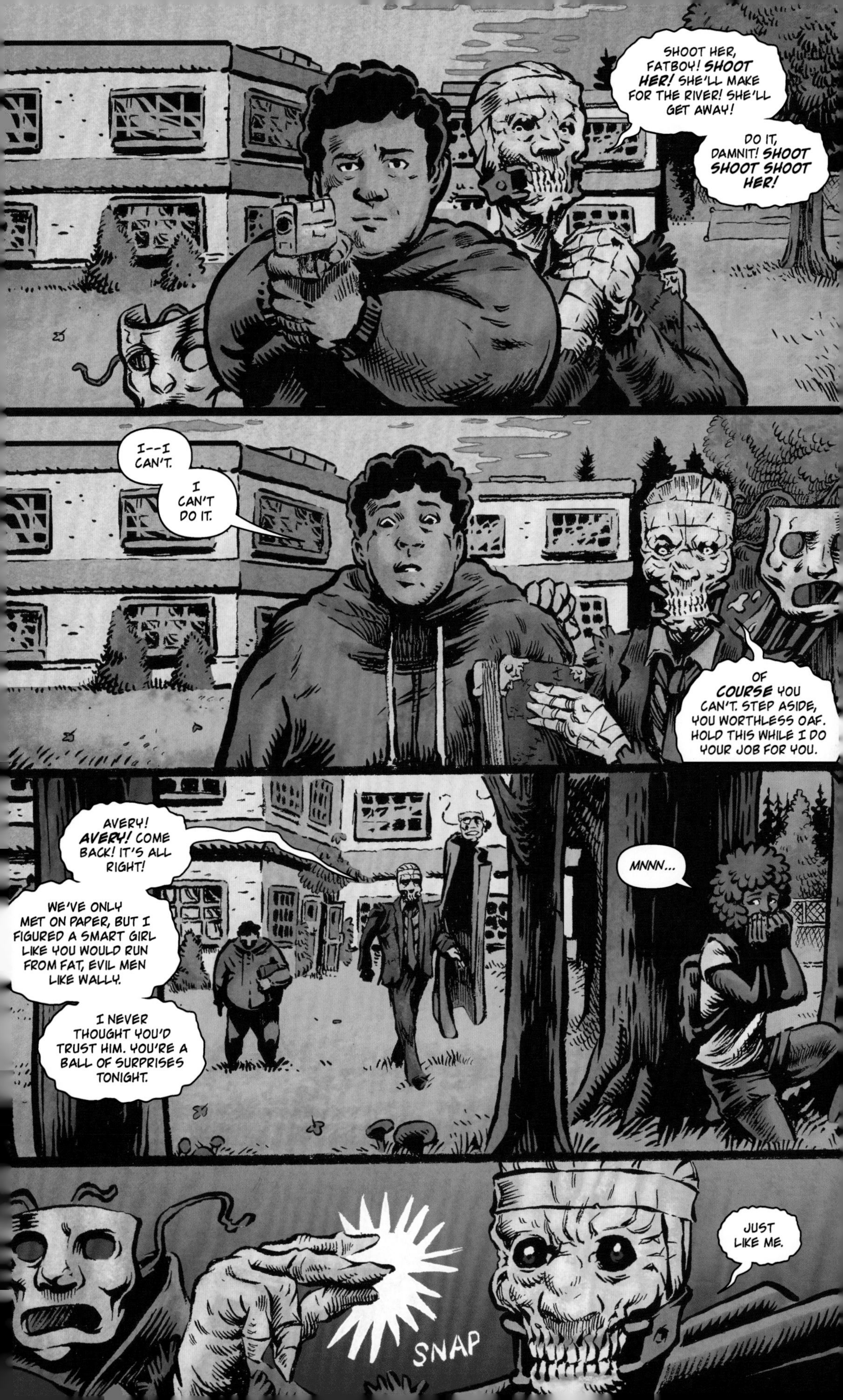
SHOOT HER, FATBOY! SHOOT HER! SHE'LL MAKE FOR THE RIVER! SHE'LL GET AWAY!
DO IT, DAMNIT! SHOOT SHOOT SHOOT HER!
I--I CAN'T.
I CAN'T DO IT.
OF COURSE YOU CAN'T. STEP ASIDE, YOU WORTHLESS OAF. HOLD THIS WHILE I DO YOUR JOB FOR YOU.
AVERY! AVERY! COME BACK! IT'S ALL RIGHT!
WE'VE ONLY MET ON PAPER, BUT I FIGURED A SMART GIRL LIKE YOU WOULD RUN FROM FAT, EVIL MEN LIKE WALLY.
I NEVER THOUGHT YOU'D TRUST HIM. YOU'RE A BALL OF SURPRISES TONIGHT.
MNNN...
SNAP
JUST LIKE ME.

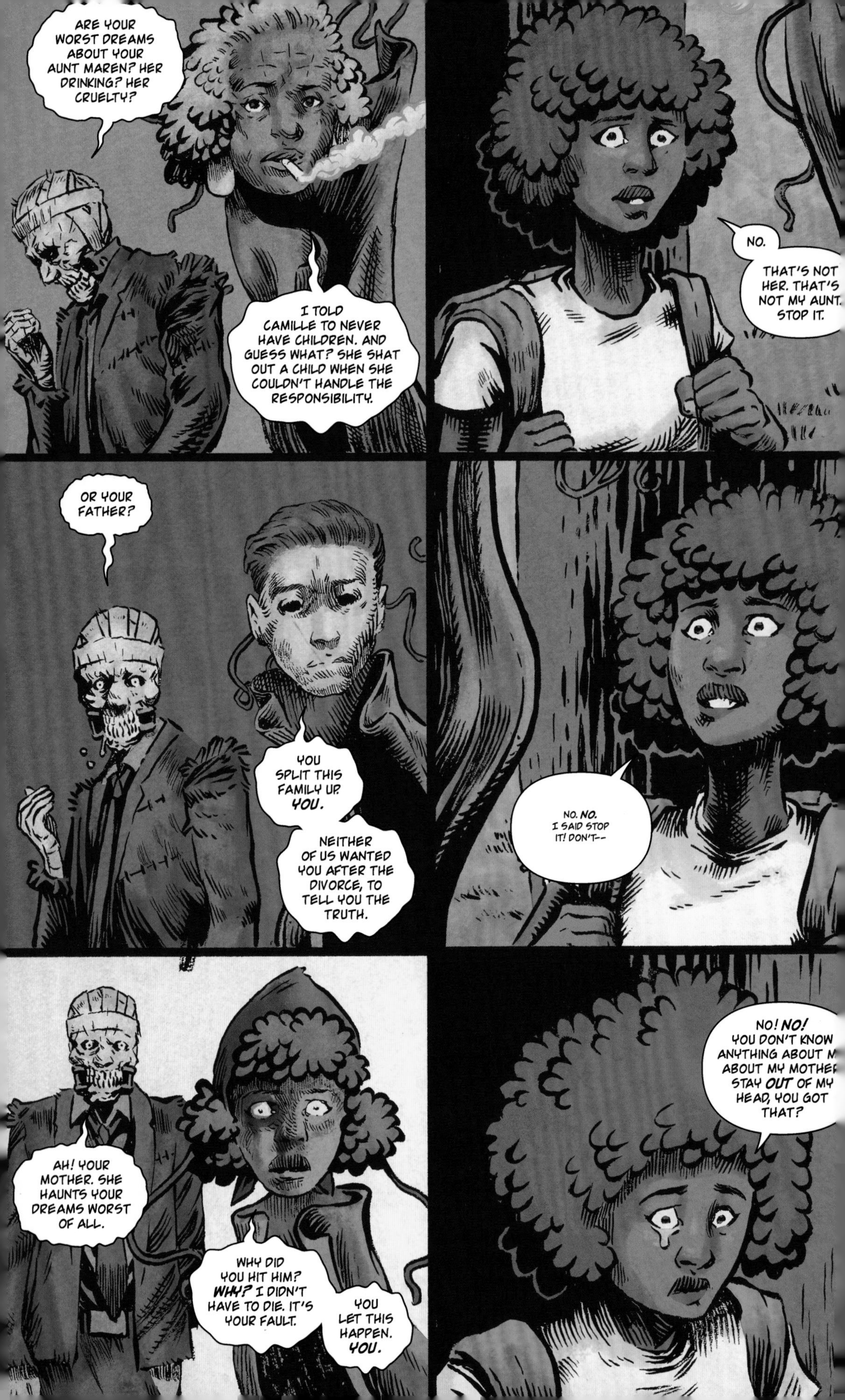
ARE YOUR WORST DREAMS ABOUT YOUR AUNT MAREN? HER DRINKING? HER CRUELTY?
I TOLD CAMILLE TO NEVER HAVE CHILDREN. AND GUESS WHAT? SHE SHAT OUT A CHILD WHEN SHE COULDN'T HANDLE THE RESPONSIBILITY.
NO.
THAT'S NOT HER. THAT'S NOT MY AUNT. STOP IT.
OR YOUR FATHER?
YOU SPLIT THIS FAMILY UP. *YOU.*
NEITHER OF US WANTED YOU AFTER THE DIVORCE, TO TELL YOU THE TRUTH.
NO. *NO.* I SAID STOP IT! DON'T--
AH! YOUR MOTHER. SHE HAUNTS YOUR DREAMS WORST OF ALL.
WHY DID YOU HIT HIM? *WHY?* I DIDN'T HAVE TO DIE. IT'S YOUR FAULT.
YOU LET THIS HAPPEN. *YOU.*
NO! *NO!* YOU DON'T KNOW ANYTHING ABOUT M ABOUT MY MOTHER STAY *OUT* OF MY HEAD, YOU GOT THAT?

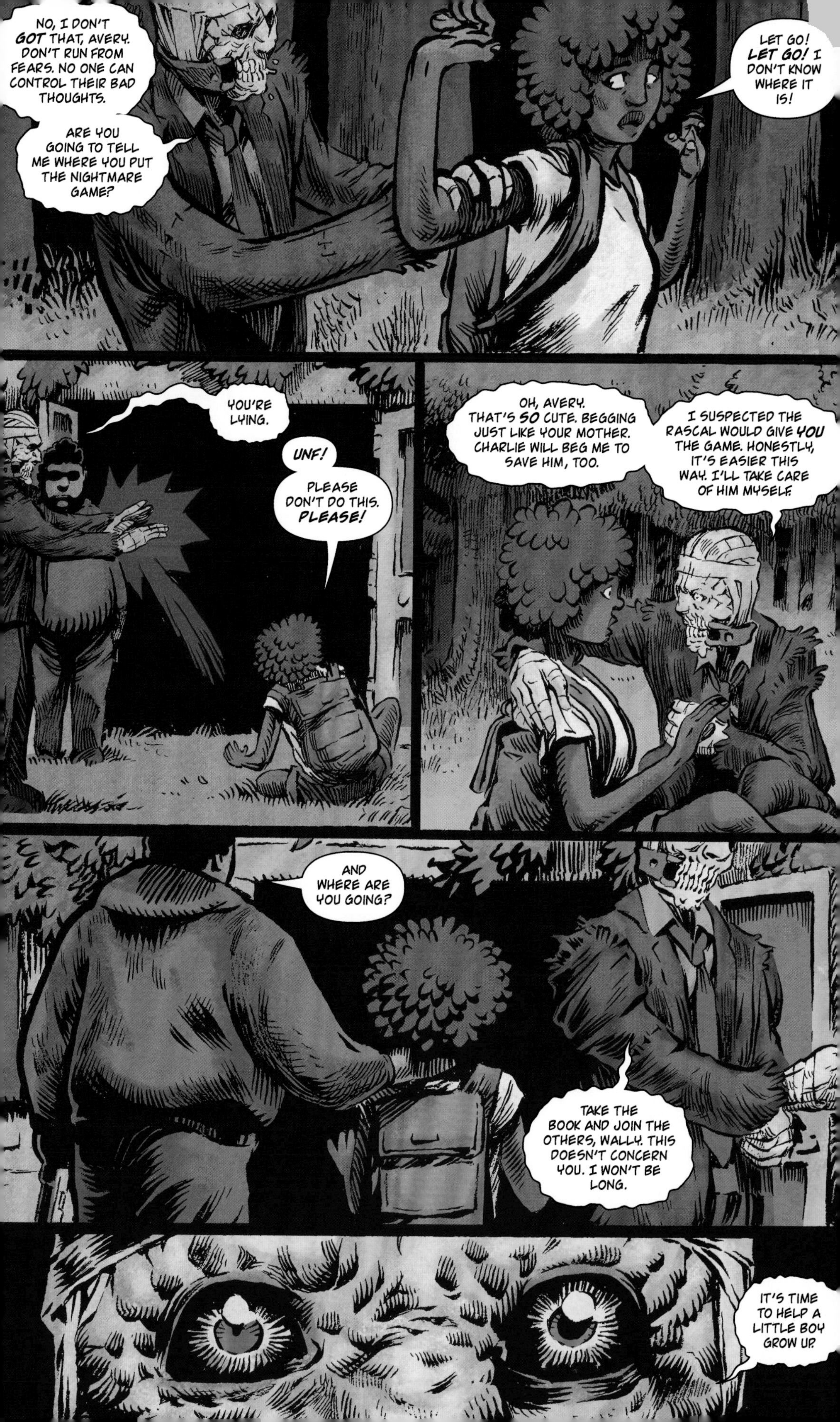
NO, I DON'T GOT THAT, AVERY. DON'T RUN FROM FEARS. NO ONE CAN CONTROL THEIR BAD THOUGHTS.
ARE YOU GOING TO TELL ME WHERE YOU PUT THE NIGHTMARE GAME?
LET GO! LET GO! I DON'T KNOW WHERE IT IS!
YOU'RE LYING.
UNF!
PLEASE DON'T DO THIS. PLEASE!
OH, AVERY. THAT'S SO CUTE. BEGGING JUST LIKE YOUR MOTHER. CHARLIE WILL BEG ME TO SAVE HIM, TOO.
I SUSPECTED THE RASCAL WOULD GIVE YOU THE GAME. HONESTLY, IT'S EASIER THIS WAY. I'LL TAKE CARE OF HIM MYSELF.
AND WHERE ARE YOU GOING?
TAKE THE BOOK AND JOIN THE OTHERS, WALLY. THIS DOESN'T CONCERN YOU. I WON'T BE LONG.
IT'S TIME TO HELP A LITTLE BOY GROW UP.

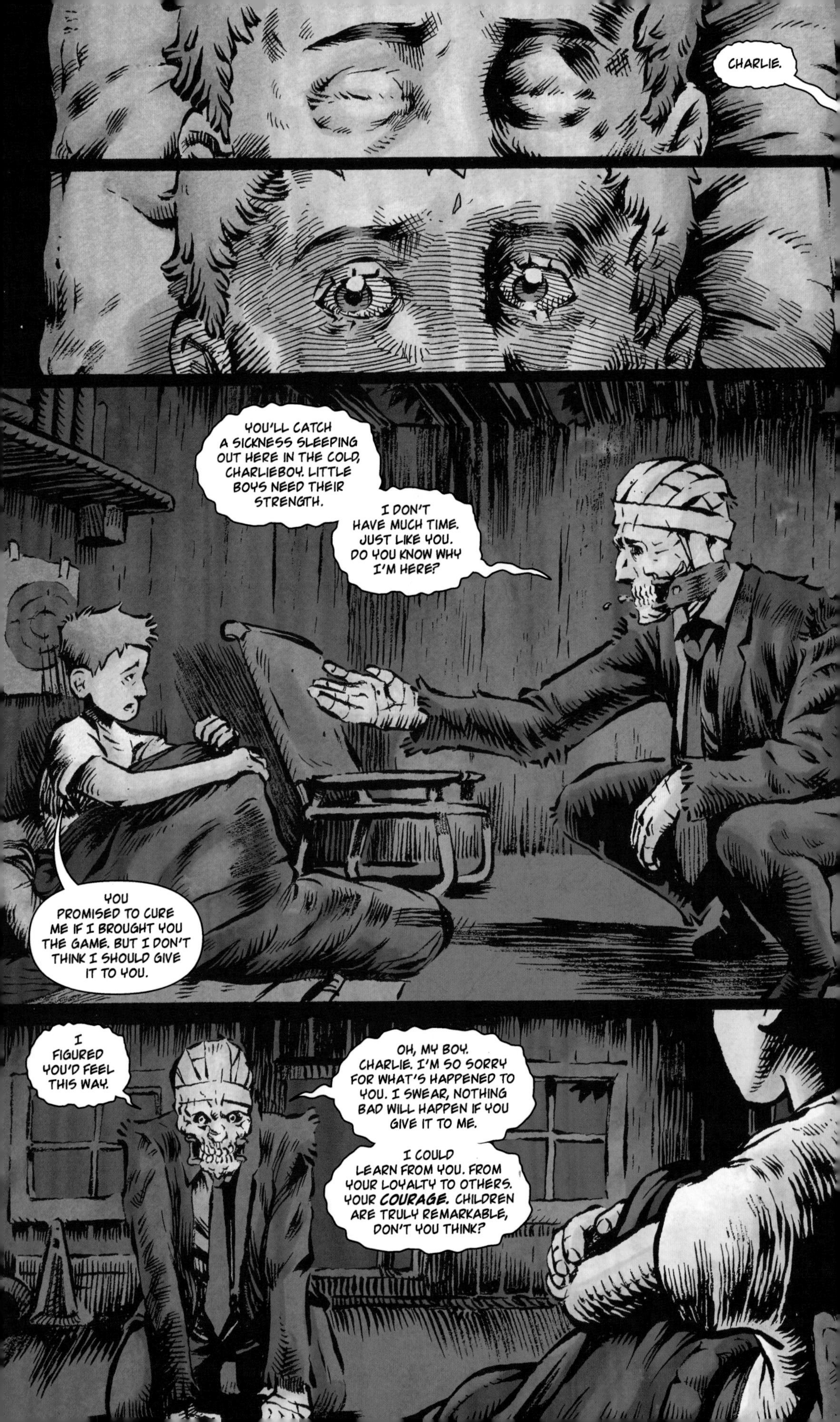
CHARLIE.
YOU'LL CATCH A SICKNESS SLEEPING OUT HERE IN THE COLD, CHARLIEBOY. LITTLE BOYS NEED THEIR STRENGTH.
I DON'T HAVE MUCH TIME. JUST LIKE YOU. DO YOU KNOW WHY I'M HERE?
YOU PROMISED TO CURE ME IF I BROUGHT YOU THE GAME. BUT I DON'T THINK I SHOULD GIVE IT TO YOU.
I FIGURED YOU'D FEEL THIS WAY.
OH, MY BOY. CHARLIE. I'M SO SORRY FOR WHAT'S HAPPENED TO YOU. I SWEAR, NOTHING BAD WILL HAPPEN IF YOU GIVE IT TO ME.
I COULD LEARN FROM YOU. FROM YOUR LOYALTY TO OTHERS. YOUR **COURAGE.** CHILDREN ARE TRULY REMARKABLE, DON'T YOU THINK?

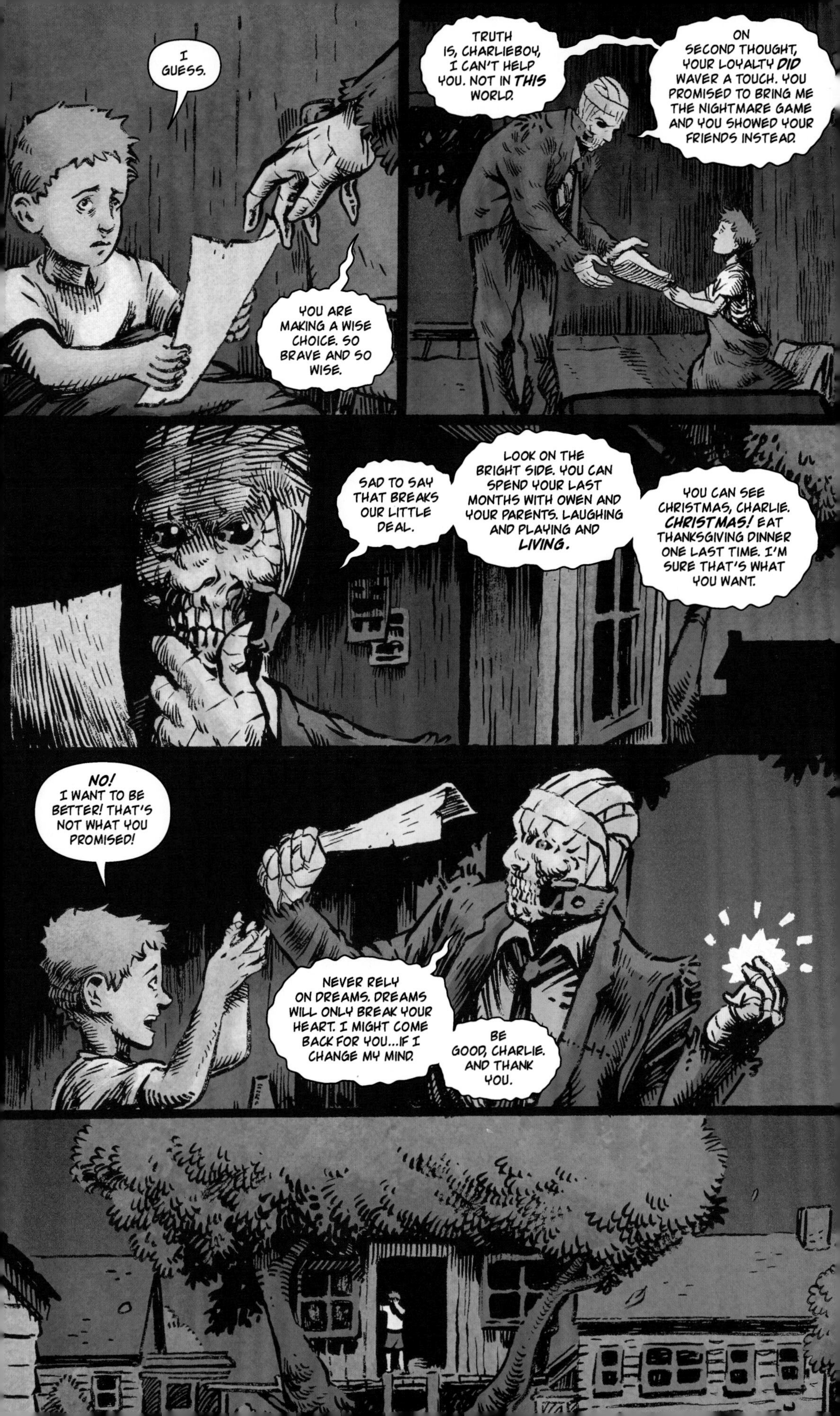
I GUESS.
YOU ARE MAKING A WISE CHOICE. SO BRAVE AND SO WISE.
TRUTH IS, CHARLIEBOY, I CAN'T HELP YOU. NOT IN *THIS* WORLD.
ON SECOND THOUGHT, YOUR LOYALTY *DID* WAVER A TOUCH. YOU PROMISED TO BRING ME THE NIGHTMARE GAME AND YOU SHOWED YOUR FRIENDS INSTEAD.
SAD TO SAY THAT BREAKS OUR LITTLE DEAL.
LOOK ON THE BRIGHT SIDE. YOU CAN SPEND YOUR LAST MONTHS WITH OWEN AND YOUR PARENTS. LAUGHING AND PLAYING AND *LIVING.*
YOU CAN SEE CHRISTMAS, CHARLIE. *CHRISTMAS!* EAT THANKSGIVING DINNER ONE LAST TIME. I'M SURE THAT'S WHAT YOU WANT.
NO! I WANT TO BE BETTER! THAT'S NOT WHAT YOU PROMISED!
NEVER RELY ON DREAMS. DREAMS WILL ONLY BREAK YOUR HEART. I MIGHT COME BACK FOR YOU...IF I CHANGE MY MIND.
BE GOOD, CHARLIE. AND THANK YOU.

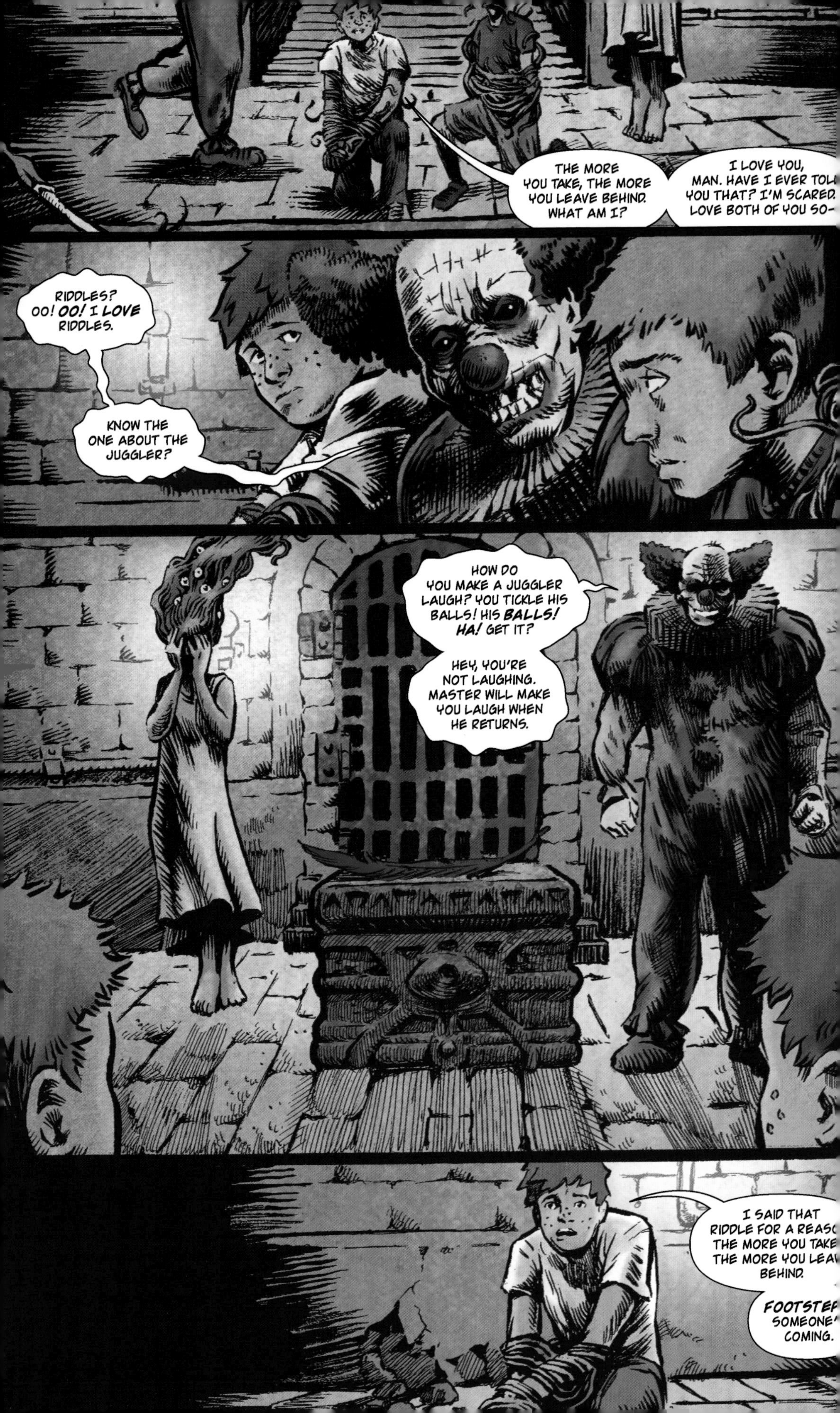
THE MORE YOU TAKE, THE MORE YOU LEAVE BEHIND. WHAT AM I?
I LOVE YOU, MAN. HAVE I EVER TOL YOU THAT? I'M SCARED. LOVE BOTH OF YOU SO-
RIDDLES? OO! OO! I LOVE RIDDLES.
KNOW THE ONE ABOUT THE JUGGLER?
HOW DO YOU MAKE A JUGGLER LAUGH? YOU TICKLE HIS BALLS! HIS BALLS! HA! GET IT?
HEY, YOU'RE NOT LAUGHING. MASTER WILL MAKE YOU LAUGH WHEN HE RETURNS.
I SAID THAT RIDDLE FOR A REAS THE MORE YOU TAKE THE MORE YOU LEA BEHIND.
FOOTSTE SOMEONE' COMING.

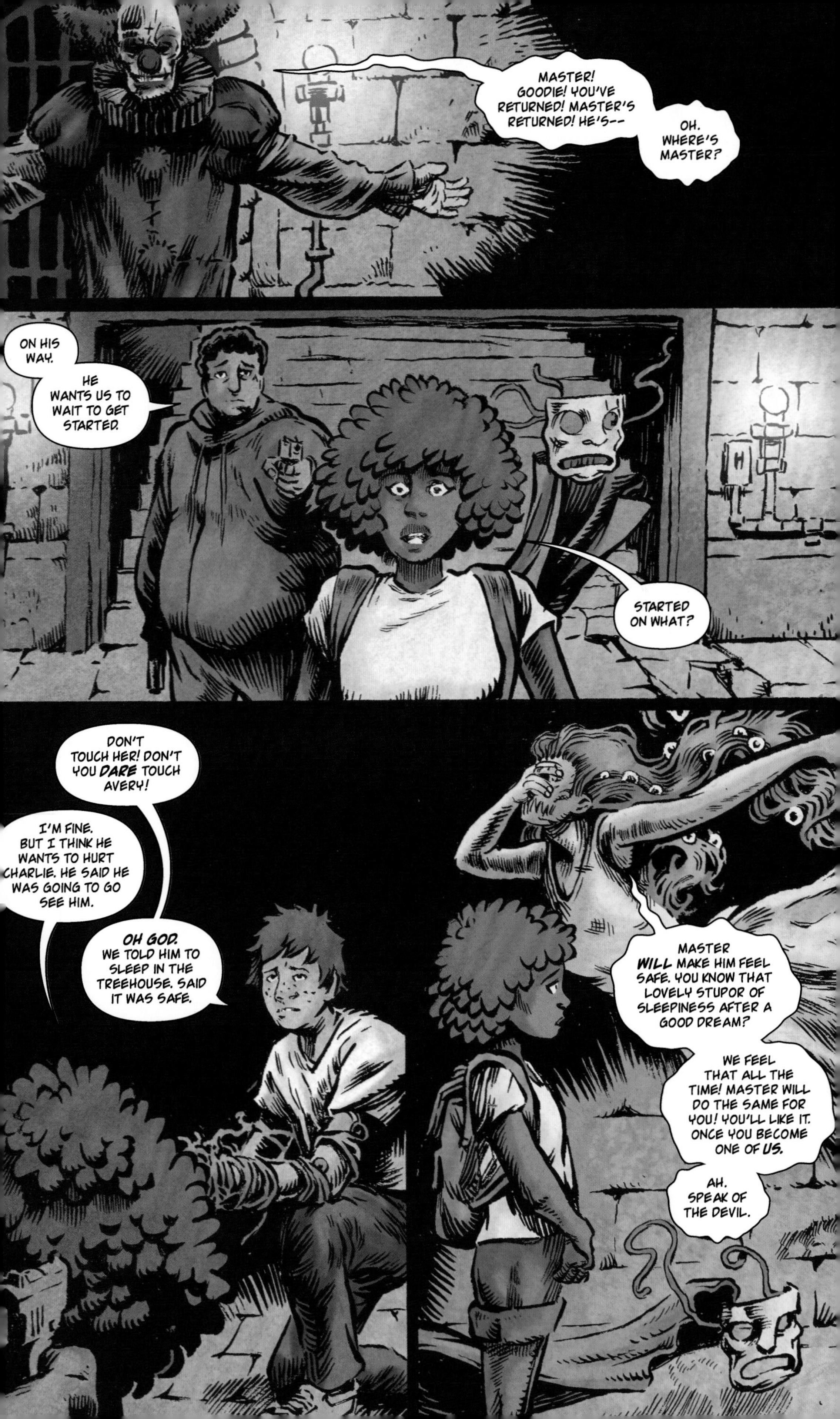
MASTER! GOODIE! YOU'VE RETURNED! MASTER'S RETURNED! HE'S--
OH. WHERE'S MASTER?
ON HIS WAY.
HE WANTS US TO WAIT TO GET STARTED.
STARTED ON WHAT?
DON'T TOUCH HER! DON'T YOU *DARE* TOUCH AVERY!
I'M FINE. BUT I THINK HE WANTS TO HURT CHARLIE. HE SAID HE WAS GOING TO GO SEE HIM.
OH GOD. WE TOLD HIM TO SLEEP IN THE TREEHOUSE. SAID IT WAS SAFE.
MASTER *WILL* MAKE HIM FEEL SAFE. YOU KNOW THAT LOVELY STUPOR OF SLEEPINESS AFTER A GOOD DREAM?
WE FEEL THAT ALL THE TIME! MASTER WILL DO THE SAME FOR YOU! YOU'LL LIKE IT. ONCE YOU BECOME ONE OF *US.*
AH. SPEAK OF THE DEVIL.

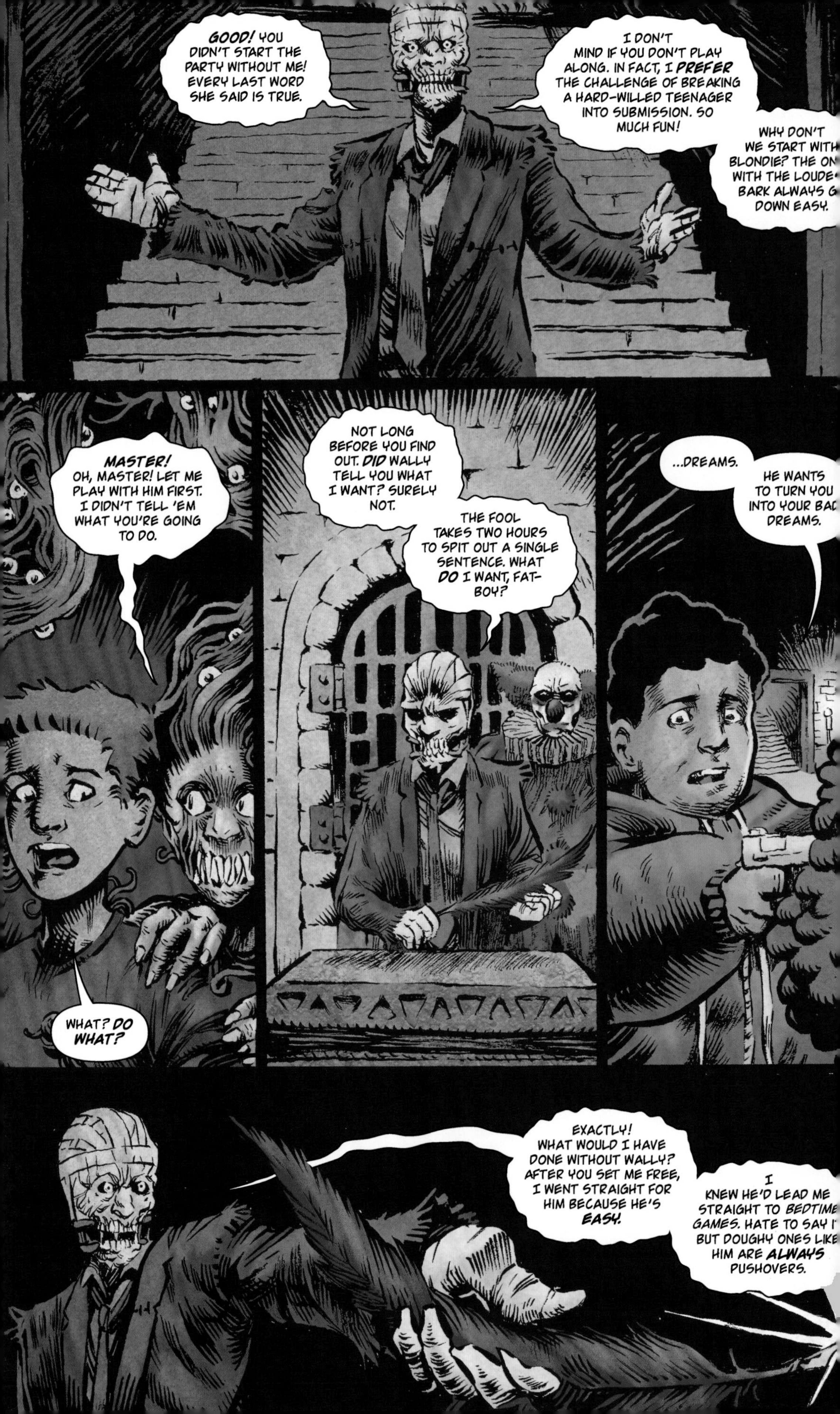
GOOD! YOU DIDN'T START THE PARTY WITHOUT ME! EVERY LAST WORD SHE SAID IS TRUE.
I DON'T MIND IF YOU DON'T PLAY ALONG. IN FACT, I PREFER THE CHALLENGE OF BREAKING A HARD-WILLED TEENAGER INTO SUBMISSION. SO MUCH FUN!
MASTER! OH, MASTER! LET ME PLAY WITH HIM FIRST. I DIDN'T TELL 'EM WHAT YOU'RE GOING TO DO.
WHAT? DO WHAT?
NOT LONG BEFORE YOU FIND OUT. DID WALLY TELL YOU WHAT I WANT? SURELY NOT.
THE FOOL TAKES TWO HOURS TO SPIT OUT A SINGLE SENTENCE. WHAT DO I WANT, FAT-BOY?
...DREAMS.
EXACTLY! WHAT WOULD I HAVE DONE WITHOUT WALLY? AFTER YOU SET ME FREE, I WENT STRAIGHT FOR HIM BECAUSE HE'S EASY!

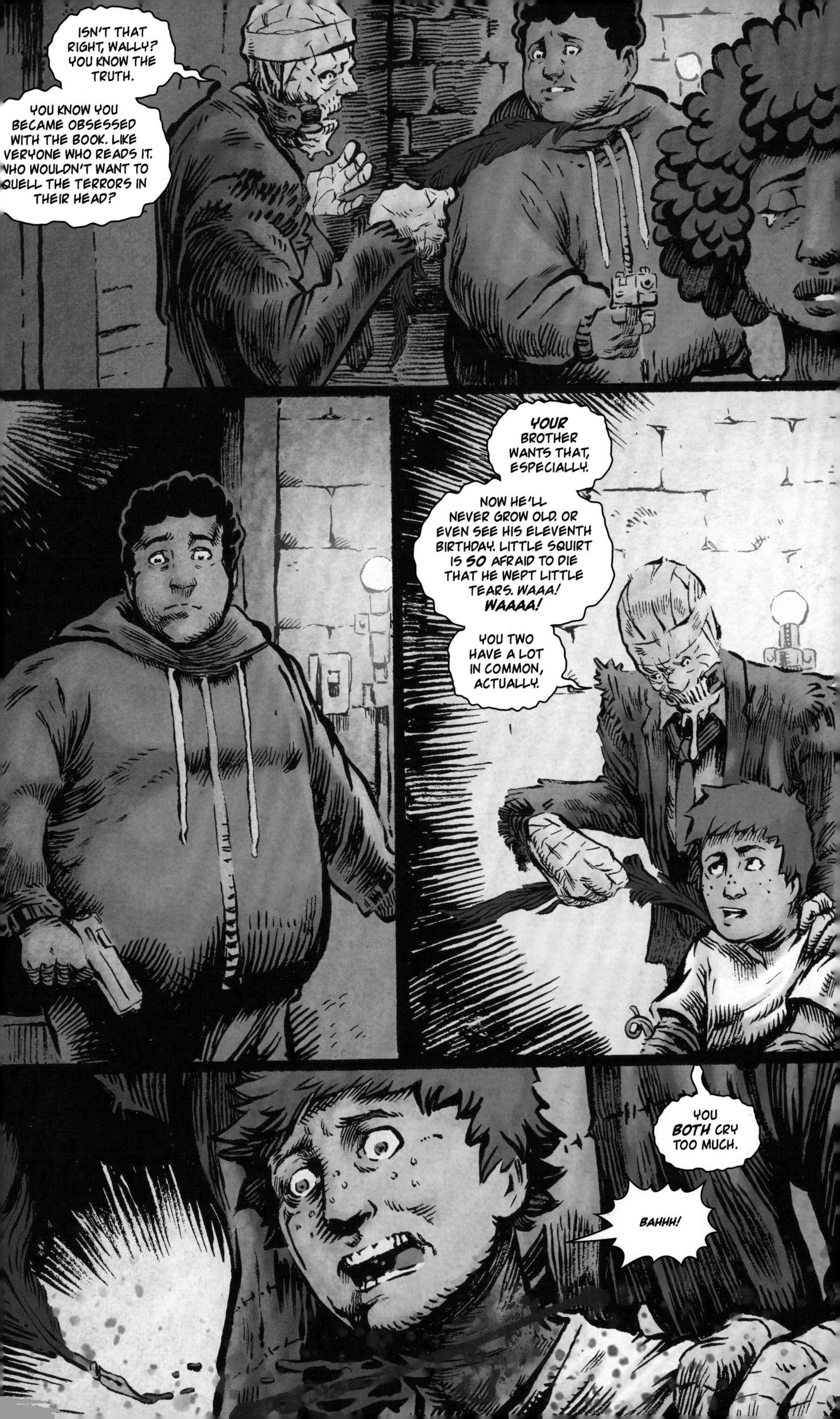
ISN'T THAT RIGHT, WALLY? YOU KNOW THE TRUTH.
YOU KNOW YOU BECAME OBSESSED WITH THE BOOK. LIKE VERYONE WHO READS IT. WHO WOULDN'T WANT TO QUELL THE TERRORS IN THEIR HEAD?
YOUR BROTHER WANTS THAT, ESPECIALLY.
NOW HE'LL NEVER GROW OLD. OR EVEN SEE HIS ELEVENTH BIRTHDAY. LITTLE SQUIRT IS SO AFRAID TO DIE THAT HE WEPT LITTLE TEARS. WAAA! WAAAA!
YOU TWO HAVE A LOT IN COMMON, ACTUALLY.
YOU BOTH CRY TOO MUCH.
BAHHH!

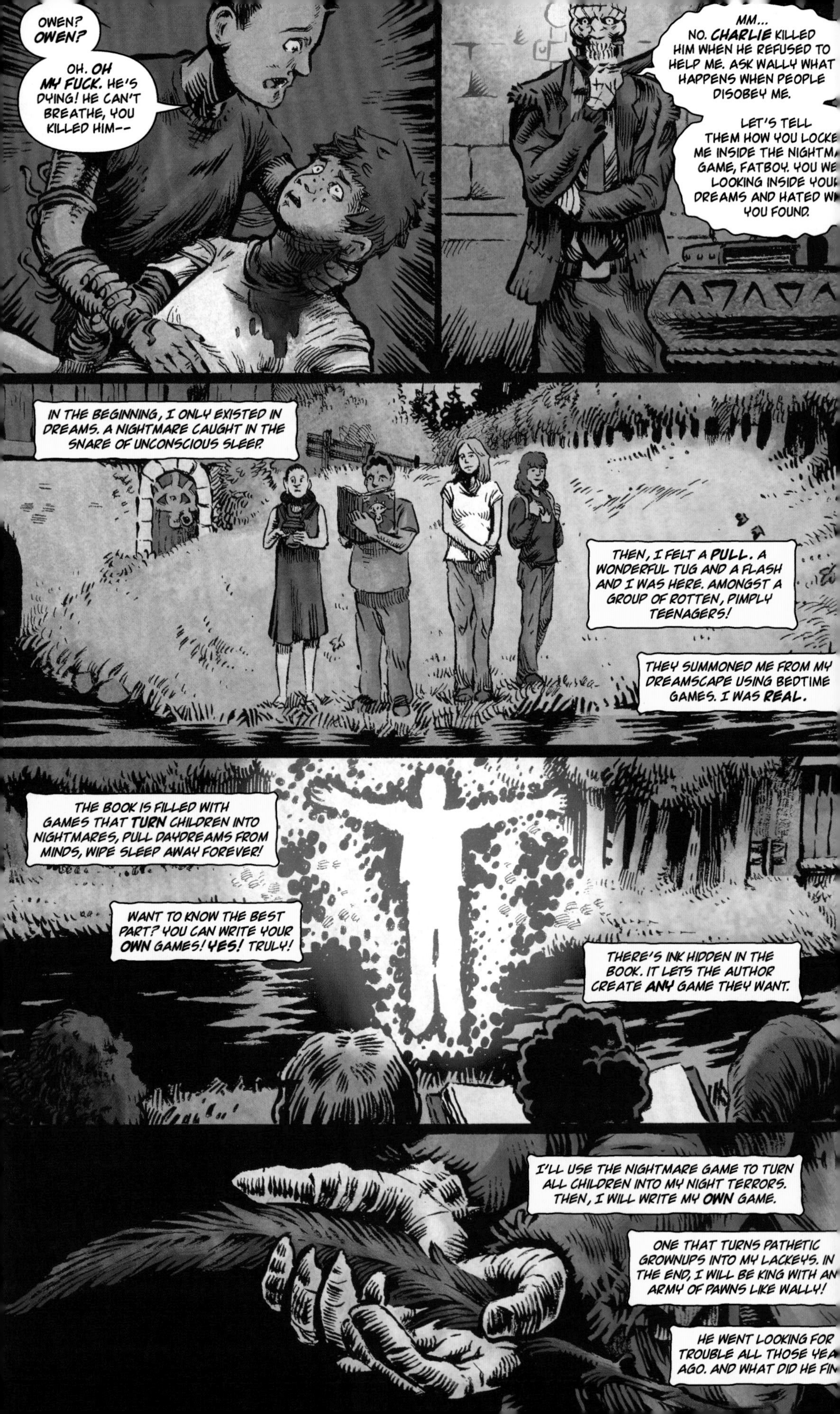
OWEN? OWEN?
OH. OH MY FUCK. HE'S DYING! HE CAN'T BREATHE, YOU KILLED HIM--
MM... NO. CHARLIE KILLED HIM WHEN HE REFUSED TO HELP ME. ASK WALLY WHAT HAPPENS WHEN PEOPLE DISOBEY ME.
LET'S TELL THEM HOW YOU LOCKE ME INSIDE THE NIGHTM GAME, FATBOY. YOU WE LOOKING INSIDE YOUR DREAMS AND HATED W YOU FOUND.
IN THE BEGINNING, I ONLY EXISTED IN DREAMS. A NIGHTMARE CAUGHT IN THE SNARE OF UNCONSCIOUS SLEEP.
THEN, I FELT A PULL. A WONDERFUL TUG AND A FLASH AND I WAS HERE. AMONGST A GROUP OF ROTTEN, PIMPLY TEENAGERS!
THEY SUMMONED ME FROM MY DREAMSCAPE USING BEDTIME GAMES. I WAS REAL.
THE BOOK IS FILLED WITH GAMES THAT TURN CHILDREN INTO NIGHTMARES, PULL DAYDREAMS FROM MINDS, WIPE SLEEP AWAY FOREVER!
WANT TO KNOW THE BEST PART? YOU CAN WRITE YOUR OWN GAMES! YES! TRULY!
THERE'S INK HIDDEN IN THE BOOK. IT LETS THE AUTHOR CREATE ANY GAME THEY WANT.
I'LL USE THE NIGHTMARE GAME TO TURN ALL CHILDREN INTO MY NIGHT TERRORS. THEN, I WILL WRITE MY OWN GAME.
ONE THAT TURNS PATHETIC GROWNUPS INTO MY LACKEYS. IN THE END, I WILL BE KING WITH AN ARMY OF PAWNS LIKE WALLY!
HE WENT LOOKING FOR TROUBLE ALL THOSE YEA AGO. AND WHAT DID HE FIN

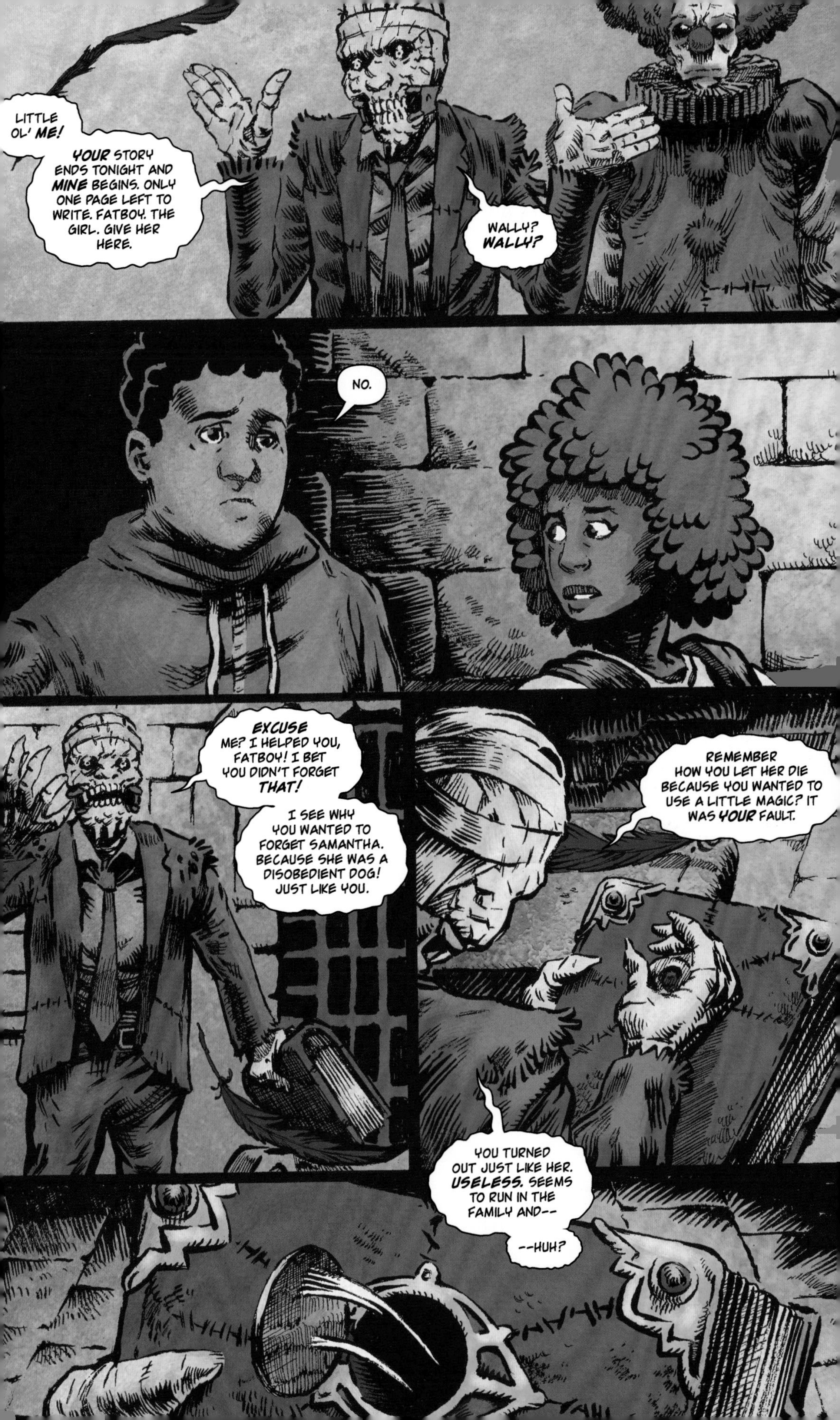
LITTLE OL' ME!
YOUR STORY ENDS TONIGHT AND MINE BEGINS. ONLY ONE PAGE LEFT TO WRITE. FATBOY. THE GIRL. GIVE HER HERE.
WALLY? WALLY?
NO.
EXCUSE ME? I HELPED YOU, FATBOY! I BET YOU DIDN'T FORGET THAT!
I SEE WHY YOU WANTED TO FORGET SAMANTHA. BECAUSE SHE WAS A DISOBEDIENT DOG! JUST LIKE YOU.
REMEMBER HOW YOU LET HER DIE BECAUSE YOU WANTED TO USE A LITTLE MAGIC? IT WAS YOUR FAULT.
YOU TURNED OUT JUST LIKE HER. USELESS. SEEMS TO RUN IN THE FAMILY AND--
--HUH?

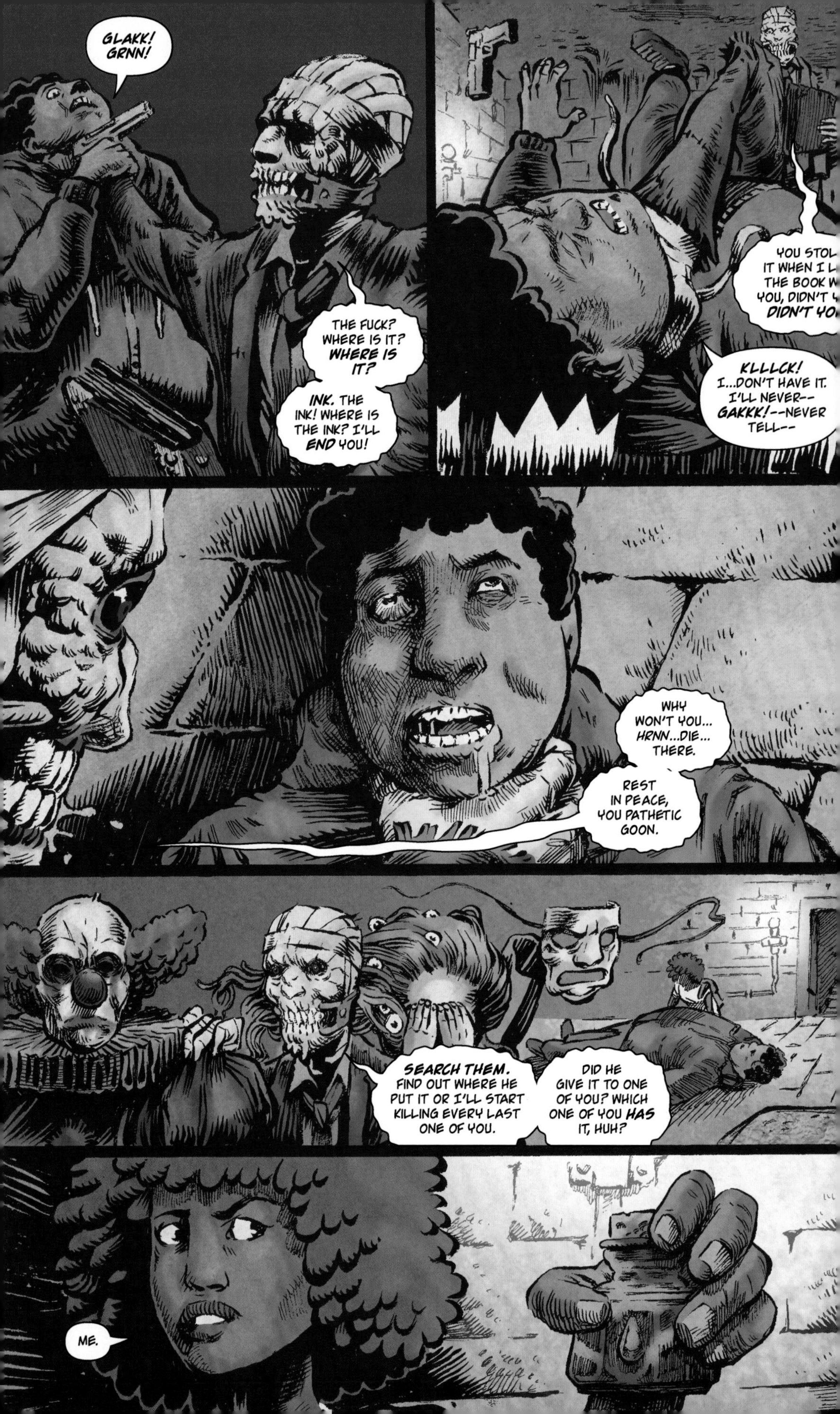
GLAKK! GRNN!
THE FUCK? WHERE IS IT? WHERE IS IT?
INK. THE INK! WHERE IS THE INK? I'LL END YOU!
YOU STOL IT WHEN I L THE BOOK W YOU, DIDN'T Y DIDN'T YO
KLLLCK! I...DON'T HAVE IT. I'LL NEVER-- GAKKK!--NEVER TELL--
WHY WON'T YOU... HRNN...DIE... THERE.
REST IN PEACE, YOU PATHETIC GOON.
SEARCH THEM. FIND OUT WHERE HE PUT IT OR I'LL START KILLING EVERY LAST ONE OF YOU.
DID HE GIVE IT TO ONE OF YOU? WHICH ONE OF YOU HAS IT, HUH?
ME.

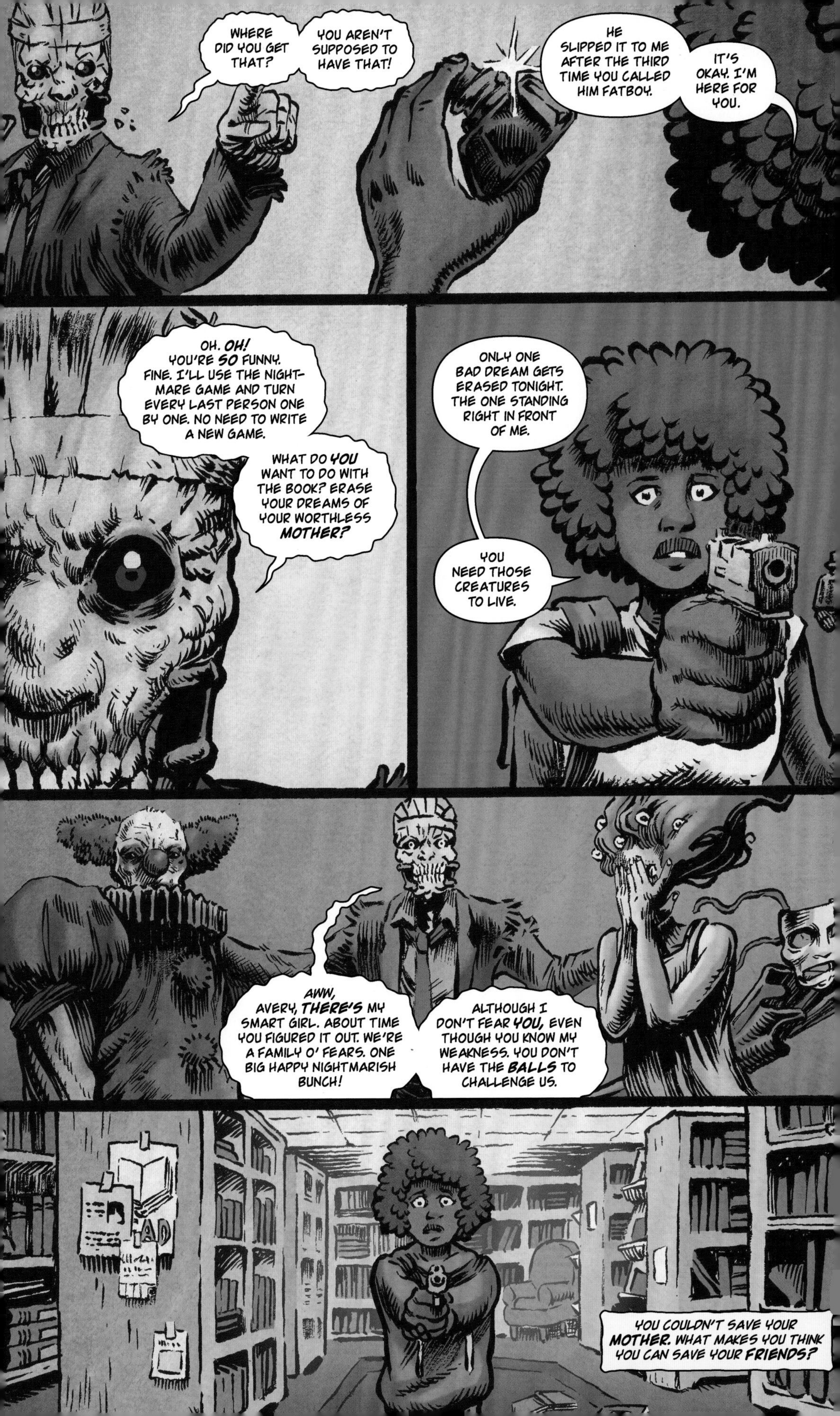
WHERE DID YOU GET THAT?
YOU AREN'T SUPPOSED TO HAVE THAT!
HE SLIPPED IT TO ME AFTER THE THIRD TIME YOU CALLED HIM FATBOY.
IT'S OKAY. I'M HERE FOR YOU.
OH. OH! YOU'RE SO FUNNY. FINE. I'LL USE THE NIGHT-MARE GAME AND TURN EVERY LAST PERSON ONE BY ONE. NO NEED TO WRITE A NEW GAME.
WHAT DO YOU WANT TO DO WITH THE BOOK? ERASE YOUR DREAMS OF YOUR WORTHLESS MOTHER?
ONLY ONE BAD DREAM GETS ERASED TONIGHT. THE ONE STANDING RIGHT IN FRONT OF ME.
YOU NEED THOSE CREATURES TO LIVE.
AWW, AVERY, THERE'S MY SMART GIRL. ABOUT TIME YOU FIGURED IT OUT. WE'RE A FAMILY O' FEARS. ONE BIG HAPPY NIGHTMARISH BUNCH!
ALTHOUGH I DON'T FEAR YOU, EVEN THOUGH YOU KNOW MY WEAKNESS. YOU DON'T HAVE THE BALLS TO CHALLENGE US.
YOU COULDN'T SAVE YOUR MOTHER. WHAT MAKES YOU THINK YOU CAN SAVE YOUR FRIENDS?

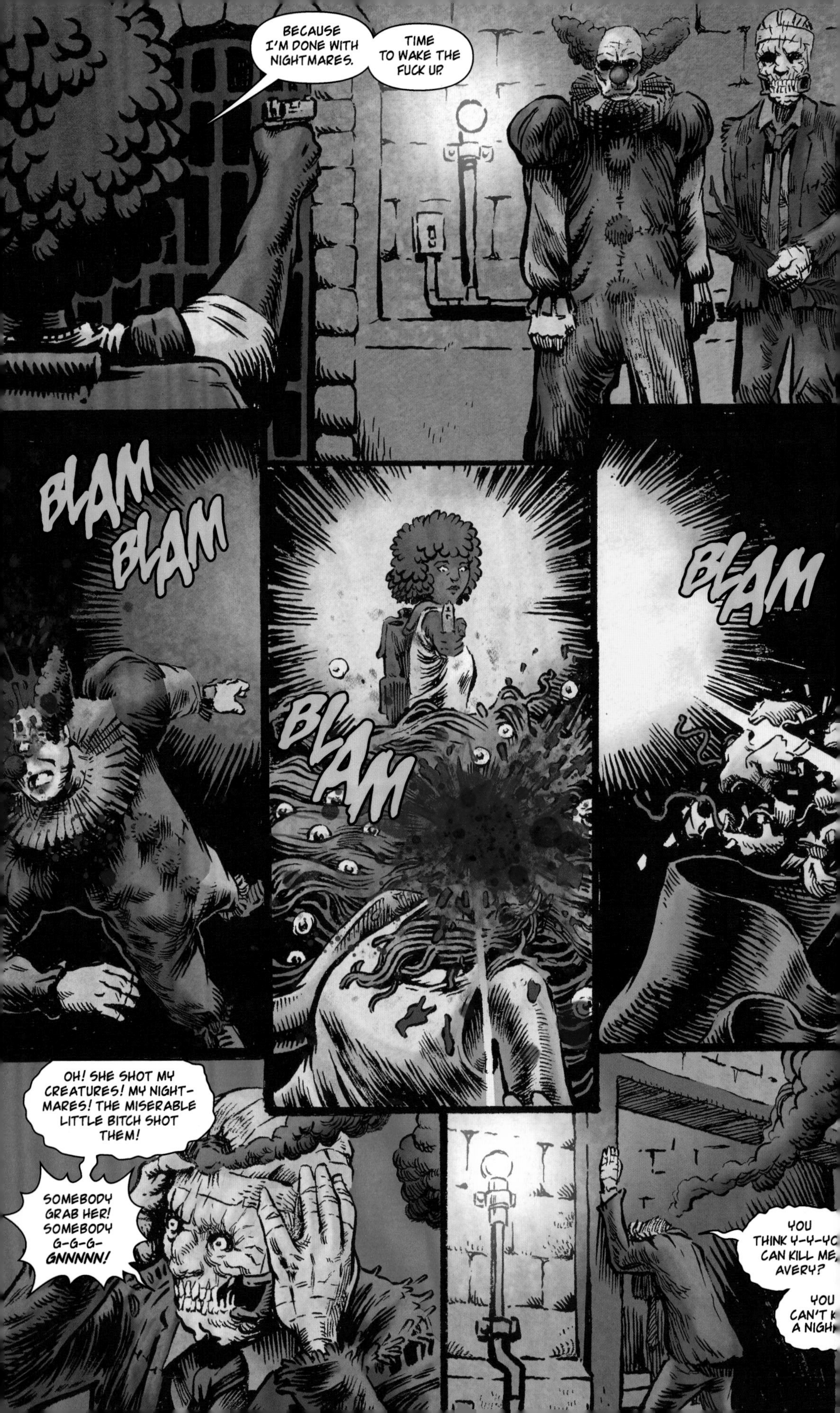
BECAUSE I'M DONE WITH NIGHTMARES.
TIME TO WAKE THE FUCK UP.
BLAM BLAM
BLAM
BLAM
OH! SHE SHOT MY CREATURES! MY NIGHT-MARES! THE MISERABLE LITTLE BITCH SHOT THEM!
SOMEBODY GRAB HER! SOMEBODY G-G-G-GNNNNN!
YOU THINK Y-Y-YO CAN KILL ME, AVERY?
YOU CAN'T K A NIGH

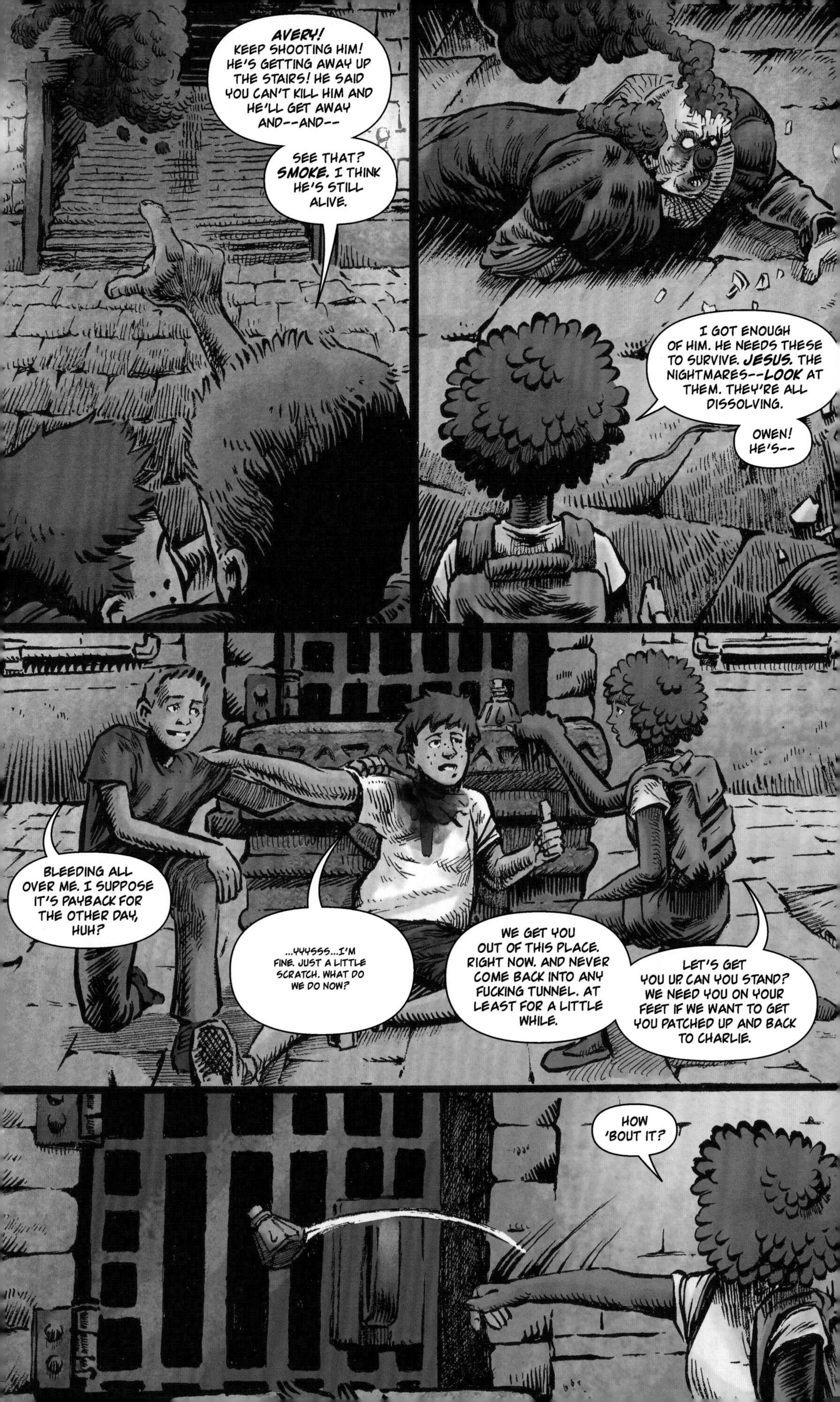
AVERY! KEEP SHOOTING HIM! HE'S GETTING AWAY UP THE STAIRS! HE SAID YOU CAN'T KILL HIM AND HE'LL GET AWAY AND--AND--
SEE THAT? SMOKE. I THINK HE'S STILL ALIVE.
I GOT ENOUGH OF HIM. HE NEEDS THESE TO SURVIVE. JESUS. THE NIGHTMARES--LOOK AT THEM. THEY'RE ALL DISSOLVING.
OWEN! HE'S--
BLEEDING ALL OVER ME. I SUPPOSE IT'S PAYBACK FOR THE OTHER DAY, HUH?
...YYYSSS...I'M FINE. JUST A LITTLE SCRATCH. WHAT DO WE DO NOW?
WE GET YOU OUT OF THIS PLACE. RIGHT NOW. AND NEVER COME BACK INTO ANY FUCKING TUNNEL. AT LEAST FOR A LITTLE WHILE.
LET'S GET YOU UP. CAN YOU STAND? WE NEED YOU ON YOUR FEET IF WE WANT TO GET YOU PATCHED UP AND BACK TO CHARLIE.
HOW 'BOUT IT?

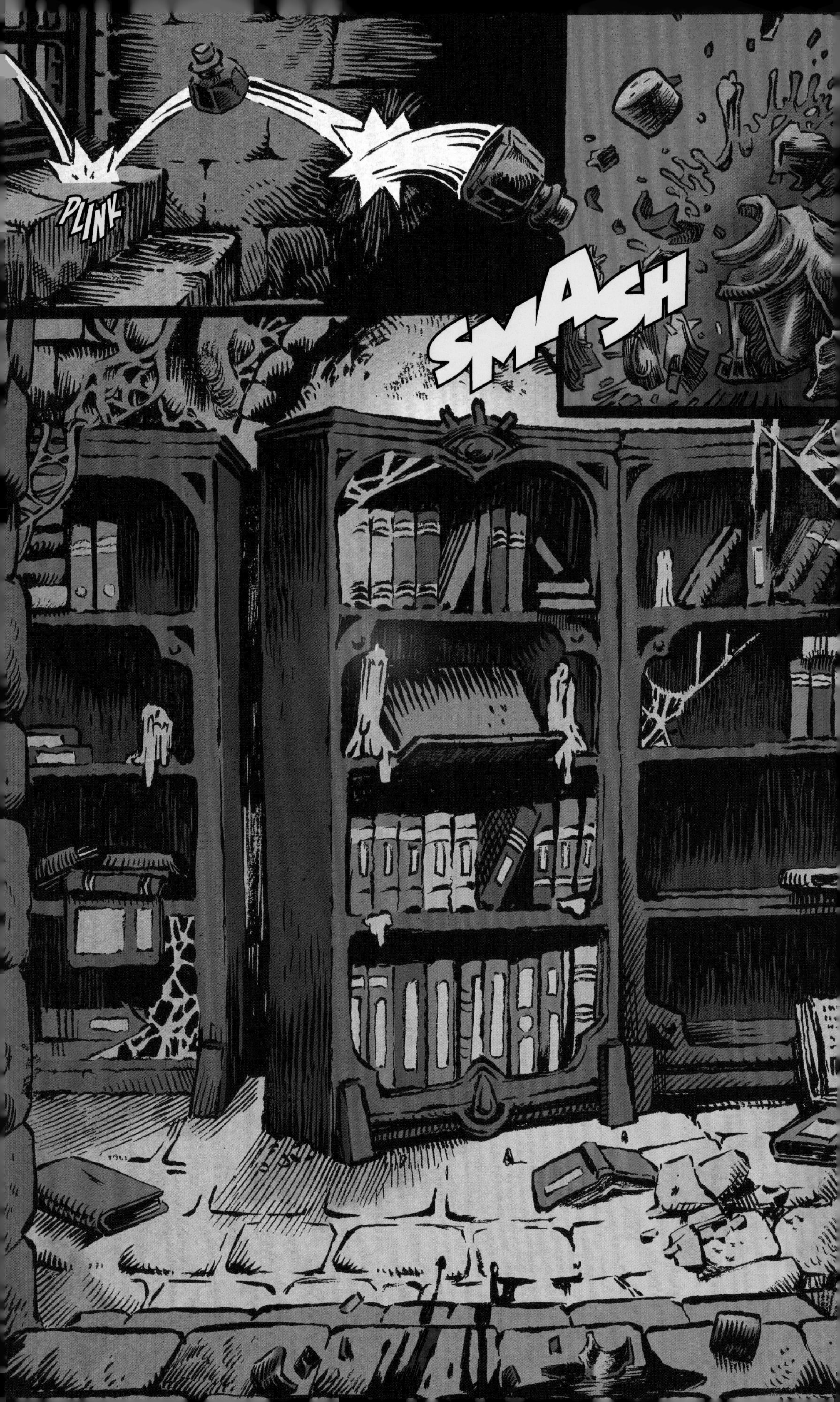
PLINK
SMASH

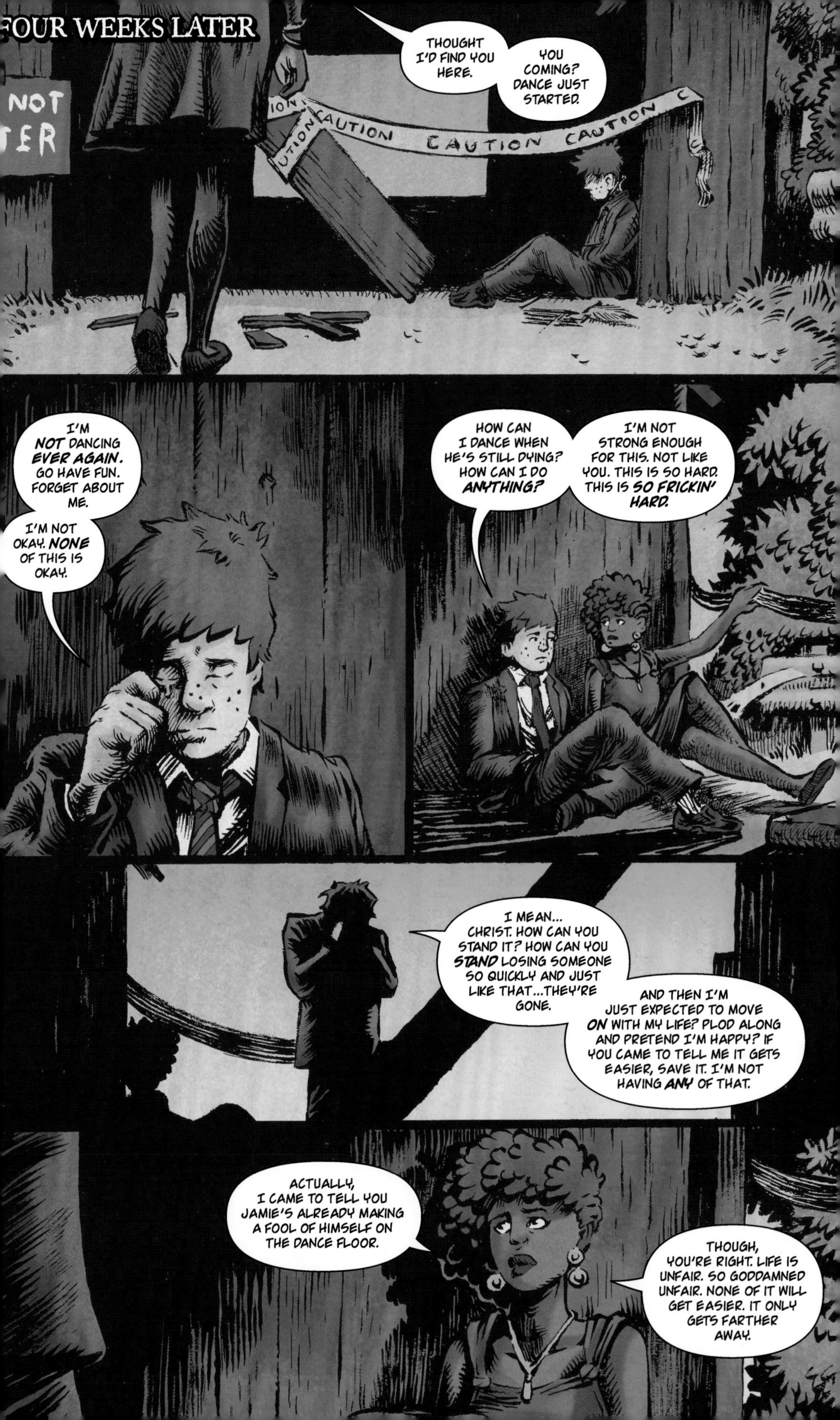
FOUR WEEKS LATER
NOT
ER
THOUGHT I'D FIND YOU HERE.
YOU COMING? DANCE JUST STARTED.
CAUTION CAUTION CAUTION CAUTION
I'M NOT DANCING EVER AGAIN. GO HAVE FUN. FORGET ABOUT ME.
I'M NOT OKAY. NONE OF THIS IS OKAY.
HOW CAN I DANCE WHEN HE'S STILL DYING? HOW CAN I DO ANYTHING?
I'M NOT STRONG ENOUGH FOR THIS. NOT LIKE YOU. THIS IS SO HARD. THIS IS SO FRICKIN' HARD.
I MEAN... CHRIST. HOW CAN YOU STAND IT? HOW CAN YOU STAND LOSING SOMEONE SO QUICKLY AND JUST LIKE THAT...THEY'RE GONE.
AND THEN I'M JUST EXPECTED TO MOVE ON WITH MY LIFE? PLOD ALONG AND PRETEND I'M HAPPY? IF YOU CAME TO TELL ME IT GETS EASIER, SAVE IT. I'M NOT HAVING ANY OF THAT.
ACTUALLY, I CAME TO TELL YOU JAMIE'S ALREADY MAKING A FOOL OF HIMSELF ON THE DANCE FLOOR.
THOUGH, YOU'RE RIGHT. LIFE IS UNFAIR. SO GODDAMNED UNFAIR. NONE OF IT WILL GET EASIER. IT ONLY GETS FARTHER AWAY.

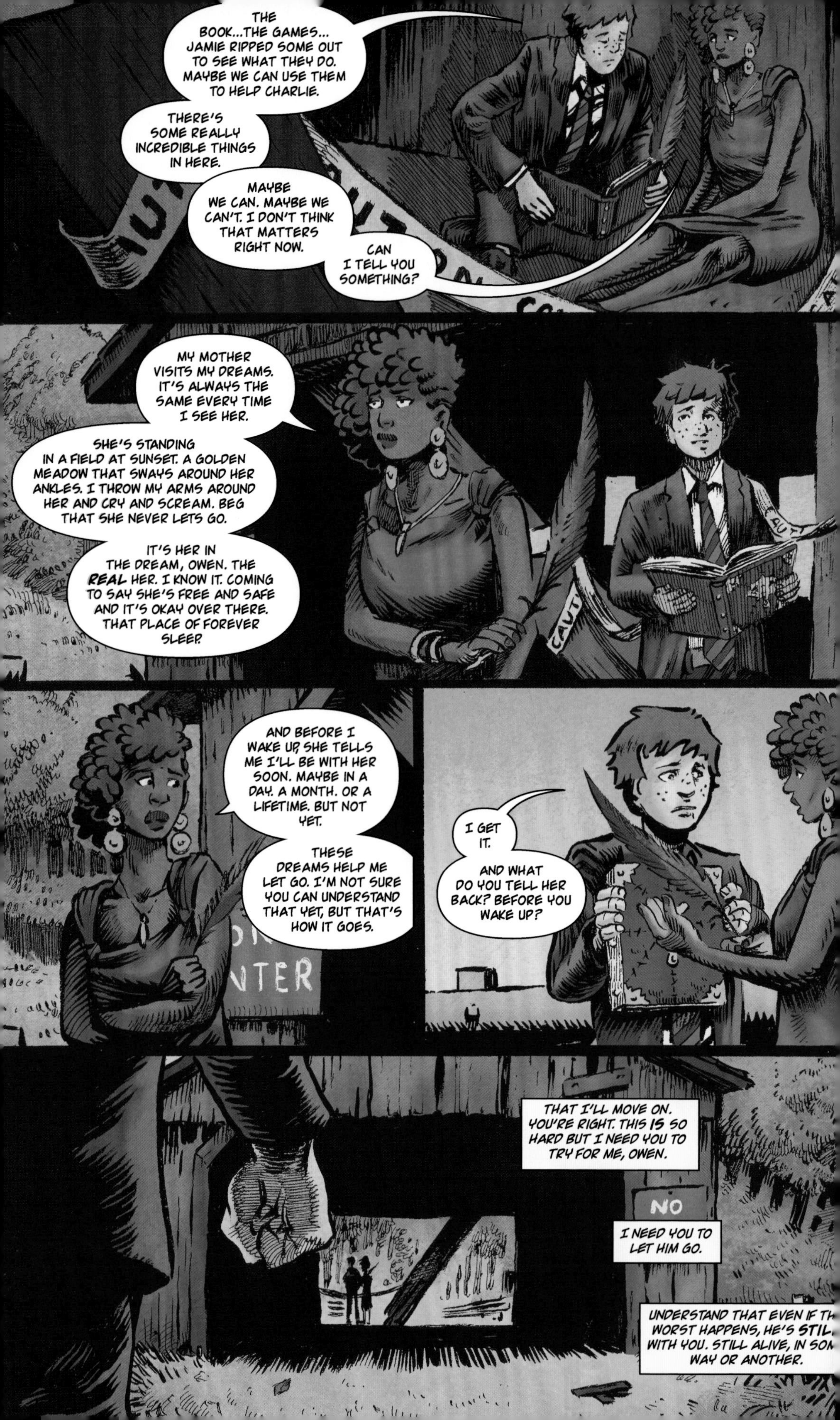
THE BOOK...THE GAMES... JAMIE RIPPED SOME OUT TO SEE WHAT THEY DO. MAYBE WE CAN USE THEM TO HELP CHARLIE.
THERE'S SOME REALLY INCREDIBLE THINGS IN HERE.
MAYBE WE CAN. MAYBE WE CAN'T. I DON'T THINK THAT MATTERS RIGHT NOW.
CAN I TELL YOU SOMETHING?
MY MOTHER VISITS MY DREAMS. IT'S ALWAYS THE SAME EVERY TIME I SEE HER.
SHE'S STANDING IN A FIELD AT SUNSET. A GOLDEN MEADOW THAT SWAYS AROUND HER ANKLES. I THROW MY ARMS AROUND HER AND CRY AND SCREAM. BEG THAT SHE NEVER LETS GO.
IT'S HER IN THE DREAM, OWEN. THE **REAL** HER. I KNOW IT. COMING TO SAY SHE'S FREE AND SAFE AND IT'S OKAY OVER THERE. THAT PLACE OF FOREVER SLEEP.
AND BEFORE I WAKE UP, SHE TELLS ME I'LL BE WITH HER SOON. MAYBE IN A DAY. A MONTH. OR A LIFETIME. BUT NOT YET.
THESE DREAMS HELP ME LET GO. I'M NOT SURE YOU CAN UNDERSTAND THAT YET, BUT THAT'S HOW IT GOES.
I GET IT.
AND WHAT DO YOU TELL HER BACK? BEFORE YOU WAKE UP?
THAT I'LL MOVE ON. YOU'RE RIGHT. THIS **IS** SO HARD BUT I NEED YOU TO TRY FOR ME, OWEN.
NO
I NEED YOU TO LET HIM GO.
UNDERSTAND THAT EVEN IF TH WORST HAPPENS, HE'S **STIL** WITH YOU. STILL ALIVE, IN SOM WAY OR ANOTHER.

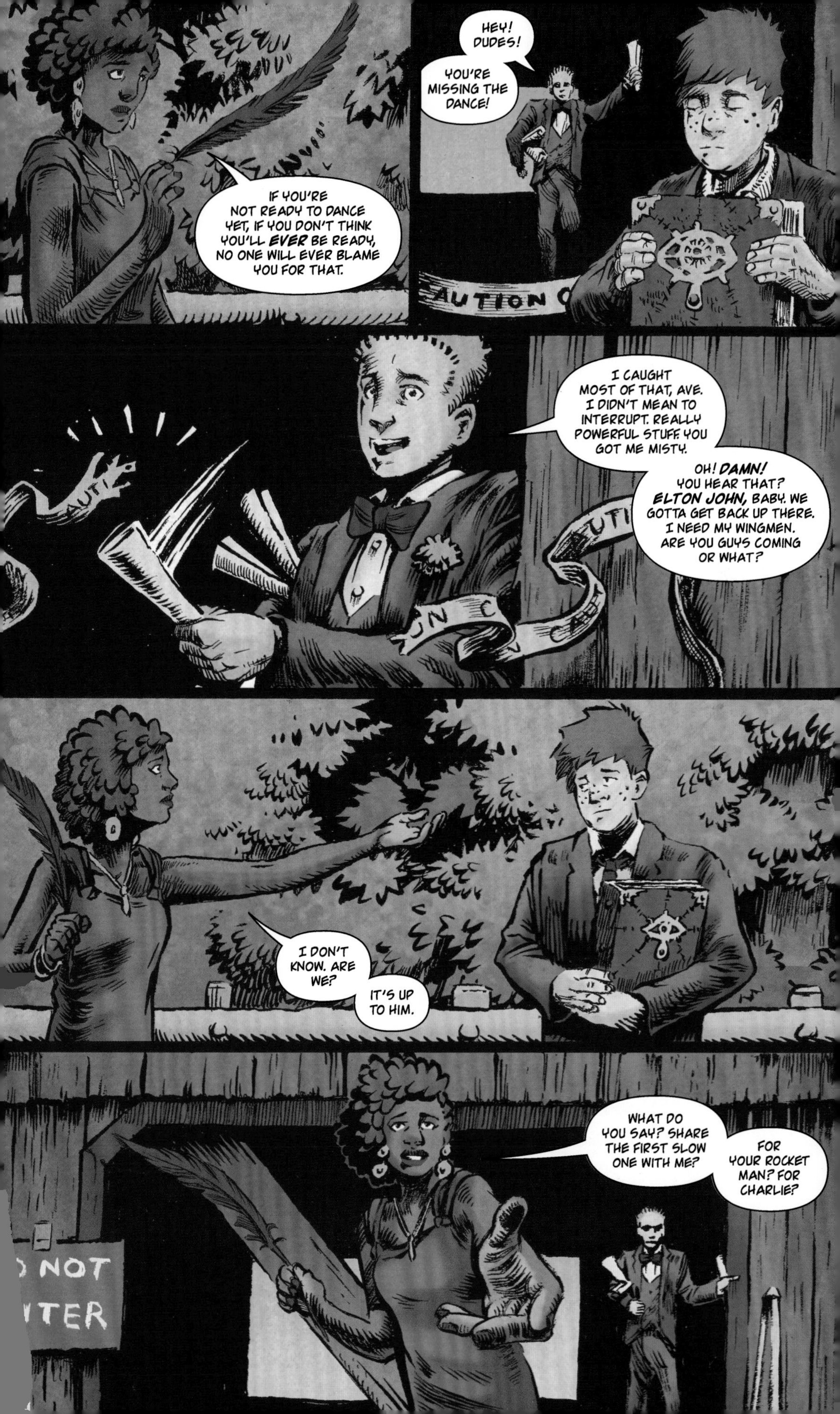
IF YOU'RE NOT READY TO DANCE YET, IF YOU DON'T THINK YOU'LL *EVER* BE READY, NO ONE WILL EVER BLAME YOU FOR THAT.
HEY! DUDES!
YOU'RE MISSING THE DANCE!
AUTION C
I CAUGHT MOST OF THAT, AVE. I DIDN'T MEAN TO INTERRUPT. REALLY POWERFUL STUFF. YOU GOT ME MISTY.
OH! *DAMN!* YOU HEAR THAT? ***ELTON JOHN,*** BABY. WE GOTTA GET BACK UP THERE. I NEED MY WINGMEN. ARE YOU GUYS COMING OR WHAT?
I DON'T KNOW. ARE WE?
IT'S UP TO HIM.
WHAT DO YOU SAY? SHARE THE FIRST SLOW ONE WITH ME?
FOR YOUR ROCKET MAN? FOR CHARLIE?
O NOT
TER

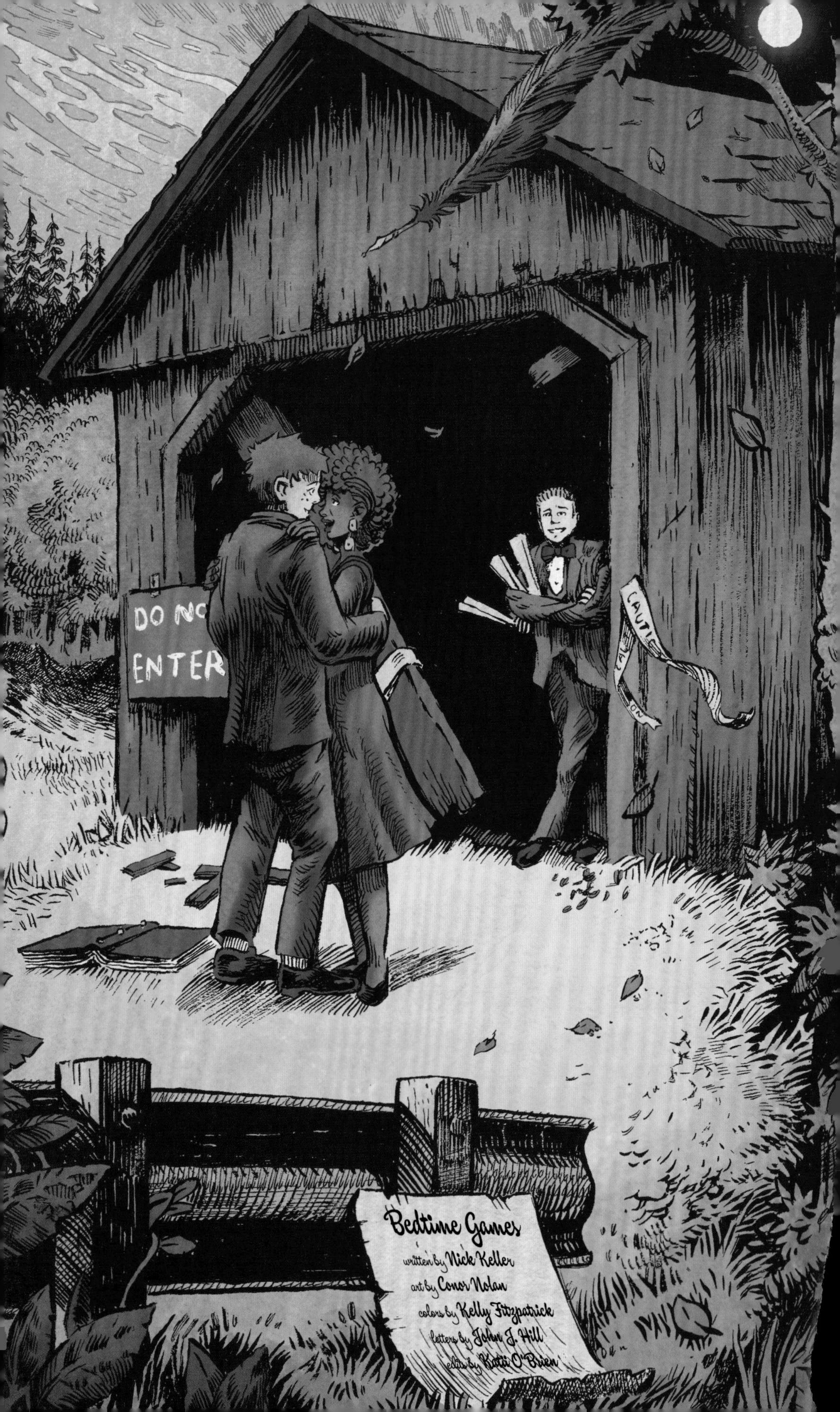
DO NO
ENTER
CAUTI
Bedtime Games
written by Nick Keller
art by Conor Nolan
colors by Kelly Fitzpatrick
letters by John J. Hill
edits by Katii O'Brien

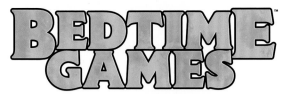

BEDTIME GAMES™

SKETCHBOOK

NOTES BY **CONOR NOLAN**

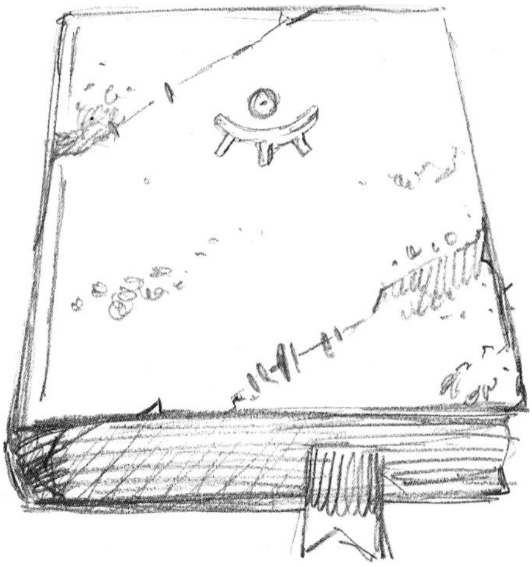

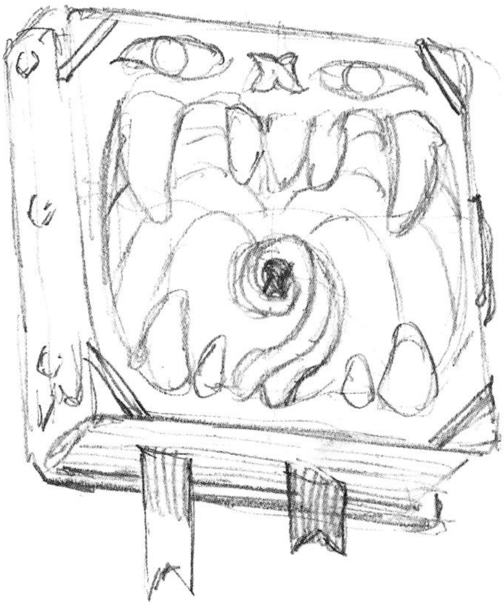

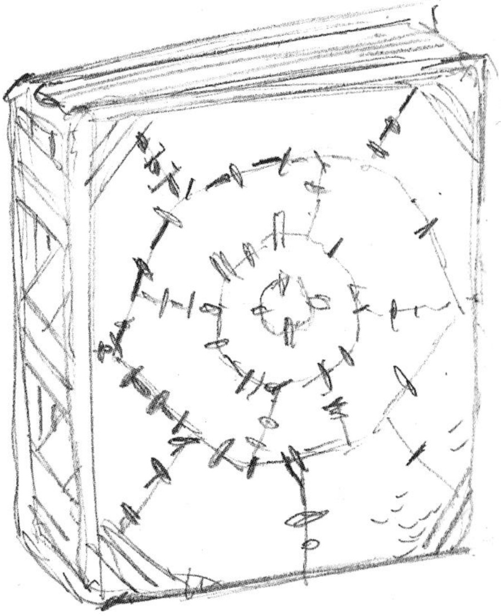

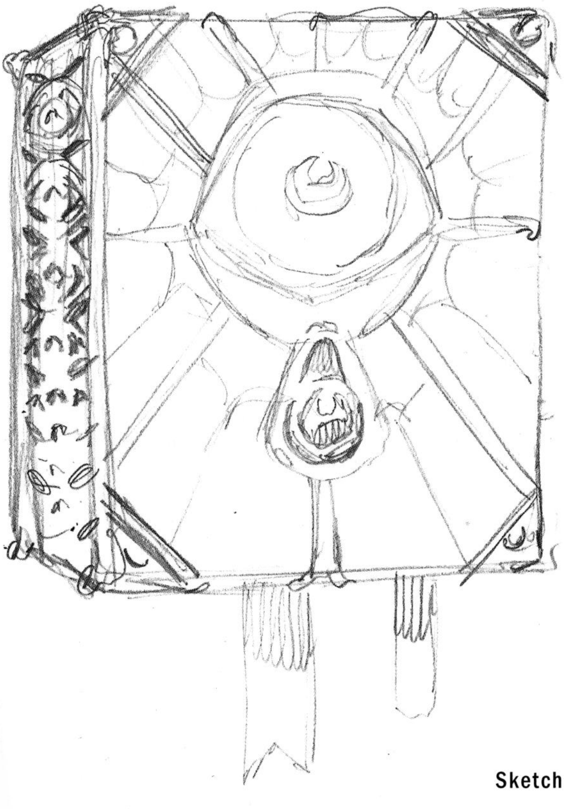

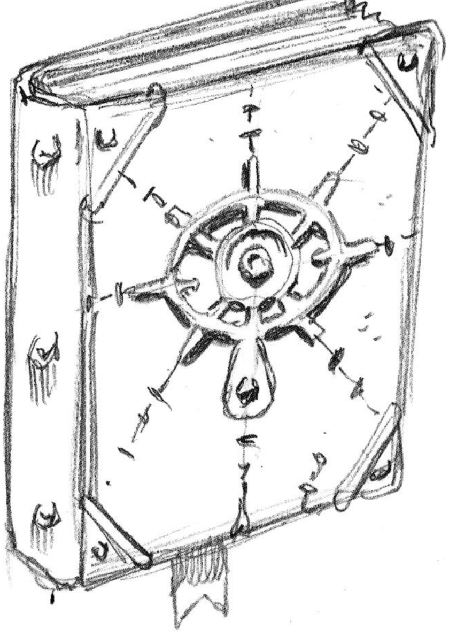

Sketches for *Bedtime Games.*

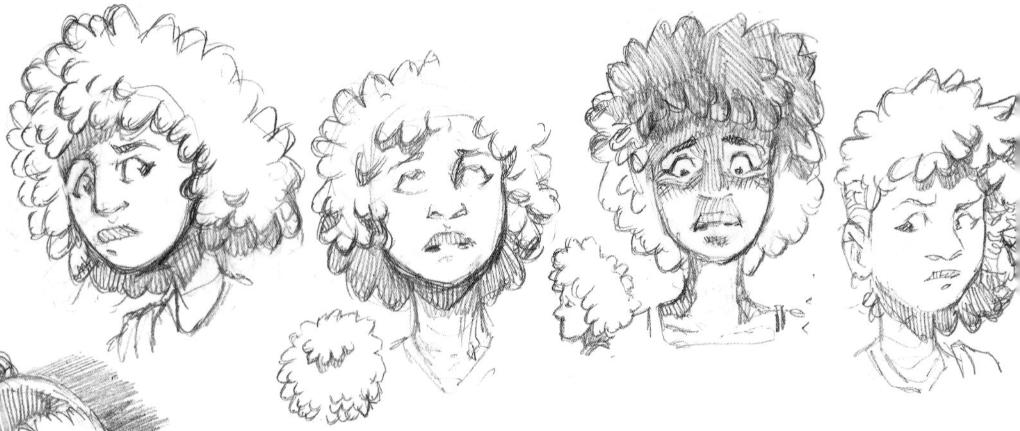

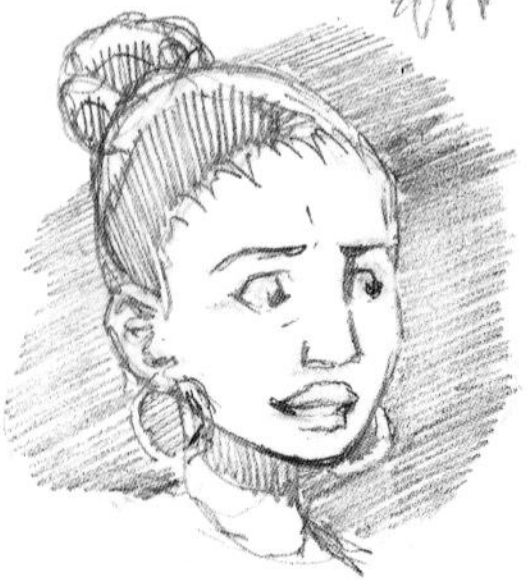

Avery was, to me, the unspoken leader of the pack. She had to look the part and I wanted confidence to play a big part in that. I enjoyed drawing her most if I had to choose. With her I tried to find the perfect combo of beauty and toughness.

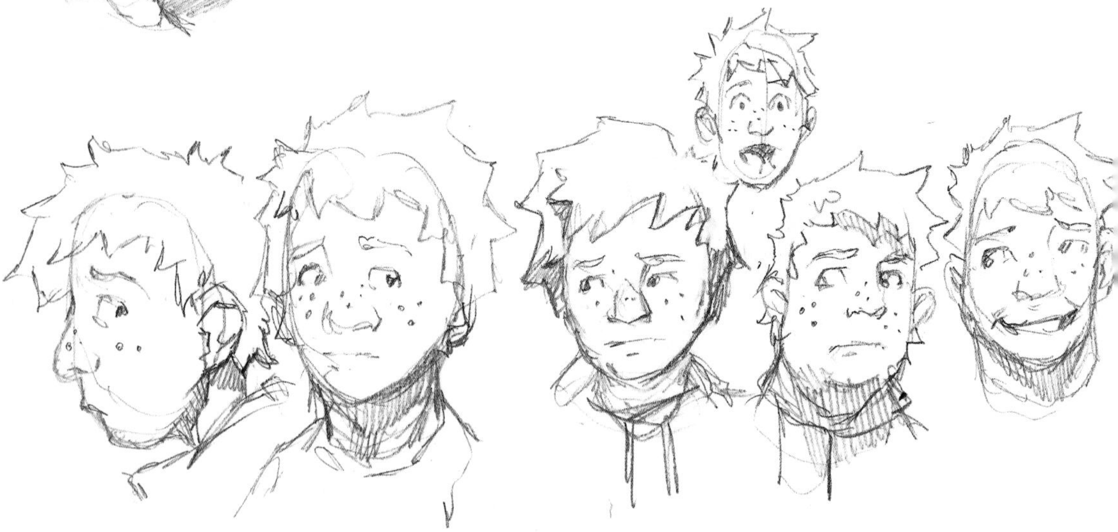

I imagined Owen's character caught in the wild throes of puberty. His general appearance should be soft and harmless. His hair is unkept, and his clothes maybe a little outdated. His corners are a little rounded, but his weight isn't his defining feature.

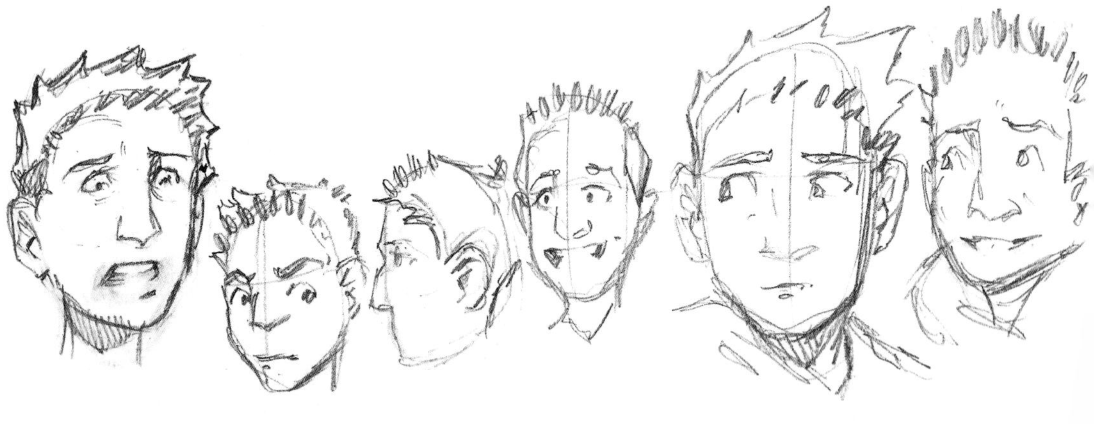

Jamie looks a little like I did at his age, especially the hair. I wanted to have him imb a cool, skater boy vibe. A teenage rebel with a soft core. A pubescent, lesser James De

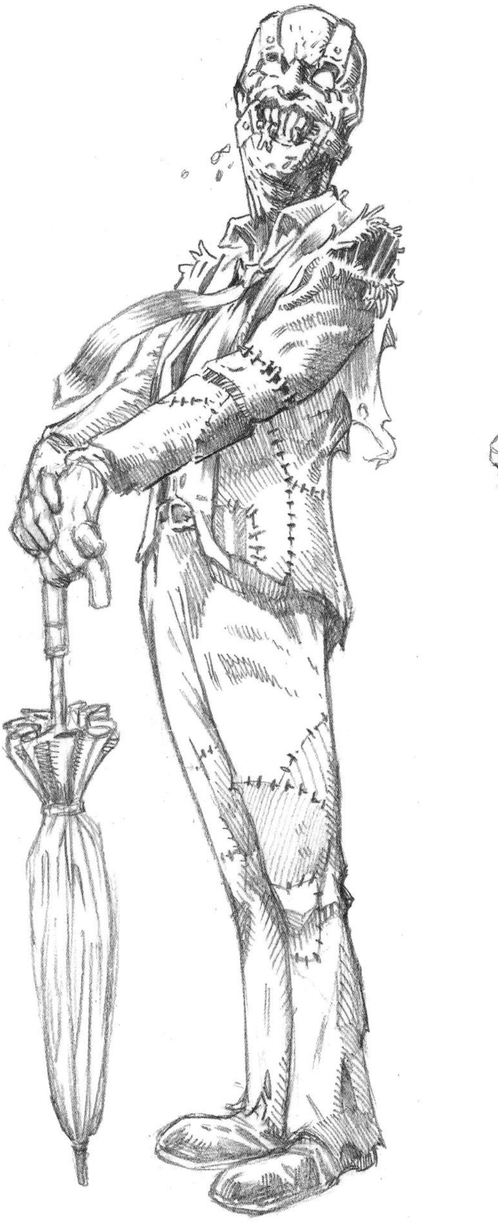

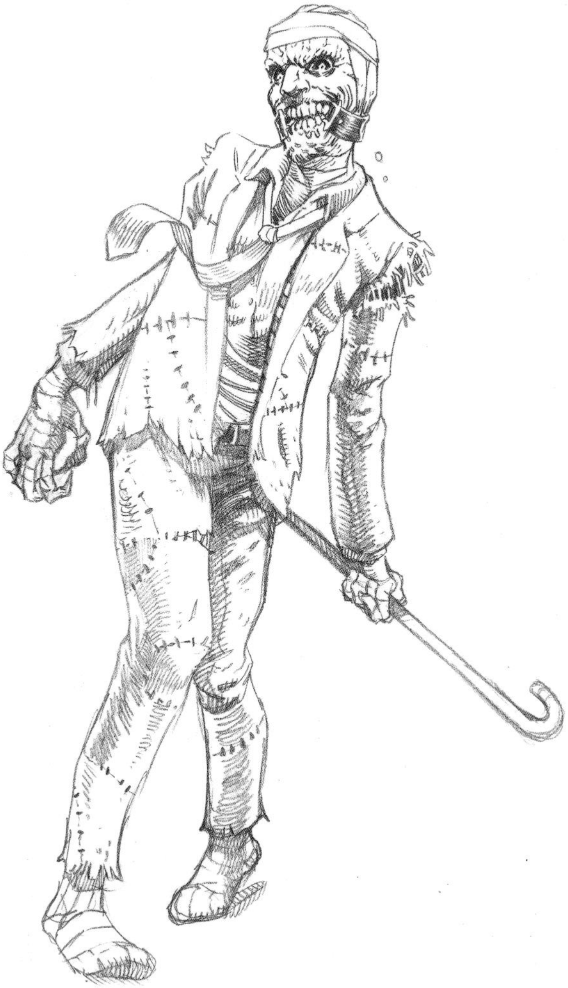

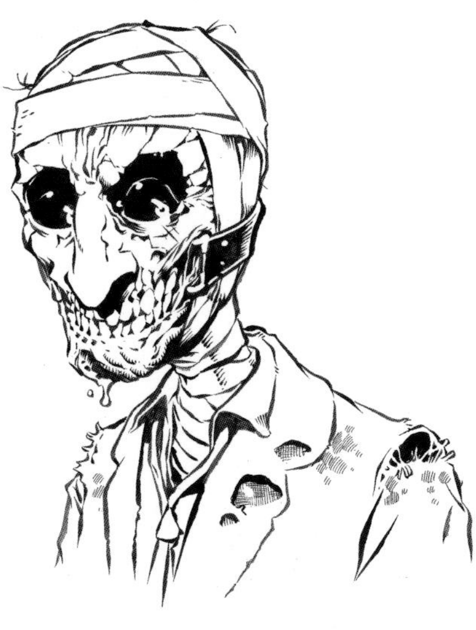

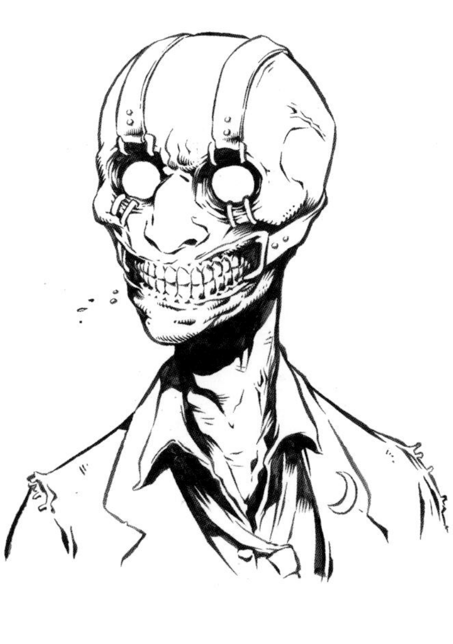

Nick and I discussed Mr. Bedtime's design at length. What we came up with is that we wanted a wolf dressed as a lamb, but barely keeping it together, if at all. The entirety of him literally unravelling away, fraying at the seams. The smile, the suit, and general demeanor are hooks to draw you in, but once he has you, you belong to him.

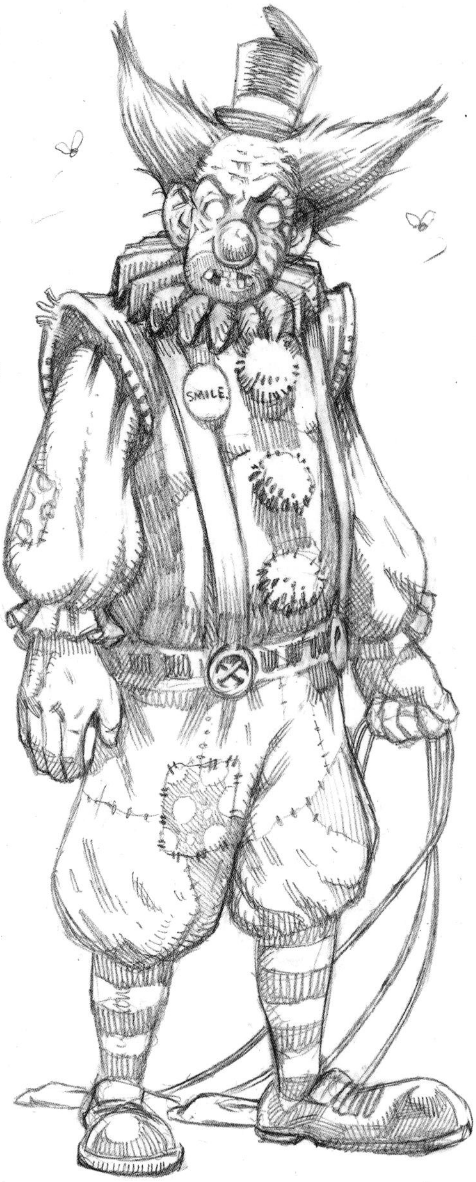
SMILE.

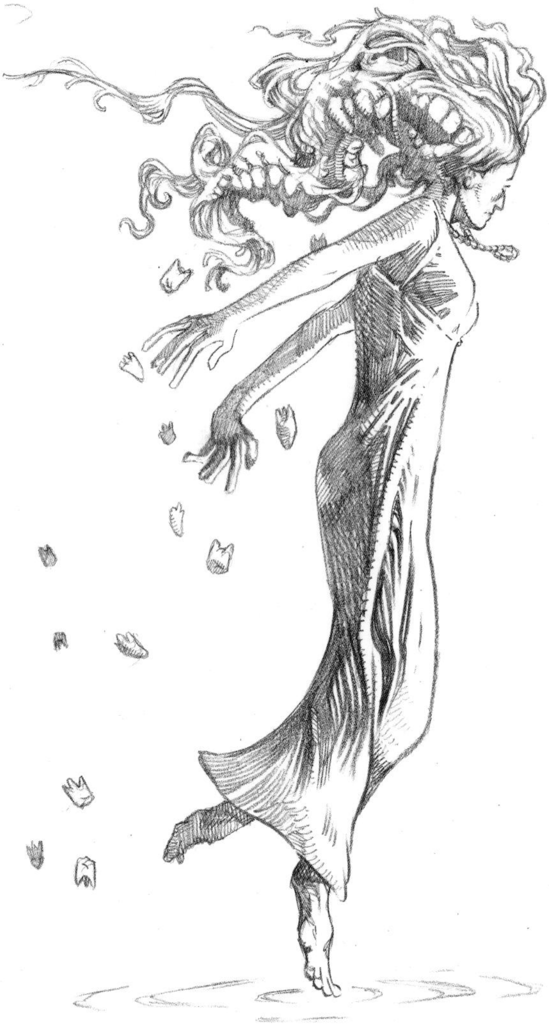

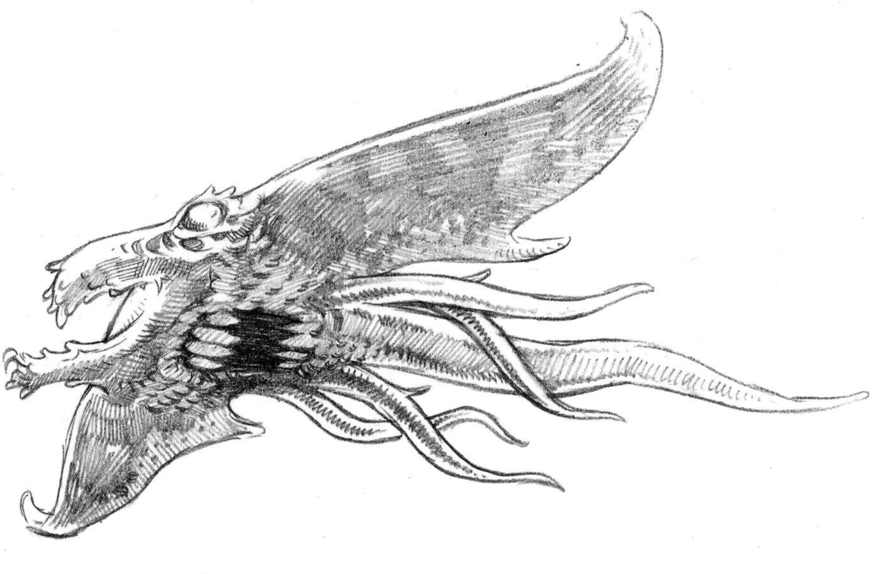

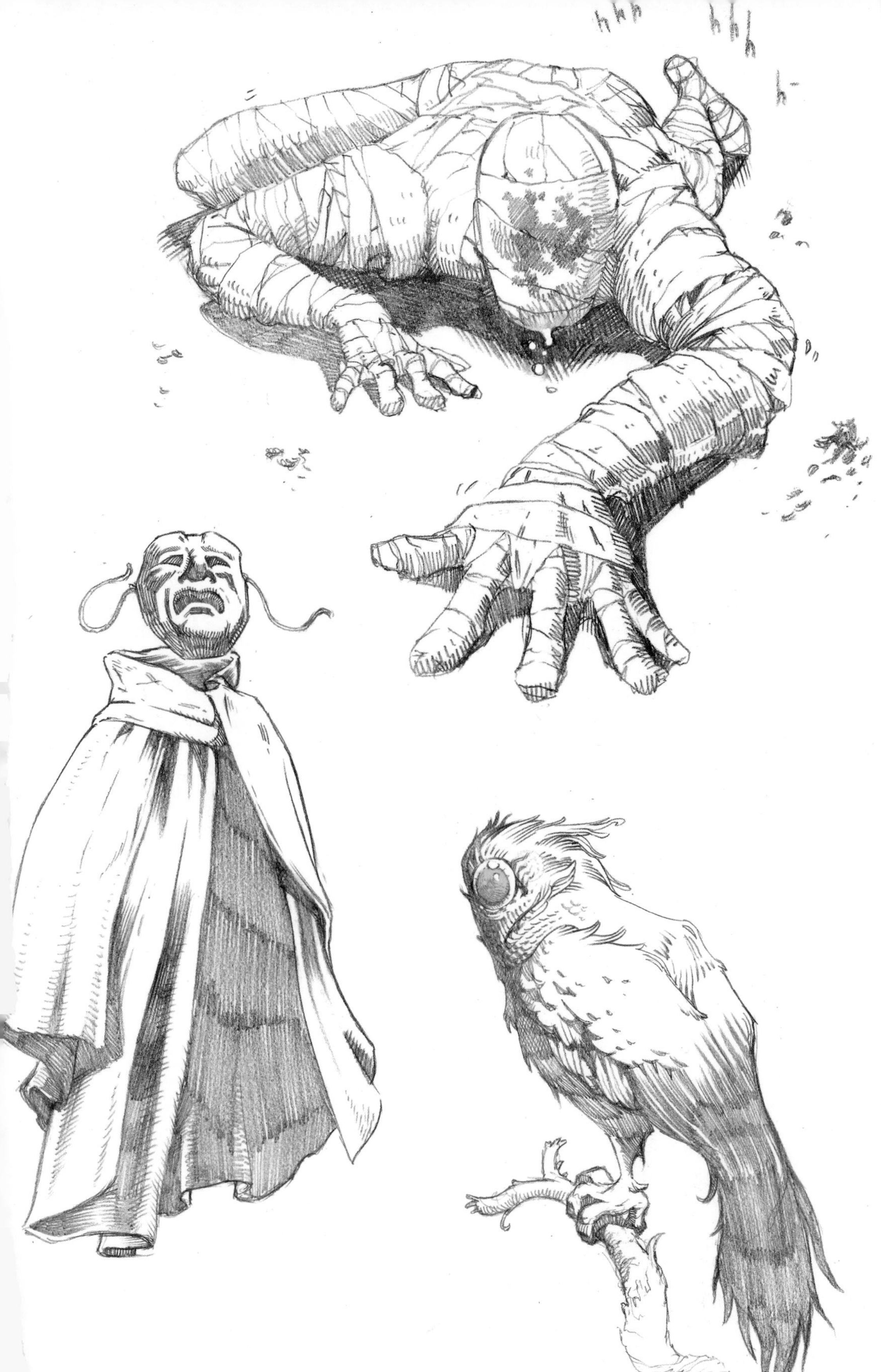

Nightmare sketches.

RECOMMENDED READING

DEATH HEAD
Zack Keller
Nick Keller
Joanna Estep
Kelly Fitzpatrick

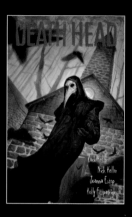

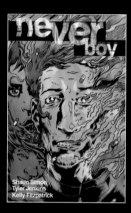

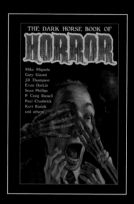

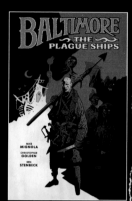

DEATH HEAD TPB
Zack Keller, Nick Keller, Joanna Estep, & Kelly Fitzpatrick
9781616559045
$19.99

never boy
Shaun Simon
Tyler Jenkins
Kelly Fitzpatrick

NEVERBOY TPB
Shaun Simon, Tyler Jenkins, Kelly Fitzpatrick, & Conor Nolan
9781616557881
$19.99

THE DARK HORSE BOOK OF
HORROR
Mike Mignola
Gary Gianni
Jill Thompson
Evan Dorkin
Sean Phillips
P. Craig Russell
Paul Chadwick
Kurt Busiek
and others

THE DARK HORSE BOOK OF HORROR HC
Mike Mignola, Gary Gianni, Jill Thompson, & others
9781506703725
$19.99

BALTIMORE
THE PLAGUE SHIPS
MIKE MIGNOLA
CHRISTOPHER GOLDEN
BEN STENBECK

BALTIMORE VOLUME 1: THE PLAGUE SHIPS TPB
Mike Mignola, Christopher Golden, Ben Stenbeck, & Dave Stewart
9781595826770
$18.99

OMNIBUS VOLUME 1
HELLBOY
SEED of DESTRUCTION
MIKE MIGNOLA • JOHN BYRNE

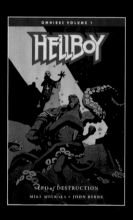

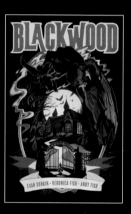

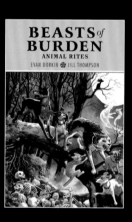

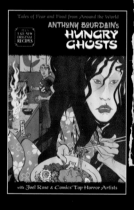

HELLBOY OMNIBUS VOL 1: SEED OF DESTRUCTION
Mike Mignola, John Byrne, Mark Chiarello, & Dave Stewart
9781506706665
$24.99

BLACKWOOD
EVAN DORKIN • VERONICA FISH • ANDY FISH

BLACKWOOD TPB
Evan Dorkin, Veronica Fish, & Andy Fish
9781506707426
$17.99

BEASTS of BURDEN
ANIMAL RITES
EVAN DORKIN JILL THOMPSON

BEASTS OF BURDEN: ANIMAL RITES TPB
Evan Dorkin & Jill Thompson
9781506706368
$19.99

Tales of Fear and Food from Around the World
ANTHONY BOURDAIN'S
HUNGRY GHOSTS
with Joel Rose & Comics' Top Horror Artists

HUNGRY GHOSTS HC
Anthony Bourdain, Joel Rose, & others
9781506706696
$14.99

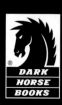